AMERICA'S ★ NEW ★ ECONOMY

ROBERT HAMRIN

AMERICA'S
★ NEW ★
ECONOMY

The Basic
Guide

1988 Franklin Watts
New York Toronto

To Krista and Kira, the dynamic duo,
who infuse each of my days with great joy.

Library of Congress Cataloging-in-Publication Data

Hamrin, Robert D.
America's new economy : the basic guide / Robert Hamrin.
p.   cm.
Bibliography: p.
Includes index.
ISBN 0-531-15077-1
1. United States—Economic conditions—1981–   2. United States—
Economic policy—1981–   I. Title.
HC106.8.H35   1988
330.973′0927—dc19   87-37153
CIP

CONTENTS

★

v

Contents

AMERICA'S
★ NEW ★
ECONOMY

PREFACE

★

Until now, whenever someone asked me, "What book can I read to get a good overview of today's American economy?" I had no answer. I have never found one book among the hundreds at major bookstores that told the current story about the American economy in a straightforward, easy to read, and easy to understand fashion.

This guidebook presents the major facts needed to understand the American economy of the present and future. Included are the good and the bad, the changes and the constants; the experts and the politicians interpreting facts. It is the foundation to allow you to draw your own conclusions about the performance of the American economy and where it is headed.

What makes this guidebook different from the literally hundreds of books on the economy that are published every year? Some describe; many more prescribe. The problem is that each one is just a piece of the puzzle, and even if one were to read ten, twenty, or forty of them, a clear picture of the American economy would not emerge. Indeed, it is likely that the picture would be fuzzier than ever. Why is this the case?

The answer is summed up in that classic economics joke: "Lay all economists end to end and you'll never come to a conclusion." In other words, the pieces are in conflict. Just when one piece seems to fit in place, another comes along to dislodge it. This results from a combination of the "experts' effect," the "pendulum effect," and the "hogwash effect."

The "experts' effect" is the most basic and powerful of the three:

Some economic experts have an ax to grind that prejudices their analysis and conclusions and suggests a distorted picture of the economy.

The ax grinding takes place for a variety of reasons. In some cases, it is because the economists are on a particular institution's payroll. Others may advise or serve as spokespersons for a political party. But for most, regardless of where they are employed, the fundamental reason is that they hold a particular ideological perspective. Consequently, their deepest commitment is to finding the data, the facts, the arguments that will fit most neatly with the results they wish to claim.

Economics is not value free. This is even true of economists' econometric models with their numerous equations. Although computer manipulation of the numbers is value free, the choice of the assumptions that govern the relationships of the model and of the numbers that go into the model are laden with the values of the programmer and the investigator.

This "experts' effect" feeds right into the highly visible "pendulum effect":

If you hear one declarative pronouncement or see one policy enacted today, just wait awhile and you will be sure to hear its opposite.

Thus in 1981, there was a major tax cut, and in 1982, a tax increase; in the early 1980s, one saw the "decline of American industry" but in the mid-1980s, "America had come back"; in early 1985, the dollar was soaring out of sight, while in early 1987 there were fears that the dollar had sunk too far; in 1980, oil was going to $100 a barrel, but by mid-1986, it stood at $12 a barrel; in 1982 the U.S. was in the worst recession since the Great Depression, while in 1987, it was concluding the fifth year of recovery and the stock market was setting new records.

The seeming impossibility of understanding the American economy is enhanced by the "hogwash effect":

Throw enough economic hogwash at people and at some point they are bound to throw up their hands in despair or simply run away.

Consider a few of the statements that have been forcefully articulated in the past few years. "America has lost its industrial might." "There will be a balanced budget by 1983" (made in 1980). "Inflation is here to stay." "Cut taxes significantly and deficits will be reduced." If leading economists and economic policy makers can make ridiculous predictions, who can be believed?

I believe there is quite a lot of hope. If I did not, I would not have written this book. The format of the book has been devised to counter the three effects described above to make the economy understandable to you. The simple three-step format for each chapter is:

1. To introduce the key questions and issues.
2. To present the basic economic facts.
3. To provide the major competing interpretations of the facts.

Thus, each chapter begins with a brief introductory Issues section that highlights the key questions, issues, and areas of controversy. Next, the basic facts about the chapter's topic are presented in their pure, unadulterated form in the Facts section. This means that the favorite numbers of the conservatives, of the liberals, and of all those in between are presented. Importantly, this section will probe beneath the surface of national figures to get at the microstatistics on our cities and states, subgroups of individuals, and individual industries—the figures that really give you an accurate picture of what is going on in this vast mosaic known as the American economy.

Think for a few moments about what the facts say to you before you go on to the Interpretation section, which presents the interpretation of the numbers by leading economists, policy makers, and business and labor leaders. This will allow you to check your assumptions, insights, and conclusions against those of the experts and other economic commentators. It is likely that this exercise will lead you to discover a great deal about yourself and about the experts. For instance, you may find that when you look at *all* the basic numbers, it is difficult to maintain a hard-line position. You are almost certain to find that the economic world is neither so neat nor so simple that it can be comfortably fitted into any ideological box. The economic world is messy, it is constantly changing, and it is full of surprises. To illustrate this point, and to see what numbers alone can say, consider the following records that were established in the first half of the 1980s:

- Interest rates surpassed all previous highs as the prime rate hit 21 percent in 1980.

- The unemployment rate hit a post-Depression record of 10.8 percent in 1982.

- In 1986, the federal budget deficit soared to over $220 billion—more than triple the pre-1980s record level.

- The trade deficit, nonexistent in the pre-1980s surplus days, reached the undreamed-of level of $156 billion in 1986.

- Start-up fever struck as never before with the creation

of 635,000 new businesses in 1984 (double the number in 1974).

- In 1986, a record number of 61,232 businesses went bankrupt, almost double the 31,334 of 1983.
- The U.S. became in 1985 a debtor nation for the first time in this century to the tune of $107 billion.
- In 1984, businesses merged at the record-breaking rate of eleven a day.
- Farm income was down $11 billion in 1983, its largest one-year drop in history.
- In 1985, more banks failed than in any year since the Great Depression.
- More people were living in poverty in 1983, 35.4 million, than in any year since the War on Poverty was launched in 1964.

* * *

The three-part Issues, Facts, and Interpretation format is used for every chapter of the book except the first and last. Chapter 1 is where I present my own interpretation of the facts, not issue by issue but what they all add up to—The Big Picture. The last chapter serves as an economic scorecard of the basic strengths and weaknesses in the economy, in business, and for workers.

Trying to keep in focus the big picture has been my primary interest throughout my thirteen years of economic policy experience in Washington. I quickly learned the truth of the old adage, "You can't see the forest for the trees," as for nearly four years I watched the country's leading economists testify before the Joint Economic Committee of Congress with only a partial, and usually short-sighted, vision of the full array of economic challenges confronting the nation. Thus, a policy prescription to cure one economic illness through the law of unintended consequences worsened other illnesses or even brought on an entirely new illness. Thus was born my passion for "seeing the forest."

It should be clear in the light of what I said earlier that I am not claiming to be value free. On the contrary, I adhere to a very deeply held set of values that largely determine what I would like to see the American economy accomplish. Importantly, however, I try not to allow them rigidly to prescribe an unalterable set of goals or policies for the economy, but to remain open to modify my thinking in view of changing facts and accumulating evidence.

Take the problem of poverty as an example, something of concern for both practical and moral reasons. In the late 1960s, I was a champion of the big-government, War-on-Poverty approach to eliminate poverty. As the years went on and the expenditures mounted into the hundreds of billions of dollars with no significant decrease in the number living in poverty, I recognized that this approach was not the full answer. Did that mean I rode the pendulum over to the laissez-faire "let-growth-do-it" approach and embrace it as the full answer? No, because although there had been quite healthy growth in most years, the poverty rate still was not decreasing. Thus, the facts made me feel uncomfortable with both the liberal and conservative solutions. It was time to seek another way.

To sum up, in this book I am not out on a personal crusade to document or to present a conservative or liberal perspective. I consider myself neither and frankly do not care for labels. Nor am I out to present my policy precriptions for the economic ills of the country. I am out to set the American economy before you (in Chapters 2 to 27) and to let you judge its performance and the challenges it faces. I also want to present to you (in Chapter 1) what I consider to be the most critical features of today's economy—what the numbers point to as "The Ten Great Myths" and "The Big Constants and Big Changes."

In reading through the book, you are likely to develop a quite different set of ideas from my interpretation. But I hope in so doing that you will have arrived at your own personal understanding of the economy because the economy is very personal. Nothing affects people's lives more pervasively, day in and day out, than the economy. It largely determines: job hirings and firings; choosing when and whether to buy a new home, move up to a better one, or refinance an existing home; deciding when to start a new job, new career, or new business; deciding to place savings in a money market fund, stocks, or gold; deciding where to retire and estimating your retirement standard of living; and much more. On a much broader scale, the individual economic well being of literally hundreds of millions of people around the globe is intimately linked to the health and well being of the American economy.

My overall goal for this book is to make the new American economy "come alive" to people in all walks of life and for it to be recognized and appreciated for what it is: interesting, intriguing, and vitally important.

PART
I

★ I ★

America's
Economy

Its Performance
and Its Policies

CHAPTER
★ 1 ★

The Big
Picture

The world's largest, most powerful, and most influential economy is the American, but it is incredibly misunderstood.

Much of what is "known" about the American economy—the prevailing conventional wisdom—is nothing but a series of myths. And, much of what should be known about it—the fact that we are living in a period of sweeping economic change, greater than any experienced before—is not known.

There is hardly a lack of basic information. In every daily metropolitan newspaper and on every TV channel we are bombarded with economic information. A bits-and-pieces approach to understanding the economy assumes that if you grab enough snatches of information, it will all add up to a coherent whole. Unfortunately, it does not and it will not. It will only add up and begin to make sense when your objective is to see and understand "the Big Picture." A basic problem is that the current Big Picture is entirely different from the one that existed a generation ago (and changed from the picture ten years ago), yet we persist in trying to fit the "bits and pieces" into the obsolete frame. To understand today's economic picture, one must look at today's economic facts in their present context.

The course of action is clear. If we want to see and understand the current Big Picture of America's economy, we must first sweep away the elements of the old frame. These are the myths referred to at the outset. They arise when facts that do not fit our old assumptions are concealed or misused. As the myths accumulate and begin to crowd in, they distort our understanding of the economy's strengths and weaknesses, its good and bad points. Such misunderstanding leads to economic policies that at best are ineffective or, at worst, quite costly to consumers, workers and, ultimately, the economy as a whole.

The Ten Great Myths

Myth #1: All Is Well with the Economy

This, the greatest of the great myths, exists because the three yardsticks normally used to judge the economy's performance are doing fairly well. If the past five years are viewed from a 1988 nation-wide vantage point, economic growth is up, inflation is way down, and unemployment has been reduced. Since the big three are all plusses, what could be wrong?

These yardsticks overlook serious problems: the federal budget deficit was at an all time high in 1986, as was the trade deficit; the U.S., which was the world's largest creditor nation in 1982, became the largest debtor nation in 1985 and increased its global debt substantially in 1987; over 32 million people were living in poverty in 1986. There is more.

Myth #2: Most Americans Prospered in the Early 1980s

A single shocking statistic: two-thirds of American house-holds experienced a decline in purchasing power from 1980 to 1983. There was a decline in real after-tax income for those in the lower-, middle-, and even upper-middle income levels. Only the top fifth of households gained purchasing power over the period. The biggest gainers were the top 5 percent of households—those with incomes over $60,000—who gained an average of $4,250 in after-tax, inflation-adjusted income.

Myth #3: A Rising Tide Lifts All Boats

Translated, economic growth will benefit everyone, including the poor. This sounds logical until one considers that a rising tide will only lift those boats in the water or near the beach edge. Those boats that have sunk to the bottom or are beached too far from shore will stay where they are. Thus, after fourteen years of strong economic growth during the past twenty years, essentially the same percentage of the U.S. population lives in poverty as before the growth began.

Myth #4: The Service Economy: A Nation of Hamburger Franchises

This is shorthand for the widespread impression that America's service economy is inherently weak and unsustainable. There are more myths about the service economy than any other economic issue. Among these myths are the following: a service economy will eventually produce only services; services are made up of labor intensive, low technology, and low capital activities; the growth of services detracts from the overall health and competitiveness of manufacturing industries; the growth of government is the primary reason we have become a service economy. Now consider these facts:

• During the 1970s, nearly 90 percent of the 19 million new jobs created in the United States were in services.

• Many of the fastest-growing service industries involve good jobs in architectural and engineering firms, computer firms, accounting firms, transportation, communications, and utilities that pay well above manufacturing's average wage.

• There was rapid productivity growth (5 to 8 percent) during the 1965–1980 period in a wide variety of service industries, including petroleum pipelines, air transportation, telephone communication, drug and proprietary services, and gasoline service stations.

• Services and manufacturing are closely interwoven as about one-fourth of the GNP consists of services used as input by goods-producing industries.

The service economy is not without its weaknesses and problems, but clearly these facts display a dynamism and underlying strength to belie the myth.

Myth #5: High Tech: America's Invincible Arena of Dynamism and Dominance

While this myth was basically true in 1980, the experience of the past few years should set to rest any notions that high tech in America is immune to domestic setbacks and foreign competition. These are leading symptoms of hard times in high tech:

• U.S. high tech trade moved from a sizable surplus in the early 1980s to its first-ever deficit in 1986.

• America's leadership is eroding rapidly in every major electronics market.

• In 1984, for the first time, the nation's electronics sector, long a positive contributor to the U.S. trade balance, went into the red, chalking up a massive $6.8 billion deficit.

- The U.S. share of worldwide computer sales is holding relatively firm at more than 80 percent, but trade figures by U.S. companies are taking a nosedive because a growing percentage of this equipment is purchased abroad.

- The semiconductor industry had collective losses of $2 billion in 1985 and 1986.

- In 1985, U.S. semiconductor manufacturers suffered the most dramatic drop in demand in two decades and capacity utilization plummeted to below 70 percent (the lowest rate ever), all this in a generally healthy economy.

- The U.S. semiconductor industry is losing more and more of the worldwide market for random-access memory (RAM) chips to Japan, with the Japanese having 90 percent of the 256K market and a one-year lead on the one-megabyte RAM.

Myth #6: Reagan's Economic Performance Is Far Better Than Carter's

The numbers on Reagan's first six years versus Carter's four address this myth:

	(Annual averages)	
	Carter (1977–1980)	Reagan (1981–1986)
Real Growth in Gross National Product	3.3%	2.5%
Inflation	10.4%	5.1%
Unemployment	6.4%	8.5%
Increase in Number of Jobs	12.5% (total)	8.6% (total)
Budget Deficit	$45.2 billion	$134.8 billion

Myth #7: Reagan Has Dismantled Much of America's Welfare State

Despite the declaration of Budget Director David Stockman early in the Reagan presidency that "substantial parts" of the Great Society would have to be "heaved overboard," most of the programs that existed in 1981 remain in place. Programs have been pared, not pulled out by the roots. Thus, Reagan's domestic spending legacy shapes up as more of a retrenchment than the revolution it is often called.

Myth #8: Unemployment Is Not a Serious Problem

Unemployment has declined from its post-Depression peak of 10.8 percent in December 1982. Despite substantial improvement in the 1983–1986 period, over 7 million Americans remain unemployed in 1987. Moreover, this four-year period of improvement masks a number of subsurface trends. In a striking departure from past patterns, over half the rise in the unemployment rate in the 1981–1982 recession was caused by permanent separations, as opposed to seasonal or otherwise temporary layoffs. Of the 5.1 million displaced workers in the recession, 46 percent were eventually able to find only part-time work or a job at a lower wage or salary rate. Far from being comfortably cushioned, almost two-thirds of the country's unemployed in 1985 and 1986 received no unemployment compensation benefits because of cutbacks in benefits and more people remained unemployed for long periods.

Myth #9: Protectionism Is Good for U.S. Industries

Protectionist trade policies, designed to restrict the flow of foreign goods into the U.S., help to save some American jobs (in the protected industries) and that is why they are advocated and many have been enacted over the past two decades. This benefit is clearly visible. What goes unseen is the fact that protectionist trade policies carry a very high cost. First, they hurt other nations, many of them developing countries with high debt that is largely owed to American banks. If our restrictions keep them from servicing the debt, the U.S. ends up paying a steep price. Second, they could lead to protectionist legislation in other countries, hurting U.S. agriculture and export industries. Finally, there is the cost to the American consumer which is usually much more than the wages paid to workers whose jobs are saved. The cost to consumers per job saved runs quite high: $241,000 from voluntary restraints on Japanese cars; $240,000 from tuna tariffs; $43,000 from textile quotas; and $114,000 from steel quotas.

Myth #10: The U.S. Is a Fair Nation

The U.S. is quite fair in providing equality of opportunity so that all have a fair chance at sharing in the country's abundance. But the key measure of a country's fairness is its income distribution. The fairness ratio is defined as the ratio of income going to the top and to the bottom 20 percent of the population. Using the fairness ratio, the United States ranks eighteenth among the twenty-four major countries in the world and *last* among all principal industrialized nations.

The Big Constants

Despite these negatives, there is a good deal to be optimistic about. Most of the "big changes" in the economy point the way to a good future. In focusing on these changes, one can see new opportunities and identify new challenges.

In a country mesmerized by "future shock" and "megatrends," and fascinated by change, we must not lose sight of the very clear fact that the force of inertia is strong and that continuity often prevails. This is certainly true in the economy, where six unheralded "big constants" have remained remarkably unshakeable in the general economic turbulence of the last fifteen to thirty years. Since these are covered in various "Facts" sections, a list will suffice at this point:

1. The poverty rate (14.7 percent in 1966 and 14.4 percent in 1984)
2. Women/men earnings ratio (between 57 percent and 64 percent over the last thirty years)
3. High nonwhite to white unemployment ratio (2.0 to 2.5 in all but four of the last thirty years)
4. Income distribution (over the past thirty years, the bottom 20 percent received about 5 percent of total income and the top 20 percent received about 40 percent)
5. Deficits in federal budget (in all but one of the last twenty-two years)
6. Steadily rising unemployment rates (rate up in each postwar decade)

The Big Changes

From the quiet of the constants, one turns to the cacophony of the changes. Ten "big changes" can be grouped under three broad transformational themes: (1) a new knowledge-intensive, human resource-based economy; (2) a reshaped business landscape; (3) the growing realities of global economic interdependence. Changes of this character and magnitude combine to create a fundamental transformation.

A New Knowledge-Intensive, Human Resource-Based Economy

For most of this century, America's economic base has been the "basic" or "heavy" industries—autos, steel, chemicals, and petroleum. These were the symbols of American economic might. Yet today, these and virtually all other basic industries are experiencing both declining jobs and output.

By now, most Americans have heard the story of the decline, but the nature of what is taking the place of these basic industries is not well or widely understood. Many people have heard that the U.S. is developing into a service economy, but the image embedded in their minds by leading public opinion makers is of the person behind the counter at the fast-food shop or the clerk entering data into a Japanese computer.

The reality is that America's economy in the 1980s comprises heavy and light manufacturing industries, service industries, and high tech industries. The common denominator is that information technologies—robots, computers, microprocessors, and CAD/CAM (computer-aided design/computer-assisted manufacturing)—are beginning to transform them.

The implications of this transition to a knowledge-intensive economic base include the following:

- The formulas, data bases, economic theories, policies, and conventional wisdom of the industrial era may no longer be applicable to the services/information economy.

- America's future prosperity will increasingly shift from a reliance on large factories in Detroit and Pittsburgh to the new ideas and technologies developed in the hundreds of "Silicon Valleys" throughout the United States.

- Knowledge must be seen as a strategic resource that requires investment and development just as physical and natural resources do.

- Education and training are critical, requiring a long-term commitment to resupport and reorient the American system of education and to revamp our approach to retraining workers displaced by technological change.

Change #1: The Transforming Power of Information Technologies and Biotechnology Is Just Beginning to Be Appreciated For most of this century, we lived in the Age of Industrial Technologies. We are now in the Age of Information Technologies. It is likely that during the next decade, certainly by the year 2000, we will be living in the Age of Biotechnology.

The Age of Industrial Technologies (the roughly one hundred-year-long period when steel, chemicals, and electrical machines formed the core technologies of our lives) began to draw to a close thirty to forty years ago. Combined with the assembly-line mode of production, these technologies gave products as diverse as automobiles, plastics, textiles, and tanks.

In the 1960s and 1970s, the leading transforming technologies became the information technologies—computers, telecommunications, and robotics. Up to now, the Information Revolution principally has been a hardware revolution—a revolution in the technologies themselves. This is really only the tip of the iceberg, for we are just beginning to journey into the really revolutionary age of applications. The factory of the future and the office of the future, where sophisticated computers and computer networks control the flow of production of goods and information, are swiftly coming upon us.

So, also, are smart consumer electronics. Work and leisure will never be the same when virtually all major home appliances and recreational equipment will incorporate computer brains.

All this is but the prelude to the major technological show that is coming. That show is biotechnology. It ultimately will dwarf the information technologies in its scope and impact.

We are on the verge of letting an entirely new genie out of the bottle. The most recent genie—microelectronics—with its semiconductors, microprocessors, supercomputers, robots, and so forth had a lot of new fancy features, but its basic character was well known. In a sense, it can be viewed as the culmination of the era of physics which had shaped the modern Western World.

Ever since the discovery of fire, mankind has twisted, pulled, stretched, pulverized, fired, cooled, polished, mixed, and separated *inorganic* materials. All of the marvelous inventions from the wheel to supercomputers have involved some new way of shaping inorganic materials for people's use.

What makes the biotechnology revolution utterly different is that organic materials—living matter—will be manipulated through an infinite variety of means to serve people's needs. It seems quite certain that such major industries as pharmaceuticals and chemicals, as well as agriculture, will be transformed. Gene-splitting may lead to the synthesis of new substances to substitute for oil, coal, and other raw materials to become the key to a self-sustaining society. There is also tremendous potential for significant ethical questions to arise, particularly in the area of human genetic engineering.

To see the future—and understand how industries, the economy, and ultimately society will be transformed—closely watch the developments taking place in the application of the information technologies and the biological sciences. These developments will surely present our country with unprecedented political, scientific, economic, and most importantly, moral and spiritual challenges. They will present us, as individuals, with the challenge to rethink the way we work, play, communicate, consume, invest, and yes, even think.

Change #2: Services Are America's Dynamic Economic Base There are three basic facts about the U.S. economy that must become better, and more widely, understood:

- We live in, and have lived in for forty years, a service economy.

- The service sector is growing and dynamic, it makes

numerous positive contributions to goods-producing industries and to the U.S. economy, and it is vital to future
economic growth and progress.

- The U.S. currently is the world's preeminent service
  economy, but the leadership gap is closing as our service
  industries face government constraints while foreign
  competitors receive government support.

Let us focus on the service economy's growing, dynamic
nature. Misconceptions about the definition of a service
economy stem from some of America's most forceful opinion
shapers. They provide a steady diet of vivid imagery which,
too often, powerfully distorts the picture of the U.S. economy. For instance, a front-page *New York Times* story, "Big
Mac Supplants Big Steel," suggests that the alternative to a
troubled steel industry is a hamburger franchise. A national
labor leader implies that a service economy offers young
people nothing but jobs in fast-food outlets and video arcades. The head of one of the nation's largest banks describes
a service economy as one where we take in each other's
laundry.

A service economy is not just personal services, such as
barbershops, restaurants, and video arcades. This perception
is refuted by the fact that in the 1980s only around 2 percent
of the Gross National Product (GNP) stems from such service activities.

To understand today's service economy, one must venture
into its major growth sectors: banking, insurance, telecommunications, accounting, advertising, engineering and
architectural services, health care, education, computer and
data processing, and other high technology services. This
heterogeneous group of economic activities has little in common other than that their principal outputs are for the most
part intangible products.

Basically, services act as facilitating agents, the grease so
to speak, that enable manufacturing, agriculture, mining,
and trade to take place. For example, without banking or

insurance or transportation—all of which are services—not a single factory would be able to operate.

The contribution of services to manufacturing can be seen from many angles and at many different levels. Starting with the most aggregate, about one-fourth of the GNP consists of services used as input by goods-producing industries. Also, many high tech manufacturing companies derive 30 to 60 percent of their revenues from services. Some go so far that they become service companies. Numerous industrial companies have left the *Fortune* 500 in the 1980s to become service companies. This quiet but dramatic evolution underway in American business makes distinguishing between service and nonservice firms more difficult and somewhat artificial.

The overall dynamism and dominance of services can be seen in looking at the facts regarding employment, the GNP, and trade:

- There has been an increase from thirty service workers out of 100 workers at the turn of the century to seventy-five out of 100 workers today.

- About fifteen new service jobs have been created for each new manufacturing job throughout the entire post-World War II era.

- Services have been the dominant contributor to the GNP for over three decades, growing steadily from a 61 percent contribution in 1950 to 69 percent in 1986.

- Each year from 1972 to 1983, the U.S. showed a positive balance of trade in services and investment income, a surplus that was responsible for pulling the overall trade balance into surplus in five of those years.

Clearly, the fundamental importance of the service sector to the U.S. economy is indisputable as it constitutes the largest share of the GNP and employment and it is an increasingly critical component of what traditionally has been classified as the manufacturing and goods sector.

Change #3: The Feminization of the Labor Force   The most striking change in U.S. labor market during this century has been the large increase in working married women. At the beginning of the century, only a tiny fraction of married women were employed outside the home. This fraction grew steadily until the 1950s, when its growth began to accelerate. Today, more than one-half of all married women are working. Stated differently, women were about 15 percent of the labor force in 1890, a little more than 25 percent in 1950, over 40 percent in 1980, and 44 percent in 1986. While employment has declined in most industrial countries, the U.S. has created jobs at breakneck speed—20 million in the past ten years alone. Many experts seem baffled by this phenomenon, but the reason is simple—women.

Women are flooding into the job market, boosting economic growth, and helping to reshape the economy dramatically. And they have been the linchpin in the shift toward services and away from manufacturing.

Because a rapidly expanding labor force is a principal element in propelling an economy onto a fast-growth track, the influx of women into the job market may be the major reason that the U.S. has emerged so much healthier than other countries from the economic shocks (principally the oil price hikes of 1973 and 1979) of the 1970s. Real gross national product has risen faster in the U.S. than in all other major industrialized nations, with the exception of Japan, during the past decade and job growth has been the greatest.

In recent decades, women have filled about two-thirds of all jobs added to the economy. As a result, the number of white males dipped below half the labor force for the first time ever in 1983. Such large-scale entry by women into the workforce would not have been possible in an economy dominated by autos, steel, machine tools, and petrochemicals. Indeed, the trend line for women participating in the labor force tracks quite closely with the declining importance of brawn in jobs. The Information Revolution and the fact that three out of four jobs are now in services as broadly defined are tailor-made developments to meet the growing need and desire of many women to join the paid labor force.

The consolidation of the service economy will continue to work in favor of higher female employment. Of the ten fastest-growing lines of work, many are areas where women traditionally have predominated: nursing, teaching, secretarial work, waitressing, office jobs, and as nursing aides. The Bureau of Labor Statistics estimates that in 1995 the female labor participation rate will average just over 60 percent, compared with 55 percent in 1986. Today's U.S. female labor force-participation rate exceeds that of almost all industrialized nations. It is surpassed only by Sweden, where the rate is about 80 percent. In Japan, the proportion of the female population at work has dropped since 1970, from 49 percent to 47 percent, while in West Germany the participation rate has been about constant, at 38 percent for the past decade.

What this all boils down to is this one remarkable fact: in the 1990s, one in every two American workers will be a woman.

Change #4: Freeing the Employee—Greater Discretion, Greater Participation   It started innocently enough. The idea was to get the workers more involved and, in the 1970s, a handful of companies set up quality circles.

From this small beginning came the seeds of a potential full-scale revolution in the workplace. The watchwords of the revolution are *participative management, employee discretion*, and *commitment*.

Participative management has been defined, by one of its gurus, Robert Townsend, in this way: "By whatever means, creating an environment in which everybody brings their enthusiasm, imagination, and brains to work with them." By Townsend's reckoning, perhaps 6,000 companies are practicing some form of participative management, often led by an entrepreneur who left a large company out of frustration with its regimented control over its employees.

The Conference Board, a business-sponsored research organization, found in its 1984 survey that fifty-two leading corporations are encouraging workers "to participate more directly in the management of their work and the overall goals of their companies." Techniques being used to spur change include: financial rewards to workers for gains in productivity, problem-solving groups and quality circles, autonomous work teams with power to change production methods, and formal agreements between labor and management to cooperate in improving shop conditions and productivity.

Yale University professor Rosabeth Moss Kanter asserts in *The Change Masters* that the key to improving U.S. businesses is the development of "participation management" skills and environments that incorporate the ideas of the firm's employees. After examining the search for innovation at General Electric, General Motors, and Wang Laboratories, Kanter concluded that individuals can make a difference as long as they are permitted to take the initiative to innovate.

Giving employees the opportunity to innovate is a basic idea behind quality circles. It has been estimated that over 90 percent of the *Fortune* 500 companies now have quality circle programs. These programs are actively used by such highly regarded companies as IBM, TRW, Honeywell, Westinghouse, Digital Equipment, and Xerox.

Closely related to participative management is what Daniel Yankelovich, management consultant and author, calls the high discretion workplace. Yankelovich argues that new jobs, new technologies, and new values all combine to create a higher discretion workplace. He notes that more than two-fifths of the members of the workforce say that they have "a great deal of freedom about how to do their jobs," while only about one-fifth (21 percent) say they have very little control. As workers gain greater discretion at the workplace, the human resource factor—people—comes to occupy a position of critical strategic importance in the task of economic revitalization.

This transformation is also a move from control to commitment in the workplace. Harvard Business School professor Richard Walton makes the case that throughout American industry a significant change is under way in long-established approaches to the organization and management of work. At the heart of the traditional "control" model is the wish to establish order, exercise control, and achieve efficiency in the application of the workforce. In the new commitment-based approach to the workforce, jobs are designed to be broader than before, to combine planning and implementation, and to include efforts to upgrade operations, not just maintain them. Individual responsibilities are expected to change as conditions change, and teams, not individuals, often are the organizational units accountable for performance.

The commitment strategy has been tried at the plant level since the early 1970s. The more visible pioneers—such as General Foods at Topeka, Kansas; General Motors at Brookhaven, Mississippi; Cummins Engine at Jamestown, New York; and Procter and Gamble at Lima, Ohio—have, according to Walton, "begun to show how great and productive the contribution of a truly committed work force can be."

A Changing Business Landscape

In the 1960s, American multinationals were feared throughout the world. They were perceived as being able to dictate to whatever market they entered. Since then, the position of big business has been eroded, and many conglomerates that failed to perform are now selling off the various companies to get back to their "core" business. The multinational corporate power now feared is Japanese, not American. For two decades, both the profitability and market share of

America's big businesses have declined. Now deregulation has made it possible for hundreds of new corporations to gain a share of the once-regulated industries. Competition has been increased by entrepreneurs and small businesses. They, not big business, are heralded as the major new job generators and the source of most innovations.

Change #1: Manufacturers That No Longer Manufacture   For more than a decade manufacturers in industry after industry have been closing up shop or curtailing their operations to become marketing organizations for other, mostly foreign, producers. Some of the markets in which the U.S. is losing dominance or out of which it has been driven are autos, steel, machine tools, video recorders, industrial robots, fiber optics, and semiconductor chips. More markets are destined to feel the bite of foreign competition.

The result is the evolution of a new kind of company: the manufacturer that does little or no manufacturing and that is increasingly service oriented. It may perform a host of profit-making functions from design to distribution but it lacks its own production base. In management jargon, these new corporations are "vertically disaggregated," since they rely on other companies for manufactured goods and many crucial business functions. They are coming to be known as network corporations.

Although few large corporations have completely become network organizations, many big companies that continue, for now, to do most of their own manufacturing are edging toward disaggregation. The high cost of developing products and penetrating world markets is turning these large companies to foreign sources for finished products. Others are forming joint ventures and temporary alliances overseas. General Motors, a prototypical vertically integrated company, is engaged in all these activities. Such industrial giants as Firestone, 3M, and General Electric sell finished products bought from foreign companies.

Even IBM, which once prided itself on making virtually everything it sold, adopted a disaggregated format when it decided to enter the personal computer market in 1981. IBM set up its Entry Systems Division (ESD) in Boca Raton, Florida, far from its Armonk, New York, headquarters. IBM relied heavily on off-the-shelf components and contract manufacturers to get its popular PC to market quickly and to keep costs down. ESD provided another plus, too: it fostered the entrepreneurial spirit so prized but so hard to cultivate at large corporations.

Nevertheless, it is smaller companies that best illustrate the network corporation: Nike, makers of athletic shoes with $1 billion in revenues, has 100 manufacturing employees out of 3,500; Liz Claiborne, in apparel with $570 million in revenues, has 250 manufacturing employees out of 2000; Sun Microsystems, in computers with $150 million in revenues, has 200 manufacturing employees out of 1400 (above figures are U.S. employees in 1985).

The basic problem is that today's deindustrialization goes far beyond that of the 1960s and early 1970s when many companies exported blue-collar jobs to low-wage countries. That trend continues but now U.S. companies are also shifting far more valuable things overseas: fundamental technology, management functions, and even the design and engineering skills that are crucial to innovation. If this trend continues, companies may gradually become less adept at understanding how new technology can be exploited and eventually may lose the ability to design. Thus, the sum of all these moves —each of which makes perfect sense for an individual company—could spell ultimate disaster for the U.S. economy as a whole.

Change #2: Going Solo—The Entrepreneurial Drive Entrepreneurs are setting up businesses in large numbers. In 1984, a record 635,000 businesses were started, nearly double the number of a decade ago. In the mid-1980s, half the jobs created have come from self-employment or the formation of new businesses. It does not appear that a let-up is in sight. Surveys of university schools of business show that over 80 percent of the students now list "starting my own business" as their long-range objective.

About six times as many women as men are starting their own ventures. Women in 1983 were already the sole proprietors of 3.2 million small businesses, which is four times greater than the number in 1980 and more than a quarter of the U.S. total. Many are entrepreneurial mothers who, rather than segmenting work and family into structured compartments, are seeking lifestyles that combine them. Exact statistics are difficult to come by, but according to some estimates, 5 million Americans now earn their keep at home, and their numbers are expected to double by 1990.

The evolution to a service economy has greatly facilitated this entrepreneurial drive. While high tech start-ups receive the most publicity, service firms are far more numerous, with particularly high growth rates in such areas as financial services, fast foods, insurance, physical fitness, legal services, and air transport.

Change #3: An Increase in Competition—Deregulation The move to deregulate, which began slowly about a decade ago, is gaining force. The results are highly visible, affecting the lives of all Americans in a personal, direct way. Long-distance airline fares, adjusted for inflation, have declined by almost 50 percent since 1979. Many trucking rates have skidded down 30 percent in real terms since 1980. The cost of buying stock for small investors using discount brokers is 60 percent below the commissions charged by old-line houses.

Most importantly, deregulation has revitalized the critical American industries of finance, telecommunications, and transportation. This $250 billion chunk of the American economy is experiencing a burst of competition, which is encouraging innovation, increasing productivity, and reducing prices. The ripple effects extend into virtually every corner of the American economy since transportation, telecommunications, and the financial system are critical components of the country's infrastructure. Transportation and communication systems provide the efficient movement of goods, services, and information. A freer financial system allows capital to flow to the most productive economic endeavors.

There are short-term costs from deregulation. More than 300 trucking companies, many of them sizable, have gone bankrupt. Braniff and a number of smaller airlines have failed.

These costs must be seen against a broader backdrop. For example, 10,000 small, new operators have entered the trucking industry, and 14 new airlines have been launched since 1978, when Congress eased entry and granted more pricing and route flexibility. The financial industry is treating the public to a breathtaking explosion of products and services—particularly new types of investment funds—offered by a growing number of new institutions.

Change #4: Acquisitions and Divestitures   In the mid-1980s, mergers were occurring in American industry at the rate of 11 every working day. In 1984, 2,543 deals were struck for a stupendous $122 billion. In 1985, the price tag rose to $138 billion and 128 transactions took place valued at more than $100 million each. In 1986, there were over 4,000 deals with a total value of $190 billion.

At the same time, companies have been selling many of their divisions in order to raise cash to pay off debts accumulated in takeovers and to concentrate on their core business. In 1984, U.S. companies sold some 900 divisions and subsidiaries, a 40 percent increase in four years. The dollar value of spin-offs nearly doubled to $29 billion. The centrifugal and centripetal forces of corporate America contribute significantly to the making of the new American economy.

Oil companies, financial service companies, paper companies, indeed almost every industry is affected by these changes in ownership. Among the recent examples:

- *Communications.* IBM sold its portion of Satellite Business Systems to MCI Communications in exchange for up to a 30 percent stake in MCI. MCI got broad new capabilities in data transmission and IBM acquired new muscle in the communications business.

- *Transportation.* United Airlines took a step toward becoming a broad transportation company by acquiring the Hertz Corporation from RCA for $587.5 million. Texas Air became an international carrier in absorbing Trans World Airlines.

- *Banking.* With the Supreme Court's sanction of regional interstate banking, bank marriages are blossoming.

Many of the most recent mergers (1985) were megabuck transactions: Phillip Morris acquiring General Foods ($5.75 billion); Royal Dutch/Shell Group acquiring Shell Oil ($5.67 billion); General Motors acquiring Hughes Aircraft ($5.20 billion); Allied acquiring Signal ($5 billion); R. J. Reynolds acquiring Nabisco Brands ($4.90 billion).

A driving force behind almost all the mergers is the rush to become more competitive in the global marketplace. In many cases, this was the result and the acquisitions made sense, providing economies of scale or good strategic pairings. Many shareholders reaped huge profits on what had been undervalued assets. Among the success stories: Nabisco and Standard Brands, Allied and Bendix, and Heinz and Weight Watchers.

But for every success, there was, remarkably, more than one failure. According to studies cited in *Business Week* in 1985, somewhere between one-half and two-thirds simply did not work. One out of three acquisitions is later undone.

Some of the biggest debacles have been takeovers of mining companies. These businesses commanded fantastic prices when inflation and commodity prices were high. When metals prices drop, mining companies are pariahs to their parents. Atlantic Richfield, for one, took a $785 million write-off in 1984 to close Anaconda Minerals. Amoco spun off Cyprus Mines. General Electric sold off Utah International in 1984 after six years of disappointing performance.

How costly can failed acquisitions be? Ask Mobil. In 1976, the oil giant bought Marcor, parent of Montgomery Ward and Container Corporation of America, for $1.8 billion. Since then, Mobil has sunk $609 million more into Ward in the form of cash infusions and debt forgiveness. Its return: Ward's net profits since Mobil bought it totaled just $17 million through 1985. Mobil plans to take a $500 million write-down on assets and to shrink Ward, probably setting the stage for its eventual sale or spin-off.

Management consultant McKinsey & Company put fifty-eight major acquisition programs undertaken between 1972 and 1983 to two tests: Did the return on the total amount invested in the acquisitions exceed the cost of capital? Did they help their parents outperform the competition in the stock market? The findings: twenty-eight of the fifty-eight clearly failed both tests and six others failed one. Most likely to fail: the megamergers, especially those involving companies in unrelated businesses.

The lesson seems clear: Mergers can work under the right circumstances. What is astounding is that so few companies seem to have studied the historical evidence before plunging ahead.

Spin-offs and divestitures are not necessarily a sign of hardship. The top brass at RCA are rejoicing that the company has shrunk substantially in the past few years. In 1984, it sold its CIT Financial Corporation unit for $1.5 billion after engineering six other spin-offs. After three years of trying, in 1985 it sold Hertz Corporation, its rental car subsidiary. These moves left RCA a straightforward electronics and broadcasting company, a return to the old Radio Corporation of America it was before setting out to diversify nearly two decades ago.

A growing number of companies that once thought diversification and expansion were vital are abruptly changing course. They are slimming down and narrowing their focus, lopping off divisions, and selling assets and product lines. Some companies are even liquidating all their assets—not out of failure but to maximize return to shareholders.

This quantity of voluntary restructuring is something the U.S. has never seen before. Many conglomerates jettisoned bad acquisitions in the early 1970s, but the current, far more pervasive sell-off is different. Companies are making moves to spin-off and scale down healthy businesses to concentrate on what they do best. The most spectacular players in the spin-off game are still the old-line conglomerates. They started to squeeze down soon after their heyday in the 1960s, but they are now restructuring and emerging better positioned for their key markets.

Perhaps the blue-ribbon for spin-offs goes to superconglomerate Gulf + Western Industries. It spun-off some sixty-five diverse subsidiaries from 1983 to 1986 worth more than $4 billion. The word "conglomerate" can be understood when one looks at some of Gulf + Western's recent selloffs (dates are for acquisition and sale): Marquette Company, cement (1977, 1982); E. W. Bliss, industrial equipment (1968, 1983); Consolidated Cigar Company (1968, 1983); Racetracks (1978, 1983); Sega Enterprises, arcade and video games (1970, 1984); Simmons Brands, bedding and furniture (1979, 1985); Automotive Products and Services (1960–70, 1985); Kayser-Roth, apparel (1976, 1985).

All such divestitures and acquisitions create a giant auction market in which almost every dollar of corporate assets seems to be on the block. More and more U.S. businesses are becoming "pure" companies concentrating on just one or two fields that they know well. It is a situation which suits a Wall Street disenchanted with conglomerates.

A study by Frederic M. Scherer, a Swarthmore College economist, of fifteen operations that large companies divested from 1970 to 1982 shows that all but one have done better under their new owners. Buyers tended to trim operating expenses, reduce inventories and receivables, and adopt more aggressive strategies for their markets.

The Growing Realities of Global Economic Interdependence

The economy of the United States is closely linked with the economies of nations throughout the world. There are an estimated 5 billion people on earth. In twenty years, it is expected that there will be more than 6 billion. The United States will account for only 250 to 270 million, less than 5 percent of the total. At the end of World War II, the U.S. economy accounted for about 50 percent of the global economic product. In 1987, the figure was less than 25 percent. Due mainly to economic progress in developing countries, this relative decline is expected to continue.

Change #1: The Impact of International Trade on the Domestic Economy   Most of the commodities we use are traded on world markets, and the prices we pay and receive are world prices. If a burgeoning world population demands more tin or chromium, we will pay higher prices for it. If marine fisheries outside this country are overfished, we will soon pay more. If Third World soils are depleted, we will pay more for such products as coffee, chocolate, tea, and bananas grown elsewhere and in more limited quantities.

The U.S. has entered into far-reaching economic relations with the rest of the world. It imports from and exports to other nations on a larger scale than ever before. As recently as 1973 exports plus imports totaled just a little over $100 billion; by 1986, the total was well over $600 billion. As illustrated by the "world car"—a car assembled from many components produced in many different countries—products are manufactured and marketed by multinational corporations without respect for national boundaries.

Several features distinguish the new foreign trade arena

from that of the past: (1) stiff competition from newly industrialized nations in traditional manufacturing, especially
autos; (2) vigorous competition from Japan and Western
Europe in high technology goods; (3) the transfer of high
technology goods and knowledge across national borders on
an unprecedented scale; (4) the large volume of services
trade; and (5) growing markets in developing nations.

The experience of the 1980s has made clear how important
trade is to U.S. employment, inflation, the value of the dollar, interest rates, and virtually all other items of economic
interest to Americans. The economic and industrial policies
being formulated today in other countries and the U.S. government's policies on exports and imports will affect where
millions of Americans will be working in the 1990s, what
investments should be made, what all Americans will be
consuming, and the prices they will pay.

*Change #2: Japan and the "New Japans" of Asia—Our Ma-
jor Trade Competitors*   Until World War II, the major European nations were the world's dominant traders. In the
1950s and 1960s, the U.S. achieved a rough parity with them
while Americans were laughing at "Made in Japan" products. Today, the story is completely reversed.

U.S. competitiveness is not deteriorating at all vis-à-vis
traditional rivals in the North Atlantic area. Most Western
European countries are suffering more than the U.S. from
high unemployment, lagging high tech industries, and the
general decline of their products in international markets.

Simultaneous with their relative decline has been the rise,
in the 1970s and 1980s, of Japan and the "new Japans" as
vigorous global competitors. Japan's rise has been widely
heralded. What is less well known is that South Korea, Taiwan, Hong Kong, and Singapore, which were industrialized
after Japan and have roughly half Japan's population, now
have a trade surplus with the United States that is 50 percent
the size of Japan's, despite numerous import restrictions.
The "new Japans" export more manufactured goods to the

United States than Britain does, about twice as much as West Germany, and four times as much as France. Their manufactured trade surplus with the U.S. is three times that of the entire European Economic Community. A recent (1985) Presidential Commission on Industrial Competitiveness bluntly observed, "Japan and the newly industrializing nations of the Pacific Basin . . . now represent our major competitive arena."

Japan's rapid and growing dominance in the international trade arena has become legendary in just two decades. Japanese companies have moved relentlessly into Western markets and swept aside the local suppliers. In the mid-1980s they produced three-quarters of the world's videocassette recorders, single lens cameras, and motorcycles. They made one-half the world's ships, two-fifths of its TVs, and a third of its semiconductors and cars.

What these facts indicate is the worldwide strength of Japanese companies. Too often the Japanese threat is viewed in the U.S. as the import penetration of our market. The fact is that the Japanese penetration of our traditional overseas markets is greater and more threatening in the long run than the penetration of the American market.

*   *   *

This brief survey of the major changes transforming America's economic landscape suggests that if you wish to understand the present and see the future of the American economy through the year 2000, you should pay particularly close attention to developments in these seven areas: computer-integrated manufacturing, biotechnology, services, participative management, deregulation, Third World markets, and East Asian competitors.

CHAPTER
★ 2 ★

Economic
Growth

The Issues

The concept of the Gross National Product (GNP) was not introduced into government statistics until 1942. The Employment Act of 1946, the nation's last clear articulation of its basic economic goals, does not even mention the word *growth*. Nonetheless the U.S. experienced a growth surge unparalleled in its history in the 1950s and 1960s—a yearly average of 4.0 percent in each decade. Consequently, Americans came to believe that as a society we *can* and *must* grow indefinitely. Hence, widespread worry developed in the past two decades as growth in the 1970s slowed to a 2.8 percent yearly average, and in the 1980s dropped dramatically to a 2.2 percent average, just over half the rate of the 1950s and 1960s.

Growth, thus, has come to occupy the preeminent place in the policy agenda of the United States. As Herbert Stein, chairman of the Council of Economic Advisers under President Nixon, said, "Growth is now the great god before whom all participants in the discussion of economic policy bow their knee. Merely to allege that a policy will promote growth is sufficient to make a case for it." (*The AEI Economist*, September 1985, p. 1.)

Despite its importance and preeminent policy position, there is still great controversy over some basic issues regarding economic growth: What causes it? What policies best promote it? Has it been a success in the 1980s? Will we have it in the future?

Definition: **Economic growth** is the increase in the country's total and per capita output. It is usually measured yearly and reflected by the Gross National Product. Real GNP growth—the most common measure—is the change in the GNP adjusted for inflation.

The Facts

Economic Growth Rates

Fact #1 *Real growth rates since 1950 exhibit very erratic behavior from year to year. However, these fluctuations with only a handful of exceptions are within a 7 percentage-point range.*

- Between 1952 and 1981, economic growth rates fluctuated between −1.3 percent and 5.8 percent, a narrow 7.1 percentage point range. (There was strong growth in 1950 and 1951, 8.5 percent and 10.3 percent respectively, while the 1982–1986 period saw extremes ranging from −2.5 percent in 1982 to 6.8 percent in 1984.)

- Each decade has had two to three years of negative

growth; the one exception is the 1960s, when growth rates never were below 2.2 percent.

• There have been no years of very strong economic growth (over 7 percent) since 1951.

• Economic growth in the low inflation period of 1954–1970 averaged 3.4 percent a year compared with 2.3 percent average per year during the high inflation period of 1971–1982.

• Economic growth in the past two decades has fallen off sharply from a healthy 4.0 percent average in both the 1950s and 1960s to 2.8 percent in the 1970s and 2.2 percent in the first seven years of the 1980s.

Fact #2   Economic growth has declined significantly in the 1970s and 1980s from the strong record of the 1960s: after inflation, the GNP grew 45.1 percent in the 1960s and 31.9 percent in the 1970s and is projected to end the 1980s at 25 percent (it was 19 percent through mid-1987).

Fact #3   It took 189 years to reach the first $1 trillion GNP mark, just over seven years to get the second trillion, around 4½ years to get the third, and only three years to get the fourth trillion ($4 trillion was exceeded in the middle of 1985).

Fact #4   Since 1950 there have been three five-year periods of fairly weak (less than 3.0 percent) real economic growth: 1955–1959 (2.9 percent), 1970–1974 (2.4 percent), and 1980–1984 (1.9 percent).

Fact #5   The 1980s expansion, the second longest in postwar history, has set both positive (inflation and interest rate reduction) and negative (surge in real imports and budget deficit increase) records.

Compared to the nine-year expansion that began in 1961 and the five-year expansion that started in 1975, the expansion of the 1980s has had:

Figure 1
Real Economic Growth Since 1950

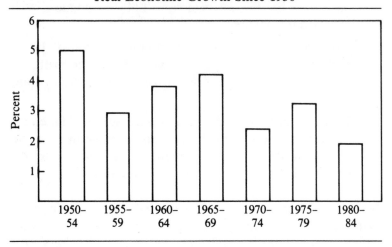

- On the positive side:
  - the greatest inflation reduction
  - a 30–35 percent drop in short- and long-term interest rates, a sharp contrast to the pattern of rising rates in the two previous upturns
  - a 13.9 percent gain in total employment, far ahead of the 11.7 percent gain of the early 1960s
  - an extraordinary rise in the stock market with the Dow Jones industrial average rising from under 1000 in 1982 to over 2700 in mid-1987

- On the negative side:
  - smaller gains in real GNP, industrial production, manufacturing employment, and nonfarm business productivity
  - a record 77 percent surge in real imports
  - the highest federal deficit as a percent of the GNP

Fact #6 *From 1950 to 1985, the percentage of the GNP generated by services increased by 14 percentage points (from 56 to 70 percent) while that from manufacturing decreased by 9 percentage points (from 29 to 20 percent).*

Table 1
Sectors Contributing to GNP
(Billions of $)

	Total GNP	Agri-culture	%	Mining	%	Con-struction	%	Manu-facturing	%	Ser-vices	%
1950	288	21	7	9	3	13	5	84	29	161	56
1960	515	22	4	13	3	24	5	144	28	309	60
1970	1015	30	3	19	2	51	5	252	25	660	65
1980	2732	77	3	107	4	138	5	581	21	1830	67
1985	3988	86	2	121	3	181	5	807	20	2792	70

Fact #7 *There have been "Two Americas" regarding economic growth in the 1980s (1981–1985): (1) the East Coast and California, with strong economic growth averaging 4.9 percent a year, and (2) the heartland states between the coasts, averaging a weak 1.4 percent a year.*

Business Cycles

Fact #1 *There have been thirty business cycles (defined as recession and recovery) in America's history. No two expansions or recessions have been identical.*

- The longest expansion, from 1961 to 1969, lasted 106 months. The shortest, in 1919–1920, was only ten months long.

- The longest recession, from 1873 to 1879, lasted sixty-five months, and the shortest, in 1980, only six months.

- The eight post-World War II expansions have averaged forty-five months while the recessions have averaged only eleven months.

- Of the eleven business slumps since 1929, only the downturns of 1929–1933 and 1937–1938 were considered sufficiently severe to be called "depressions."

- Ten of these eleven recessions were quite short, ranging between six and sixteen months.

Fact #2 *During expansions, the growth of the goods-producing sector has always exceeded that of the services sector; the difference has been especially pronounced in the 1980s expansion, where the goods sector increased 19.0 percent in 1983–1985 vs. 6.4 percent growth in services.*

Table 2

Goods vs. Services
in Postwar Expansions
(percentage growth)

First 3 Years of Expansion Beginning	Goods	Services	Total GNP
1954 II	11.6	11.2	10.8
1961 I	17.4	15.5	16.6
1970 IV	17.6	12.0	14.5
1975 I	15.9	11.0	14.3
Average of above	15.6	12.4	14.0
1982 IV	19.0	6.4	14.1

Source: Economic Report of the President, Washington, DC: U.S. Government Printing Office, 1986, p. 44.

Note: Roman numerals refer to quarters of the year.

Underground Economy

Fact #1   The official GNP figure and growth rates are understated because of the existence of a vast unrecorded "underground economy." The underground economy refers to activity, whether legal or illegal, generating income that is either underreported or not reported at all. Estimates of its size in 1982 ranged from $450 to $810 billion.

Economic Growth and Total Debt

Fact #1   For most of the post-World War II period, total debt (household, business, and all government) fluctuated between 130 percent and 140 percent of the GNP. Beginning in 1981 debt surged at a rate more than double economic growth, boosting total debt to $7.2 trillion at the end of 1986 and the percentage to a postwar high of 173 percent.

- From 1981 to 1986, household debt went from $1,578 billion to $2,452 billion, corporate debt went from $1,591 billion to $2,504 billion (virtually the same figures as household debt), and federal government debt went from $830 billion to $1,706 billion (the fastest increase).

Fact #2   The U.S. is living beyond its means in the 1980s.

- In 1981, total spending by consumers, business, and government came to 98 percent of the GNP while the other 2 percent ($65 billion) was invested abroad.

- In 1986, total spending by consumers, business, and government came to 104 percent of the GNP, the difference made up by borrowing $157 billion abroad.

- In the 1950s, 1960s, and 1970s, by contrast, total spending was always less than the GNP and thus the U.S. was able each year to invest abroad.

- In every previous decade we consumed slightly less than 90 percent of our increase in production while in the 1980s we have consumed 325 percent of it.

Figure 2

Net National Savings—International Comparison
(percent of Gross Domestic Product, 1984)

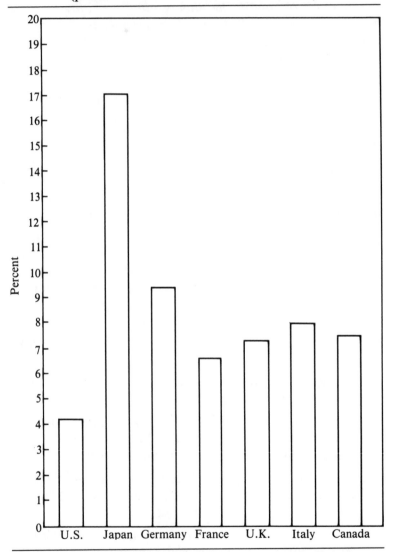

Source: Joint Economic Committee, *1987 Annual Report*, Washington, DC: U.S. Government Printing Office.

Economic Growth, National Savings, and Investment

Fact #1 The U.S. lags far behind other leading industrial nations in terms of net national savings (which feeds into investment and thus contributes to growth).

- The U.S. savings rate over the past twenty years has only been one fourth to one third that of Japan's rate. This means that Japan has considerably more internal savings to draw upon for investment, which itself contributes directly to growth.

Fact #2 The investment/GNP ratio in the U.S. is very low (14.9 percent in 1986) compared to Japan's (28 percent) and has declined since 1979 (from a 17.6 percent level).

U.S. Growth Rates in Comparison to Other Countries

Fact #1 The U.S. economic growth rate has generally been lower than that of other industrial nations and considerably lower than that of developing countries.

Table 3

Comparison of Economic
Growth Rates, 1955–1984
(Average percent change in real GNP)

Years	U.S.	Industrial Market Countries	Developing Countries
1969–1978	2.8	3.4	6.0
1979–1986	2.2	2.4	3.0

Source: International Monetary Fund, Annual Report 1987, Washington, DC, pp. 7 and 11.

Table 4

Economic Growth in Major Industrial Countries, 1970–1986
(Average annual percent change in real GNP)

Country	1970– 1980	1980– 1985	1985– 1986
United States	2.8	2.4	4.1
Canada	4.6	2.5	4.3
Japan	4.7	3.9	3.9
France	3.6	1.2	1.5
Germany	2.7	1.3	2.4
Italy	3.1	.9	2.3
United Kingdom	1.9	1.9	3.2

Source: Economic Report of the President, Washington, DC: U.S. Goverment Printing Office, 1987, p. 104.

Fact #2   U.S. economic growth lagged far behind other major industrial countries in the 1970s but has become one of the top three leaders in the 1980s recovery.

Fact #3   For the 1979–1985 period, the U.S. ranked lowest among industrial market countries in economic progress as measured by some seventeen indicators.

- The U.S. did lead in a few areas, such as employment growth and growth of gross capital investment.

- The U.S. was last in such areas as per capital economic growth, industrial productivity, average unemployment, export growth, and the savings rate.

- The U.S. was last in terms of the misery index, which combines inflation and unemployment.

Fact #4   Foreign demand (exports minus imports) actually dragged down economic growth rates in the U.S. in the first half of the 1980s. Conversely, in Japan and West Germany foreign demand stimulated economic growth.

Fact #5 *Real U.S. GNP grew by a rate of 2.1 percent a year from 1979–1986, about the same growth rate as that of the collective GNP of all other industrial nations; however, in the U.S. most of the growth (70 percent) was due to increases in the number of workers, while in the other countries, most of the growth (85 percent) was due to increases in output per worker.*

Fact #6 *The U.S. spends a much higher percentage of its GNP on defense than any other industrialized nation; in 1986 it spent 6.7 percent versus 3.1 percent in West Germany and 1.0 percent in Japan (the percentages in 1982 were closer: 6.2, 3.4, and 1.0 respectively).*

Interpretation
of the Facts

---

1. What Causes Economic Growth?

The answer you receive to this question depends on whom you ask. Ask a growth expert like Edward Denison and you will receive a lot more than you bargained for. Denison charts economic growth as shown in Table 5.

Ask the Reagan administration's experts and the answer you will receive, as expressed in the 1987 *Economic Report of the President*, will be slightly less esoteric. Table 6 illustrates their "convenient accounting progression from population growth to real GNP growth."

Most economists agree that the three primary economic variables that determine the economy's growth are (1) the size of the labor force, (2) productivity, and (3) the rate of unemployment. The relationship, expressed most simply, is: labor force growth + productivity growth = economic growth. There is also agreement that productivity is the key and the swing factor because it changes much more rapidly than the other two. Economist Pierre Rinfret points to the differences

Table 5

Sources of Economic Growth, 1929–1957— Economist's Perspective
(Contributions to growth rate in percentage points)

National income	3.02
Total factor input	1.68
Labor	1.32
Employment	1.03
Hours	−0.23
Age-sex composition	0.01
Education	0.40
Increased experience and better utilization of women	
workers	0.00
Unallocated	0.11
Capital	0.36
Inventories	0.38
Nonresidential structures and equipment	0.13
Dwellings	0.14
International assets	0.01
Land	0.00
Output per unit of input	1.34
Advances in knowledge and n.e.c.[a]	0.80
Restrictions against optimum use of resources	n.a.[b]
Improved resource allocation	0.30
Farm	0.28
Nonfarm self-employment	0.02
Dwellings occupancy ratio	0.01
Economies of scale	0.33
Irregular factors	−0.10
Weather in farming	−0.01
Labor disputes	0.00
Intensity of demand	−0.09

Source: Edward F. Denison, *Accounting for United States Economic Growth 1929–1969*, Washington, DC: The Brookings Institution, p. 346.

[a] Not elsewhere classified

[b] n.a. Not available

Table 6

Sources of Economic Growth—Reagan Administration's Perspective
(Average annual percent change)

Item	1948 IV to 1973 IV	1973 IV to 1981 III	1973 IV to 1986 IV[a]	1986 IV[a] to 1992 IV
GROWTH IN:				
1) Civilian noninstitutional population aged 16 and over	1.5	1.8	1.2	.9
2) PLUS: Civilian labor force participation rate	.2	.5	.5	.6
3) EQUALS: Civilian labor force	1.8	2.4	1.7	1.5
4) PLUS: Civilian employment rate	−.1	−.4	.1	.3
5) EQUALS: Civilian employment	1.7	2.0	1.8	1.8
6) PLUS: Nonfarm business employment as share of civilian employment	.1	.1	.2	.2
7) EQUALS: Nonfarm business employment	1.7	2.1	2.0	2.0
8) PLUS: Average weekly hours (nonfarm business)	−.4	−.6	−.1	−.1
9) EQUALS: Hours of all persons (nonfarm business)	1.4	1.5	1.9	1.9
10) PLUS: Output per hour (productivity, nonfarm business)	1.9	.6	1.1	1.9
11) EQUALS: Nonfarm business output	3.3	2.0	3.0	3.8
12) LESS: Nonfarm business output as share of real GNP	.0	−.1	.5	.3
13) EQUALS: Real GNP	3.3	2.2	2.4	3.5

Sources: Department of Commerce (Bureau of the Census and Bureau of Economic Analysis), Department of Labor (Bureau of Labor Statistics), and Council of Economic Advisers.

[a] Data for 1986 IV are preliminary.

Note: Based on seasonally adjusted data. Detail may not add to totals due to rounding.

between the 1948–1968 and the 1969–1981 periods as a firm illustration of the key role of productivity. In the earlier period, real GNP averaged 3.9 percent per year growth and GNP per employee (a productivity measure) increased 2.5 percent annually. In the later period, real GNP growth dropped to a 2 percent average and productivity barely increased. To Rinfret (and many others), the reason for the growth slowdown was quite straightforward: "We were not realizing our historical productivity gains."

2. What Economic Policies Best Promote Economic Growth?

There are four major contending schools of thought—the Keynesians, the conventional conservatives, the supply-siders, and the planners—each with their own beliefs on how to promote economic growth.

The Keynesians   The Keynesians have occupied the mainstream of economics ever since John Maynard Keynes exploded onto the scene in the 1930s with his new ideas of macroeconomic management of the economy. Most of the big names in economics since then—such as Paul Samuelson, James Tobin, and Charles Schultze—have been Keynesians.

Politically, this group was best represented in recent years in the Carter administration. The annual economic reports of the President, coming from the Council of Economic Advisers chaired by Charles Schultze, showed increasing concern about the slowdown of productivity growth and potential output. They believed that if you stimulated demand in the economy sufficiently, this would lead to full employment. In particular, they proposed tax cuts, focused on business taxes, rejecting the other principal Keynesian means of boosting demand: increased government spending. By cutting business taxes, they hoped to increase the incentive to invest and to increase the savings of business.

Conventional Conservatives   Leaders of the business and financial community were the spokespersons for this group in the 1970s. Alongside them were such well-recognized and well-respected economists as Milton Friedman, Alan Greenspan, chairman of the Federal Reserve, and Herbert Stein. Their thinking was very similar to that of the Keynesians, particularly in their pro-growth tax program, which was almost exclusively a pro-business tax program. They disagreed with the Keynesians in stressing the importance of the capital shortage (insufficent savings relative to the nation's investment needs).

The Supply-Siders   This group, which arose in the late 1970s led by economist Arthur Laffer and Representative Jack Kemp, believed the focus of policy should be the relation between tax deductions and economic growth. In their view, cutting taxes promoted growth by providing greater incentives for consumption and investment. This growth, in turn, would increase tax revenues over time and reduce or eliminate any short-term budget deficits.

The Planners   The planners first emerged as a force in the mid-1970s, advocating that more or better planning by the government could achieve broad national economic objectives, including economic growth. Their legislative vehicle was the 1978 Humphrey-Hawkins Bill, an amendment to the Employment Act of 1946 which, unlike the original act, introduced the idea of growth (and of *full* employment). In 1980, and right up through 1984, the planning approach to economic growth appeared under the concept "industrial policy." Industrial policy, like planning before it, covered a whole host of actions the government could take to stimulate economic growth, such as greater R&D incentives, increased and better targeted spending on education, favorable trade policies for industry, a national industrial development bank, and so forth.

*   *   *

Although the supply-siders have gained the most headlines in the 1980s, the Reagan administration views are best represented by conventional conservatives. The Reagan administration's position on growth-promoting policies is clearly spelled out in its 1986 *Economic Report of the President*. Its priorities are:

1. Establish Appropriate Incentives Through Relative Prices:
   It is crucial that economic policies operate to confront individuals with relative prices (i.e., market-determined) of products and factors accurately reflecting true values.

2. Maintain Reasonable Fiscal Discipline:
   Governments cannot run large and persistent fiscal deficits; the amount of public sector spending should be limited.

3. Restrain General Price Inflation:
   Successful efforts to reduce high inflation rates have usually been associated with higher real (i.e., inflation-adjusted) economic growth.

4. Maintain an Open Policy Toward International Trade:
   Internal relative prices of internationally traded goods should not diverge too far from world market prices due to import tariffs, quotas, export taxes, subsidies, or other non-free-market policies.

5. Limit Distortions of Domestic Product and Factor Markets:
   The appropriate role of government policy is to promote competition, *not* to support cartels or other anticompetitive practices.

6. Maintain Political Stability:
   A political and economic system that does not provide reasonable assurances that those who make the

sacrifices will enjoy a fair share of the reward will almost inevitably fail to generate much growth.

Despite generations of study and promises, economic growth is still never assured. This uncertainty factor was summed up by Herbert Stein:

> [W]e do not know much with confidence about how to get more economic growth. If we knew more, such diverse ideas about pro-growth policy would not persist for so long . . . our ignorance is great with respect to the efficiency-improvement contribution to growth . . . that is only the beginning of what we do not know, however. Even if we understood the contribution of the various factors to growth, we would still not know much about the policies that would increase the contributing factors . . . the problem is complicated because most policies for increasing growth require the rearrangement of the uses of a total of resources that is given at the outset. These rearrangements often have negative as well as positive consequences for growth and the direction of the net effect is hard to tell. (H. Stein, "Reflections on Growth," *The AEI Economist*, September 1985, pp. 8–9.)

As proof of this general ignorance concerning policy paths to attain and maintain growth, one has only to look to the endurance of the business cycle:

> Indeed, the [business] cycle's perseverance constitutes a distinct enhancement for the economics profession. It serves as indelible proof that the experts, whatever their stripe, have failed to deal with or even fathom the economy's intricacies. (*The Wall Street Journal*, November 1, 1984.)

3. How Successful Has Economic Growth Been in the 1980s?

The five-year expansion (1983–1987) is beyond dispute. The success of that expansion is in question. Two voices in the argument are summed up by the Council of Economic Advisers' 1986 *Economic Report of the President* and the Center for Popular Economics in *Economic Report of the People* (1986).

Judging Growth in the 1980s

A Success:
Economic Report of the President

A Failure:
Economic Report of the People

The American economy is now in the fourth year of robust expansion that has increased employment by more than 9 million, sustained the greatest advance in business fixed investment of any comparable period in the postwar era, while inflation has remained at less than a third of the rate prevailing when the Administration took office. Interest rates are at the lowest levels of this decade. Long-term interest rates, in particular, have declined 5 percentage points from their peaks in 1981, and home mortgage rates are down by 7 percentage points. Worldwide confidence in the vitality of the U.S. economy has been restored, as is reflected in the unprecedented inflow of foreign investment and the substantial appreciation of the dollar since 1980. (*Economic Report of the President*, 1986, Washington, DC: U.S. Government Printing Office, p. 23.)

But the old-time religion of the free market has not delivered the goods. Its sole success has been a pyrrhic victory over inflation, one for which the American people are paying dearly. And they will continue to pay for years to come. Nor has it reversed the long-term rise in the level of unemployment, sagging productivity, or lack of improvement in living standards. Rather, as we will show in the pages which follow, the new conservative orthodoxy has left a path of economic indebtedness and social division . . . conservative economics has not only clubbed a vast majority of Americans, widening economic disparities; it has also failed to reverse the underlying decline in U.S. economic performance. Relying on the club, it has mortgaged the future, steering the economy toward a risky, uncertain, highly-debted existence of sluggish growth and high unemployment. Conservative economics should be supplanted not only because it is unfair and undemocratic but also because it is ineffective and risky. (*Economic Report of the People*, Boston: South End Press, 1986, pp. 3–4.)

4. What Does the Future Hold?

The Congressional Budget Office is considerably less optimistic than the administration, as the most recent (August 1987) forecasts of each show.

Table 7
Forecasts of Growth
(Percentage growth rate)

Real GNP	1989	1990	1991	1992
Administration	3.4	3.4	3.3	3.1
CBO*	2.6	2.7	2.7	2.7

* Congressional Budget Office

The consensus of private economists is that real GNP should grow at an average rate of around 3 percent from 1988 to 1992. These economists believe that large problems remain unresolved, but expect the U.S. economic climate will remain fundamentally better than it was in the 1970s. The International Monetary Fund agrees, predicting a "period of sustained and better balanced growth" for all the industrial nations.

But what about the possibility of an economic collapse— another Great Depression? The vast majority of economists feel it is highly unlikely, citing changes in attitudes, institutions, and the economy's make-up, as well as closer monitoring of business activity. Arthur Burns, who served as Federal Reserve Board chairman under Presidents Nixon, Ford, and Carter, stressed the role of attitude: "I still see no new Great Depression in the cards for the simple reason that the government can prevent collapse, and the government will prevent it." Paul Samuelson, a Nobel laureate, echoes this sentiment, pointing out that the difference between now and the 1930s is that the government "will do what it has to do" to avert a collapse. Other specific factors cited by economists that make a depression highly unlikely are: (1) the expanding role of such institutions as the Federal Deposit Insurance Corporation; (2) various government income maintenance programs ranging from unemployment compensation to farm price supports; (3) the structure of employment, with over two-thirds of jobs within the service sector where jobs are more stable and inventory problems do not normally arise; (4) the improvement in resources available to policy makers in gauging the economy's course.

Finally there are the disciples of Kondratieff, a Russian economist, who believe that the economy operates in fifty- to sixty-year waves. There are, however, differences of opinion in the long-wave camp. Some see in the disinflationary environment of 1983–1986 an eerie resemblance to the 1920s when prosperity gave way to outright deflation and the Depression. Jay Forrester of the Massachusetts Institute of Technology is a leading Kondratieff bear: "We're still on the declining side of the wave, and we've got the whole debt situation to unravel before the thing is done." (*Business Week*, May 5, 1986, p. 88.) He points to an array of troubling signs: the rate of business failures set a postwar record last year and is still climbing; debt is growing twice as fast as the Gross National Product; and a slump in agriculture has caused a continuing slide in farmland prices.

Another group, led by Walt Whitman Rostow, an economic historian at the University of Texas, argues that the current price drop phase of the wave is not necessarily a downer. Far from presaging a depression, this group asserts that the price drop signals that the world is on the verge of a massive turn to new technologies and that this changeover will foster a new era of growth in productivity and incomes. Their key point is that disinflation has set the stage for a major growth cycle.

CHAPTER ★ 3 ★

Inflation

The Issues

The United States has had inflation in all but two years since the end of World War II that separates into three distinct phases. The first was the 1953–1965 period, when inflation generally ran below 2 percent per year. From 1973 to 1982 inflation in every year was greater than 6 percent, except for 1976. During the 1983–1986 period, inflation once again returned to a fairly low range of 1 to 4 percent annually.

The effects of high inflation became evident to all Americans in the late 1970s as consumers saw the prices of many basic items double, triple, or even quadruple. Business leaders saw their companies' performance figures go from positive to negative when inflation was factored in. Investors in stocks, bonds, and T-bills saw their returns dwindle compared to returns on hard assets such as gold, oil, diamonds, and farmland.

Definition: **Inflation** can be measured by changes in the Consumer Price Index (CPI), the producer price index (PPI), and the "GNP implicit price deflator." Most popular discussions of inflation focus on the CPI, which measures the price increases for a market basket of common consumer items.

The Facts

U.S. Experience: 1946–1986

Fact #1   *In the 1950s and 1960s inflation's yearly average was 2.1 and 2.4 percent, respectively. In the 1970s and 1980s (through 1987) the yearly averages were 7.1 and 5.7 percent, about triple the earlier averages.*

Fact #2   *In each of the four post-World War II decades, the inflation rate for commodities was below the overall average inflation rate, while the rate for services was above. The average inflation rate for energy (due to the OPEC oil shocks) went from 1.3 percent in the 1960s to 10.5 percent in the 1970s (an eight-fold increase) and to 8.1 percent in the early 1980s.*

Recent Experience: 1982–1986

Fact #1   *The CPI increased at a rate of only 1.1 percent in 1986, the smallest annual increase since a 0.7 percent rise in 1961 and only one-fourth the increase of the previous four years.*

Fact #2   *The low 1.1 percent inflation rate for 1986 masked a vast range of price increases (or decreases) for major consumer items.*

Figure 1

Annual Inflation Rates
(Percent change in the CPI)

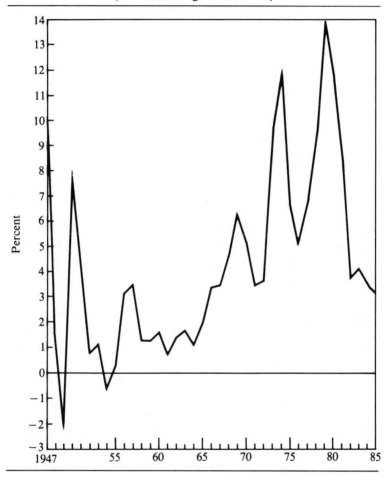

Table 1

Price Increases for Major
Consumer Items, 1986
(Percent changes)

Overall CPI	+ 1.1
Food	+ 3.8
Shelter	+ 4.6
Fuel and Other Utilities	− 5.7
Apparel and Upkeep	+ 0.9
New Cars	+ 5.8
Motor Fuel	− 30.6
Medical Care	7.7

Source: Department of Labor, Bureau of Labor Statistics

Fact #3   The low rate of inflation was due almost entirely to a sharp 20 percent drop in energy prices—the price increase, excluding energy, was 3.8 percent, just under the 4 to 4.5 percent range of the previous four years.

Fact #4   In 1985 and 1986, while the overall inflation rate rose a modest 5.3 percent, the prices of common small-ticket consumer purchases rose by 28 percent in a survey of thirty-six commonly purchased items.

Inflation's Powerful Impact

Fact #1   In just a decade (1973–1982), the prices of many basic consumption items doubled, tripled, or even quadrupled. For example, from 1973 to 1982, a loaf of bread went from $.38 to $.93, a gallon of gas from $.34 to $1.20, and a mid-sized car from $3,200 to $9,200.

Fact #2   With inflation factored in, corporate performance went from reported good results to all negative results in the early 1980s. From 1980 to 1984, sales went from a reported

Table 2

High Inflation in Basic
Small Consumer Items, 1985–1986

	Price*		Percent rise
	Jan. '85	Jan. '87	
Ground coffee (1 lb.)	$ 1.79	$ 3.19	78.2
Liquid detergent (22 oz.)	1.29	1.89	46.5
Toothpaste (5 oz.)	0.99	1.39	40.4
Round beef (1 lb.)	1.99	2.79	40.2
Taxi (2-mi. ride)	3.10	4.25	37.1
Orange juice (½ gal.)	1.69	2.29	35.5
Peanut butter (18 oz.)	1.79	2.39	33.5
Pack of gum	0.45	0.60	33.3
Ice cream (1 pt.)	1.09	1.45	33.0
Pizza (slice)	0.95	1.25	31.6
Bananas (1 lb.)	0.39	0.49	25.6
Woman's haircut	20.00	25.00	25.0
Movie	5.00	6.00	20.0
Shoe shine	1.25	1.50	20.0
Paperback book	3.75	4.35	16.0
Imported beer (bottle)	1.30	1.50	15.4
Dry cleaning of suit	6.00	6.75	12.5
Newsmagazine	1.75	1.95	11.4
Hamburger & milk shake	2.63	2.88	9.5
Sole and rubber heels	25.00	27.00	8.0

Source: Manufacturers Hanover Trust Co.

* New York City retail levels

5.6 percent to −2.1 percent after adjustment for inflation; dividends went from +4.3 percent to −3.2 percent; and profits went from −1.1 percent to −15.4 percent.

Fact #3   Investors' return on assets has been totally reversed in the 1970s from the 1970s, with real assets (such as oil and gold) going from the top to the bottom, and financial assets (such as stocks and bonds) going from the bottom to the top.

Inflation's Impact on an Individual

Mr. George Frazier, age 61, sold his small superette in 1974 and took the $60,000 proceeds along with his retirement nest egg and bought $120,000 worth of risk-free, long-term U.S. Treasury bonds with a 6 percent yield. The $7,200 of yearly income for the bond's twenty-five years seemed more than adequate. Yet in 1980, he and his wife were scrimping and scraping, having come through a period since 1974 in which inflation averaged 6.6 percent a year. To add to their misery, they find that the bonds are now worth only about 60 cents on the dollar if they are not held to maturity—an instant $48,000 erosion in their value. But things do get worse. The $72,000 value of the bonds is itself worth less than 61.5 cents on the dollar in terms of present purchasing power. Thus, inflation over just six years had reduced his 1974 $120,000 nest egg investment to a value of $44,280.

The 1980s Disinflation

Fact #1   The drastic slowing of inflation in the 1983–86 period made many people winners; but there were also many losers from such disinflation.

Inflation Throughout History

Fact #1   Stable prices are not the norm; the history of prices does not show a single era of stable prices.

Table 3
Disinflation's Impact: Winners and Losers
(1983–1986)

WINNERS	LOSERS
Savers	Farmers, farmland speculators
Companies with little debt	
Consumers with few install-ment loans	Workers dependent on cost of living raises
Investors in interest-sensitive stocks	Highly leveraged (big debt) homeowners
Investors in bonds	Some real estate speculators
Companies with high rate of productivity	Highly leveraged consumers and companies
Companies able to use tech-nology to cut prices	Capital-intensive firms with little price flexibility
People on fixed incomes	OPEC and other cartels
	Investors in tangibles

Fact #2 *Many of the leading contemporary solutions to inflation have deep historical roots: the prescription to hold the money supply down dates to John Locke (1632–1704) and David Hume (1711–1776). The history of wage and price controls can be traced to Code of Hammurabi, some 4,000 years ago.*

Inflation Around the World

Fact #1 *Widespread and persistent inflation has been a leading characteristic of the world economy since the end of World War II. The postwar generation has seen no important deflation, and prices have risen in every country reported on by the International Monetary Fund.*

Fact #2 *In the major industrial countries, inflation went from low levels in 1960 to moderate levels in 1970 to high levels in 1980 and back down to moderate levels in 1985 and 1986.*

Table 4

Inflation Rates in Major
Industrial Countries: 1960–1986

	Annual percent increase in consumer prices				
	1960	1970	1980	1985	1986
Major Industrial Countries	1.9	5.6	11.9	4.2	n.a.
United States	1.6	5.9	13.5	3.5	1.9
Japan	3.7	7.6	8.0	2.1	0.6
West Germany	1.5	3.4	5.4	2.2	−0.2
France	4.2	5.9	13.8	5.8	2.7
Britain	1.0	6.4	18.0	6.1	3.4

Sources: International Monetary Fund; Data Resources, Inc.

Table 5

Recent Inflation in Selected
Countries: 1983–1985

	(Percent increase)		
Country	1983	1984	1985
Bolivia	276	1,281	3,408
Argentina	344	627	851
Israel	146	374	407
Brazil	142	197	220
Peru	111	110	130
Mexico	102	66	65
Italy	14.7	10.8	9.3
Britain	4.6	5.0	6.1
Canada	5.8	4.3	3.7
United States	3.2	4.3	3.7
West Germany	3.3	2.4	2.5
Japan	1.8	2.3	1.6

Note: 1985 figures compare mid-year 1985 prices with those of a year earlier.

Fact #3 *In recent years, the U.S. rate of inflation has been very low relative to most countries in the world, with the main exceptions being Japan and West Germany.*

Interpretation
of the Facts

---

1. The Causes of High Inflation
in the 1970s

Despite variations and individual pet theories, analysts are divided into two major camps over the cause of inflation in the 1970s: the "cost-push" school and the "demand-pull" school. The former look at those forces that boost costs to suppliers and producers while the latter look at those forces that boost the level of demand in the economy. Those favoring the cost-push explanation blame OPEC (Organization of Petroleum Exporting Countries) price increases, monopolistic pricing strategies by big business, union-inspired wage increases, and the burden of proliferating government regulation. The demand-pullers blame overextended and materialistic consumers, a bloated public sector, or an obliging Federal Reserve Board for increasing the money supply. Another way to group the theorists is to divide them into those who blame "many sources" versus those who blame "one source." Three groups stand out: the Keynesians, the monetarists, and the "supply-shock" adherents.

The Keynesian group is by far the largest as it includes most commentators on inflation. Keynesians emphasize that inflation must be explained by a host of contributing factors. They usually emphasize, however, one or two key factors, the leading ones being federal budget deficits, excessive money growth, and union-driven wage increases.

The 1980 President's Commission for a National Agenda for the Eighties—a diverse political, ideological, and professional group—provides a dramatic example of this eclectic

Keynesian perspective. The "disagreement within the Panel on which view would be given priority in analyzing inflation" led them to submit a lengthy list of contributing causes:

- Difficulties in economic fine-tuning.

- The breakdown of the Phillips curve relationship (the presumed inverse relationship between inflation and unemployment rates).

- The disastrous results of wage-price guidelines and controls.

- Excessive rates of growth of the money supply.

- The depreciation of the dollar.

- The slowdown in the growth of productivity and the accompanying rise in unit-labor costs.

- Substantial externally-caused price increases in the four basic necessities (food, energy, housing, and medical care).

- Price shocks, such as occurred in oil and food.

- Government microeconomic policies that address the problems and needs of specific industries, areas, or population groups (such as agricultural price supports, tariffs and quotas on imports, and economic regulation that creates cartels and monopolies).

Albert Sommers, long-time chief economist of the Conference Board, well summarizes the eclectic perspective:

No effort to explain the multiple interconnections that constitute the "cause" of modern inflation can hope to be complete. Modern inflation is rooted in a social, political, technological and ethical history; in the frictions that arise at critical interfaces within the system. . . .

Most generally of all, modern Western inflation reflects a distribution of political power that is substantially more egalitarian than the natural distribution of economic power in a free-market system. . . .

The implication of this description is that there are no one-shot cures for inflation, no simple remedy or combination of remedies. Anti-inflation proposals that focus exclusively on balancing the federal budget, or containing the growth of money, or elimination of regulation, or the removal of excessive profits, or reduction in the power of unions—such proposals ignore the systematic character of inflation, and its deep roots in social history. (Albert Sommers, *Inflation: The Crucial Challenge in the 1980s*, The Conference Board, pp. 29–30.)

Monetarists maintain that too rapid a growth of the money supply is the only real cause of inflation. The intellectual leader of this school of thought is Milton Friedman, an economics professor widely known as America's leading monetarist. A leading current proponent is Beryl Sprinkel, chairman of the President's Council of Economic Advisers.

The "supply shock" adherents point to the large and rapid increase in the price of basic necessities, particularly energy and food, as the driving inflationary force of the 1970s. Gar Alperovitz and Jeff Faux, two of the country's leading liberal economists, are prime developers of this "supply shock" school of thought.

The "supply shock" and monetarist groups largely define the conventional ends of the left-right spectrum. Their argument is summarized in the following excerpts on the causes of inflation:

The Causes of Inflation

Monetarist Perspective
It is widely believed that monetarism was tried in the United States from 1979 to 1984 and that it did not work in practice. That is very far from the truth. In October 1979, the Federal Reserve in desperation adopted

"Supply Shock" Perspective
The predominant pattern of recent inflation has been made up of three distinct stages. The first stage is brought on by one or more jolts. The second stage is the transmission of the jolts into higher prices, wages, and

monetarist rhetoric. It did not then and has not since adopted a monetarist policy. . . .

A monetarist policy consists of two essential items: First, the acceptance of a monetary aggregate by the monetary authorities as their prime target; second, the adoption of policies directed at producing a stable and predictable rate of growth in that monetary aggregate. This general description covers many variants—ranging from an absolutely fixed monetary growth target such as I have favored to the use of monetary growth as a means of fine-tuning the economy. . . .

All in all, the period since the change in Federal Reserve policy, like the prior three years and the decades before that, strongly support the conclusion that erratic monetary growth produces erratic economic growth and that the monetarist prescription of steady monetary growth would mean steadier, albeit not completely steady, economic growth. (Milton Friedman in *Monetarism, Inflation, and the Federal Reserve*, Joint Economic Committee, U.S. Congress, June 27, 1985. Washington, D.C.: U.S. Government Printing Office, pp. 51, 55.)

interest rates throughout the economy. Finally, there is subsequent low productivity stemming from sluggish growth that makes the economy less productive and even more vulnerable to the next inflationary jolt. . . .

The fact that our recent inflation was largely initiated by, and concentrated in the four key sectors we have just reviewed, is not in significant dispute. The statistical facts stand for themselves. With some reservations about precisely how the housing component of the Consumer Price Index should be calculated, economists of every political persuasion have recognized this reality. . . .

Perspective in economics is as important as it is in art. The perspective of conventional inflation theory is dominated by the abstract assumptions of the competitive model and the obsession with seeing inflation solely as a phenomenon of aggregates—the general price level. The sectoral pattern of inflation is recognized but dismissed as an oddity because it does not conform to theory. (Gar Alperovitz and Jeff Faux, *Rebuilding America*, New York: Pantheon Books, 1984, pp. 163, 165, 166).

2. Inflation Remedies

Since 1946, every president except Eisenhower has constructed a policy for the "solution" of inflation. Their anti-inflation policies are known generically as wage-price policies (or income policies). They are intended to halt the wage-price spiral either through the imposition of voluntary "guideposts" or mandatory "controls."

In the immediate postwar period, Truman was compelled by the threat of high inflation to administer and then to dismantle a complex system of controls. He reapplied controls during the war in Korea. During the Eisenhower era, prices were relatively stable and no specific wage and price tools were required.

There was a rise in inflation during the Kennedy administration. The Kennedy guidelines, first applied in 1962, were shaped largely in response to price shifts in the steel industry, an industry viewed by the government as a key source of price increases in a slack economy. It was believed inflation could be controlled if wage changes reflected productivity changes and prices reflected only a pass-through of labor costs.

The Johnson administration promoted these policies, too. However, business and labor officials ignored them as economic growth and inflation accelerated. Wage settlements in the construction, airline, and metropolitan transit industries all broke the guidelines. The Kennedy guidelines were dismantled in 1967.

Four years later, wages and prices were again subject to control as the demands of the Vietnam War had overheated the economy. In 1971, an inflation rate of 5 percent, up from a 2.4 percent average in the 1960s, impelled the Nixon administration to abandon its noninterventionist approach. Solemnly announcing, "I am now a Keynesian," Nixon resorted to wage-price controls. A ninety-day freeze on all prices, rents, wages, and salaries began on August 15, 1971, as part of the Economic Stabilization Program (ESP). After the freeze, called Phase I of the ESP, comprehensive and mandatory Phase II guidelines were established. They differed from the Kennedy guideposts in that allowable wage increases were based on the trend in productivity of the overall economy rather than on an industry-specific figure. Before his resignation, Nixon was to enact two more phases of the ESP and a second freeze covering only prices.

In his first presidential address to Congress on August 12, 1974, President Ford asked Congress to reactivate the Cost of Living Council to deal with inflation. Ford stated his opposition to controls and urged Congress to create an agency to "monitor wages and prices to expose abuses." Twelve days later, he signed a bill creating the Council on Wage and Price Stability (CWPS). Although the formal powers of CWPS were quite limited, its mandate was broad: to examine wage and price behavior throughout the economy and to determine the extent to which the activities of the federal government were contributing to inflation. This marked the first time that the federal government turned the anti-inflation spotlight on itself in a systematic fashion.

In October 1978, the Carter administration announced new wage-price standards as part of a more comprehensive anti-inflation program. The new program was intended to be a voluntary effort, with CWPS performing a formal review of average wage and price increases for employee units and product lines. The program ended after two years as workers and firms appeared unwilling to moderate wage and price rises. At the time of its termination in 1980, the country was experiencing a record 13.3 percent inflation rate. This rate was the final judgment on CWPS and the wage-price standards—they had by and large failed as inflation fighters.

3. Inflation's Decline in the Early 1980s

The record testifies that despite the best efforts of six presidents, inflation kept moving stubbornly upward. It was only halted and reversed when the one solution not yet tried—

squeezing aggregate demand, that is, engineering a serious recession—was put into effect in 1981.

Contrasting the number of interpretations for the cause of the 1970s' high inflation rates, there is virtual unanimity that inflation was down in the early 1980s from 12.4 percent in 1980 to 3.9 percent in 1982 because of the money-crunch-induced recession of 1981–1982. In the more refined terminology of the Federal Reserve, it was "the slack in the economy that developed as growth in aggregate demand was constrained, primarily by a policy of monetary restraint."

The country's highest postwar inflation was halted and reversed principally by a monetary policy that substantially reduced the growth of the money supply, leading to the worst recession since the Great Depression. The large and rapid decline in the money supply growth rate in 1981 and 1982 put the economy through what a Federal Reserve Board economist described as "one of the most difficult periods of adjustment in the postwar era." The real gross national product was slightly lower in the final quarter of 1982 than it had been three years earlier. Manufacturing capacity utilization, which had peaked at 87.4 percent in early 1979, plunged to 69.5 percent toward the end of 1982. The civilian unemployment rate climbed from 5.7 percent to more than 10.5 percent over the same period. It was these types of serious "costs" that no one prior to Paul Volcker, the Federal Reserve Board chairman installed in 1979, had been willing to incur.

4. The Future

According to the U.S. government, *low inflation* will prevail for the period 1988–1992. There is an uncharacteristic display of consensus by the Reagan administration and the Congressional Budget Office (CBO) on this point. The former has the Consumer Price Index falling steadily from 4.4 percent in 1988 to 2.5 percent in 1992, while the latter has it falling from 5.2 percent in 1988 to 4.4 percent in 1992.

The administration's projection assumes monetary policy will reduce money supply growth rates while the CBO assumes that labor markets start to tighten when the unemployment rate nears 6.0 percent. Both projections do contain a considerable degree of uncertainty. The major wild cards over the next few years are: oil prices, the value of the dollar (on international exchange markets), the budget deficit, and political will.

The course of inflation will be largely determined by the degree to which the downward pull of low oil prices—which have a downward ripple effect throughout the economy—is offset by the upward push of a devalued dollar, which will increase import prices and give U.S. producers more room to raise their own prices.

Another major factor is the budget deficit. The CBO's projection of low and stable inflation assumes that both nominal and real interest rates will decline in the 1988–1992 period, reflecting the impact of lower deficits under current law. Many observers point out that with $100 billion to $200 billion in red ink likely to be an annual occurrence for the remainder of the decade, the easiest way out politically would be high inflation. The government's creditors would then be paid back in cheaper dollars. Inflation may be politically preferable to raising taxes and cutting spending, or a combination of the two. As Rudolph Penner, head of the Congressional Budget Office, warns: "The faster we increase the debt, the more temptation there will be to tax it away with inflation. One can create circumstances in which there is essentially no choice but to inflate."

What virtually all observers see as the most fundamental determinant of whether inflation will rise is the commitment of economic policy makers to its demise. The further the double-digit inflation of the 1970s recedes in the public's memory, the less political pressure will be applied for an anti-inflationary course in Washington. The Reagan administration speaks to this point in its 1986 *Economic Report of the President*:

Memories of rising inflation in the 1970s are still fresh in the public's mind. If inflation were allowed to resurge to the rates recorded in the late 1970s, inflation expectations would likely rise rapidly, and quickly and firmly become embedded in economic behavior . . . the government, particularly the Federal Reserve, has a responsibility to provide price stability. . . . The President remains committed to his original objectives of restoring price stability and sustaining economic growth.

Beyond these policy considerations, the big unknown is whether moderate inflation can be maintained. Some economists feel it is almost impossible to keep a constant inflation rate. With a 5 percent inflation rate, for example, prices will double in sixteen years. That prospect alone will force consumers to take defensive action. The CBO's Penner observed, "While those psychological expectations are there people will take actions to protect themselves against inflation, and that in itself causes inflation." Columnist Robert Samuelson noted about inflation in the 1970s: "Our fantasy was that a little bit of inflation is a good thing; but a little inflation soon feeds on itself and becomes uncontrollable."

CHAPTER
★ 4 ★

Employment and Unemployment

The Issues

Unemployment has been a key focus of American economic policy since the Great Depression of the 1930s. The major piece of economic legislation in the forty years since the close of World War II is the Employment Act of 1946, which clearly states that promoting "maximum employment" was an important national economic goal, but did not mention full employment. Throughout the 1960s and 1970s, the unemployment rate was closely watched. Whenever the rate went too far above the prevailing "full employment" rate—around 4 percent in the 1960s and early 1970s—a sizable economic policy offensive was launched to bring it down, which involved a variety of job-creation and job-training programs.

In the 1980s there has been little discussion of unemployment. It is as though the problem has disappeared. This is ironic since the average annual unemployment rate is significantly higher than in the previous three decades.

Not surprisingly, different explanations and remedies are offered for unemployment. An additional issue concerns the value of the official unemployment rate. Some analysts suggest that it seriously underestimates joblessness.

Definition: The official **unemployment rate** is calculated by dividing the number of people who are unemployed by the total number of people in the labor force. It is based on a Labor Department survey of 59,000 selected households one week every month. People are considered employed if they work full time; if they worked in their own business or profession or on a farm; or if they worked fifteen hours or more in an enterprise operated by a member of their family, whether they were paid or not. People are considered unemployed if they had no job during the survey week, provided that they also were available for work during the survey week and that they tried to find employment sometime in the four weeks prior to the survey week. Other people counted among the unemployed are those not looking for work because they were laid off and are waiting to be recalled, and those expected to report to a job within thirty days. People who have given up looking for work are not considered "unemployed."

The Facts

Basic Unemployment Rates

Fact #1   *The unemployment rate has increased in five administrations during the last four decades and has doubled since World War II. The average annual unemployment rate in each postwar decade was 4.5 percent in the 1950s, 4.8 percent in the 1960s, 6.2 percent in the 1970s, and 8.0 percent in the 1980s.*

Fact #2   The national unemployment rate at any given time spans conditions for various population subgroups ranging from boom-time rates through recession and on to depression rates.

- In September 1987, white men and women aged twenty and older were enjoying boom-time unemployment rates of 3.9 and 4.7 percent respectively.

- At the same time, all of the rest of the population—all white teenagers and blacks aged twenty and older—experienced serious recession-level rates (10–14 percent).

- At the same time, black teenagers were experiencing severe depression-level rates (31.5 percent).

Fact #3   The unemployment rate also varies greatly across industries and occupations, with service industries and white-collar rates considerably lower than nonservice and blue-collar rates.

Table 1

Unemployment Rates
by Industry, September 1987

Industry	Unemployment Rate
Nonagricultural private wage and salary workers	5.9
Mining	7.0
Construction	12.1
Manufacturing	5.7
Services	
Transportation and public utilities	4.0
Wholesale and retail trade	6.4
Finance and service industries	4.9
Agricultural wage and salary workers	8.3

Source: U.S. Department of Labor, Bureau of Labor Statistics

Table 2

Unemployment Rates
by Occupation, September 1987

Occupation	Unemployment Rate
Total	5.7
Managerial and Professional Specialty	2.4
Technical, Sales, and Administrative Support	4.4
Precision Production, Craft, and Repair	5.1
Service Occupations	7.5
Operators, Fabricators, and Laborers	7.8

Source: U.S. Department of Labor, Bureau of Labor Statistics

Fact #4   Unemployment rates for blacks and teenagers are, and have been for many years, very high.

- In the 1960s and 1970s the proportion of black Americans in the ranks of the unemployed shrank steadily, from 20 percent in the 1960s to 17.3 percent in 1975, only to rise again to a record 22.4 percent in 1985.

- From 1972 to 1986 the unemployment rate for blacks substantially exceeded the rate for whites, the ratio being from 1.9 to 2.5 times the rate for whites.

- Teenage unemployment rose two percentage points from 1979 to 1986 despite a 12 percent drop in the teenage population.

- Teenage male unemployment has for the past thirty years been three to four times as great as for adult males. White teenage females have rates two to three times those of adult females.

Fact #5   The significantly higher female unemployment rate— relative to males—of the 1960s and 1970s has all but disappeared in the 1980s.

- From 1952 to 1962, the female rate was 0.5 to 1.0 percentage points higher than the male rate.
- From 1963 to 1979, the female rate was 1.3 to 2.1 percentage points higher than the male rate.
- From 1980 to 1986, the female rate ranged from 0.7 percentage points *lower* than the male rate to 0.5 percentage points higher.

Fact #6   Unemployment rates vary significantly according to educational backgrounds; in 1986, the rate for elementary school graduates (12.7 percent) was five times that of college graduates (2.5 percent).

Employment and Job Generation

Fact #1   The United States has had by far the greatest job-generating economy in the world since the mid-1960s.

- Between 1975 and 1985, the U.S. created 21 million new jobs, more than all other Western industrial nations combined.
- Western Europe in the 1970s actually experienced a net loss of jobs.

Fact #2   While the equivalent of 9 million full-time jobs were created from 1981–1986, this represented a job creation slow-down, since the equivalent of 14 million full-time jobs were created in the previous 6 years.

Fact #3   In mid-1987, a record 61.8 percent of the civilian population was employed while the labor force participation rate reached a new high of 65.7 percent.

Fact #4   In 1986, employment rose by 2.2 million with nearly all of the new jobs coming in the service industries.

- Factories lost an additional 100,000 workers.

- Jobs in retail trade and health and business services accounted for 67 percent of the net increase in jobs during 1986.

Fact #5   In the seven-year period 1979–1986, the service-producing sector generated 14 million jobs while the goods-producing sector peaked in 1979 and had a net loss of 1.5 million jobs by mid-1987.

- Nearly three-fourths of the service-sector jobs (74.1 percent) were in the two lowest-paying categories of the service sector—retail trade and health and business services.

Unemployment and Jobs Lost

Fact #1   Manufacturing jobs have been lost in record numbers in the 1980s and manufacturing's share of employment has steadily declined since 1970.

- From 1970 to 1985, manufacturing's share of U.S. employment declined from 26.1 percent to 19.3 percent.
- From 1979 to mid-1987, 1.9 million manufacturing jobs were lost.
- In the period 1978 to 1982, the labor force grew by 8 million while the net increase in the number of manufacturing jobs (among firms with 100 or more employees) was only 77,000.
- In 1985, manufacturing lost 180,000 jobs while 3 million jobs overall were added to nonfarm payrolls.
- Less than half (45 percent) of the factory jobs lost during the 1981–1982 recession had been regained by October 1987.

Fact #2   A total of 10.8 million workers 20 years of age and over lost jobs because of plant closings or employment cutbacks over the January 1981–January 1986 period; 5.1 million had been at their jobs three years or more.

- Close to 18 percent of those displaced were unemployed when surveyed in January 1986.
- Of the 3.4 million workers who found work following the displacement, 2.7 million were working at full-time wage and salary jobs, 56 percent earning as much or more in their new jobs.

Fact #3   The number of hard-core, long-term unemployed remains high.

- In October 1987, a record low 25 percent of the unemployed received any unemployment benefits, compared to 62 percent in 1975 and 50 percent in 1980.
- Some 5.5 million unemployed persons were without jobless assistance in an average month in 1986.

U.S. Unemployment Compared to Other Industrialized Nations

Fact #1   Although the 1986 U.S. unemployment rate of 7.0 percent was historically quite high, it was considerably lower than that of most other industrialized countries.

- In 1986, unemployment rates were 7.9 percent in West Germany, 10.5 percent in France, 11.5 percent in the United Kingdom, 11.1 percent in Italy, and 9.6 percent in Canada. (Note: rates in different countries are measured differently but still roughly comparable.)

Fact #2   The only major industrialized nation in 1986 with an unemployment rate lower than the U.S. was Japan, which had a very low rate of 2.8 percent.

Future Projections

Fact #1   Unemployment pressures will diminish considerably as the U.S. heads into the "baby bust shrinkage" of the labor force.

- The powerful labor force growth rate of 2.7 percent in the 1970s has diminished to a projected 1.2 percent in the 1986–2000 period.

- From 1986 to 2000, the labor force growth rates for various demographic groups will vary considerably: whites, up 14.6 percent; blacks, up 28.8 percent; Hispanic, up 74.4 percent; and Asian and other, up 71.2 percent.

- The number of 16- to 24-year-olds entering the labor force will fall nearly 10 percent to 21.3 million by 1995 versus 1987's 23.4 million.

Interpretation of the Facts

1. Causes of Unemployment

For over thirty years, the unemployment rate has been steadily rising. In order to understand the controversy among economists regarding an apparent inability to reverse this pattern, one must first understand the three main causes of unemployment, as well as the concept of the "natural" rate of unemployment.

Frictional unemployment, the first cause, reflects the *voluntary* actions of workers who quit to look for new jobs and of persons who move in and out of the labor force with some frequency and spend short periods of time looking for work. It also involves large fluctuations in output and employment in any company due to occasional effects or other short-term factors, such as the layoff of construction workers in the winter.

The second cause, cyclical unemployment, has to do with the ups and downs of the business cycle. During downturns in the cycle and during recessions, demand in the economy is weak, businesses are unable to sell all their output, and thus workers are laid off as production is scaled back.

The Human Face of Unemployment
Frank Burton—Akron, Ohio

It could be said, though it would be stretching it, that Frank Burton is one of the "lucky" ones. He, after all, is a displaced factory worker with a job.

But how lucky is it to go from a comfortable $30,000 job building tires (like your dad and granddad before you) to a minimum wage, below-poverty $7,000 job ringing the register at a convenience store (the same basic job you held twenty-four years ago after graduating from high school)?

It's not that Frank didn't try to make good. He studied 980 hours of computer science, only to find that nobody in Akron needed his new skills.

The physical and psychic toll? The dream of sending his children to college abandoned; health problems; pension rights sold to pay debts. In his words, "I got my heart torn out."

The third cause, structural unemployment, identifies the mismatch between jobs and workers. This category includes the "hard-core" unemployed who often lack basic literacy and number skills and even the motivation to work. Racial or sexual discrimination (which are illegal) can also lead to jobs going unfilled by those available to work, even when the unemployed have the necessary skills. It results also from the mismatch between industrial or geographic distribution of jobs and workers. One city or industry may be experiencing a shortage of labor while another city may have high unemployment.

The impact of these three causes of unemployment depends on the overall health of the economy. During periods of expansion when the demand for goods and services is very strong (as in the late 1960s), jobs are easy to find and the impact of the frictional and structural causes is reduced. Structural problems become more evident during recessions as the unskilled, the young, and the disadvantaged bear the brunt of the unemployment and as certain cities and industries are hurt more than others.

2. The Inflation-Unemployment
Trade-Off

Economists have had a long-standing debate about whether there is an inflation-unemployment trade-off. In the 1960s, most economists said such a trade-off existed, based on their examination of historical evidence and the behavior of the economy in that decade. Inflation started out low and unemployment was fairly high and steadily increased as unemployment came down in the latter half of the decade.

This neat inverse relationship became considerably messier in the 1970s as both inflation and unemployment increased. Today, the trade-off debate is between those who would abandon the idea of a trade-off altogether, and those who would retain it but try to understand why the relationship it implies seems to shift over time.

The Monetarists and the Natural Rate of Unemployment   The monetarists, led by Milton Friedman, argue that a free market economy will always move toward an economically efficient level in its use of capital and labor. At this efficient point, frictional and structural sources combine to produce what Friedman called "the natural rate of unemployment." Outside disturbances can cause unemployment to deviate temporarily from this natural rate. Such disturbances, the business cycle, are caused mainly by erratic government policy. In particular, the average growth rate of the money supply over two to three years determines the rate of inflation, a time period in which there is no trade-off at all between inflation and unemployment. Thus, monetarists believe policy making need not be concerned with a trade-off.

The Mainstream Keynesians—The Short-Run Trade-Off and Demographic Causes   Most mainstream economists contend that a short-run trade-off does exist that is relevant to policy making. Put simply, squeeze the economy ("exercise policy of demand restraint") and you will get lower inflation and higher unemployment. Their rule-of-thumb, based on empirical studies, is: each percentage point of increase in the unemployment rate that is sustained for one year will reduce the inflation rate by one-half a percentage point.

Interestingly, they agree with the monetarists on the notion of a natural rate of unemployment. However, they define it differently: the natural rate is the minimum level of unemployment that can be reached by policies to stimulate demand without generating rising inflation. Thus, if unemployment falls below the natural rate, inflation will increase. The natural rate will rise or fall due to changes in the amount of structural and frictional unemployment, and the unemployment rate will rise above or fall below the natural rate due to cyclical changes.

Therefore, the natural rate of unemployment in the 1950s was 4 to 4.5 percent. As long as unemployment was close to this, low and stable inflation could persist. Solely as a result of demographic change, the natural rate rose by 2 percentage points by the late 1970s, putting it in the 6 to 6.5 percent range. This change had three major dimensions: young people, women, and blacks increased their share in labor force and unemployment. The most important factor was the increase in young people: the "baby boomers."

This explanation, however, only carries mainstream economists half the way because from the 1950s to the 1980s the average unemployment rate rose almost 4 percentage points. They explained the additional 2 percent rise as a consequence of the retreat from the goals of full employment and from an active commitment to use macroeconomic policies to reach high employment. Once this rise in the natural rate is explained, they calculate the relative importance of cyclical and structural factors in the rising trend of unemployment. First, looking at the 1.5 percentage-point rise from the 1960s to the 1970s, one major study attributes 40 percent to an increase in the amount of cyclical unemployment and 40 percent to the increase in the natural rate. As for the 1.9 percentage-point increase from the 1970s to 1980–1982, all of it was cyclical. (See Martin Neil Baily, "The Problem of Unemployment in the United States," *Jobs for the Future*, Center for National Policy, May 1984.)

The Structuralists—Focus on the Demand Side   The structuralists reject the orthodox position and believe a significant share of unemployment is due to such changes on the demand side as technology, industrial location, and the like. This school is perhaps best represented by Barry Bluestone and Bennett Harrison, major proponents of the deindustrialization thesis. To reinforce their rejection of the orthodox position they cite the following: (1) labor force participation rates have actually declined among minorities, especially black men, since the early 1970s; (2) the female unemployment rate is now less than the male rate; and (3) in the past fifteen years, the average unemployment rates for white male adults have been rising, indicating growing joblessness for this dominant group as well as for the other segments of the labor force.

3. Underestimating the Unemployment Rate

A growing number of observers of the official unemployment rate put out monthly by the Bureau of Labor Statistics (BLS) feel that it grossly underestimates the level of joblessness in America. The most vigorous opponents of the official rate are Ward Morehouse and David Dembo of the Council on International and Public Affairs. They have developed a jobless rate which they feel more accurately reflects the true extent of joblessness. Their rate for 1986 was 13.9 percent, nearly double the official rate of 7.0 percent. Indeed, going back to 1969, they found that the jobless rate was between 1.8 and 2.6 times as high as the official rate.

Morehouse and Dembo cite two major factors for the difference between their figures and the government's: the

Table 3

Cyclical Trends in Unemployment
and Jobless Rates, 1969–1986

	1969	1970	1971	1972	1973	1974	1975	1976	1977
					(Percent)				
Civilian Unemployment Rate	3.5	4.9	5.9	5.6	4.9	5.6	8.5	7.7	7.1
Morehouse-Dembo Jobless Rate	10.2	11.1	12.7	11.9	11.3	12.0	15.7	14.8	14.4

	1978	1979	1980	1981	1982	1983	1984	1985	1986
Civilian Unemployment Rate	6.1	5.8	7.1	7.6	9.7	9.6	7.5	7.2	7.0
Morehouse-Dembo Jobless Rate	12.9	12.5	14.4	14.9	17.9	17.8	15.0	14.3	13.9

Source: Based on U.S. Department of Labor, Bureau of Labor Statistics, *Employment and Earnings*, various issues from 1970–1986, cited in Ward Morehouse and David Dembo, "Joblessness and the Pauperization of Work in America," Council on International and Public Affairs, May 1986, May 1987.

increase in part-time employees and the increase in those who want jobs but cannot find them.

The BLS counts anyone as fully employed who has worked one hour or more in a week. In early 1986, some 25 million people (21 percent of the civilian labor force) worked less than 35 hours a week, with 20 hours per week about the average. Since a substantial number of these part-timers want full-time work but cannot find it, Morehouse and Dembo use a full-time equivalent employment calculation.

The category "those who want jobs but cannot find them" surged from 5.8 million in 1981 to 6.6 million in 1982 and 6.5 million in 1983. Even after four years of recovery, it was above the 1981 level. Unlike Morehouse and Dembo, the BLS stops counting these millions of persons as part of the labor force and therefore as unemployed if they have not tried to find work in the preceding four weeks.

4. Joblessness in the Future

Will America's incredible "job-creation machine," as it has been called, produce jobs in the decade ahead for all who want them? The prevailing consensus is that it will, but there are a few dissenters.

The official government projection comes from the BLS, which projects that the American economy will create 21.4 million new jobs in the 1986–2000 period versus a labor force increase of 20.9 million. Taking issue with this sanguine assessment are Gail Garfield Schwartz and William Neikirk in their book *The Work Revolution* where they estimate that the economy will produce 12 million fewer jobs than will be needed by 1990.

CHAPTER
★ 5 ★

The Budget,
the Deficit, and
the National Debt

The Issues

Many people are enraged by the $200 billion-plus deficits (in three of the four years from 1983 to 1986) and the $2 trillion-plus national debt. Some blame government "handouts," beginning with President Johnson and his Great Society program. Others blame the war machine, beginning with the "give-away" to the military under President Reagan. However, others shrug the deficit off as they have for years.

What are the facts on federal spending, the deficit, and the debt? Just how high are they compared to ten, twenty, and thirty years ago? What has caused the increase? How do they compare to other nations? The three most important questions are: (1) How serious a threat is the national debt? (2) Is the Gramm-Rudman balanced budget bill the right answer? and (3) What does the future hold?

The Facts

The Federal Budget

Fact #1   In the relatively short period from 1965 to 1986, federal spending rose an astronomical 737 percent: entitlements, including retirement, health and welfare programs, were up 1,159 percent, interest payments were up 1,481 percent, national defense was up 440 percent, and nondefense discretionary spending (such as spending for transportation and the environment) was up 436 percent.

- During the 1965–1986 period, entitlements increased their share of the GNP substantially, from 5.2 percent to 11.0 percent, while defense decreased from 7.5 percent of the GNP to 6.6 percent.

Fact #2   Government spending as a percent of GNP has actually risen in the 1980s. It began at 22.2 percent in 1980, hit a record 24.3 percent in 1983, and declined slightly to 23.7 percent in 1986, still above the 1980 figure.

- Federal spending percentage increases declined every year (with the exception of 1985) from 1980 to 1986. In 1986 they only rose 4.4 percent, the smallest rise since 1969.

Fact #3   Differences in government spending increases in the 1980–1986 period are startling: interest payments soared 163 percent, national defense was up 104 percent, entitlements were up 63 percent, and nondefense discretionary spending rose only 12 percent (the price level during this period rose 32 percent).

- In the 1980s, defense spending increases started very high but declined dramatically:

    1981, up 13%
    1982, up 12%

1983, up 8%
1984, up 5%
1985, up 6%
1986, down 2%
1987, down 2%

Fact #4   *In 1986, $455 billion (or 46 percent of total federal spending) was spent on benefits payments to individuals; about $360 billion was for cash payments and the rest consisted of in-kind payments (e.g., health care, food stamps, and rental assistance).*

Fact #5   *In entitlements, nearly 70 cents of every dollar goes for retirement programs (Social Security, Medicare, and "other retirement and disability"); only 15 cents of each dollar is for means tested programs (e.g., welfare, Aid to Dependent Children).*

Fact #6   *In entitlements, the major growth in the past decade (1976–1986) has come in the two health categories, with Medicare up an astounding 336 percent and Medicaid up 191 percent. (These two health categories constitute 38 percent of all entitlements, excluding Social Security.)*

Deficits

Fact #1   *The size of budget deficits, and hence increases to the national debt, were not of particular significance or concern until 1975; the severe escalation began in 1982, with three of the four deficits in 1983–1986 exceeding $200 billion.*

Fact #2   *The record deficit prior to 1975 was $25.2 billion in 1968. Since then, the deficit has averaged $109 billion.*

Fact #3   *In FY 1987, the deficit did decline sharply, by $73 billion, to $148 billion; much of the decline was due to a one-time boost from the 1986 tax law.*

Fact #4   In the thirty-two years from 1950 to 1981, there was only one year (1976) in which the federal deficit rose above 3.6 percent of the GNP. In the five years, 1982–1986, the respective percentages were 4.2 percent, 6.4 percent, 5.2 percent, 5.4 percent, and 5.3 percent.

Fact #5   There has been only one surplus ($3.2 billion in 1969) in the past twenty-six years.

National Debt

Fact #1   It took 191 years to reach the first $1 trillion of national debt: it took five years (1981–1986) to reach the second $1 trillion.

Fact #2   The national debt in the 1950s and 1960s grew by an insignificant 43 percent over a twenty-year period; in the next seventeen years (1970–1986), it grew by 457 percent.

Fact #3   The national debt in June 1986 passed $2 trillion ($2,000,000,000,000):

- Two trillion $1 bills placed end to end would stretch from the earth to the sun and back, 186 million miles.
- A $1 trillion spending spree—at a rate of $1,900 a minute—would last 2,000 years.
- It is twelve times all the cash in the land.

Fact #4   The federal debt as a share of GNP had been steadily falling from 1946 to 1981; in the next five years, it rose 15 percentage points to nearly half the GNP.

Fact #5   The national debt in 1986 amounted to nearly $8,500 for every man, woman, and child in America. It is increasing by nearly $1,000 per person each and every year.

Interest Payments on the Debt

Fact #1   *Interest payments on the national debt have soared to $136 billion in 1986, when the government spent more on interest payments on the national debt than on all its major health programs, and for every two dollars going into defense, one was spent on debt.*

Fact #2   *In just fifteen years (1970–1985), net interest payments rose over ten times. In just six years, 1980 to 1986, the annual interest payment shot up 160 percent, increasing by $84 billion from a $52.5 billion starting point.*

Fact #3   *In seven of the eight years from 1978 to 1985, net interest payments made up more than 60 percent of that year's deficit.*

Fact #4   *Paying for the debt was relatively easy from 1950 to 1981 as net interest payments never exceeded 11 percent of total government revenues; in the five years from 1981 to 1985, these payments rose from just 10.2 percent of revenues to more than 18 percent.*

- In 1980, interest consumed one dollar of each ten the federal government spent whereas in 1985, it consumed one dollar in seven.
- Nearly four dollars of each ten the government collects in individual income taxes goes to paying interest on the debt.
- Interest payments are more than twice the revenue generated by the corporate income tax.

Impact on Savings and Investment

Fact #1   *The tremendous size of recent deficits has exerted a significant adverse impact on the economy, particularly the savings-investment arena.*

- In the mid-1980s, the annual deficit was absorbing 30 percent of all capital raised in the U.S., twice the average of the 1970s.

- In 1986, the federal deficit consumed the equivalent of 90 percent of all private sector savings.

- In 1974, the national debt was only 17 percent of private debt; in 1986, it had risen to 26 percent.

Holders of the Debt

Fact #1   Individuals hold only a very small percentage (8.5 percent) of the debt; large institutions are the government's primary lenders.

Table 1
Uncle Sam's Creditors, 1985

	Amount held (Billions)	Percent of total
Government trust funds	$295.5	17.2
Individuals	$145.3	8.5
Commercial banks	$195.0	11.4
Foreign holders	$186.3	10.9
Federal Reserve banks	$161.0	9.4
Insurance companies	$84.0	4.9
Corporations	$51.9	3.0
Money market funds	$26.6	1.6
State, local governments	$165.0	9.6
Other holders	$404.5	23.5

Source: Office of Management and Budget and U.S. Department of Treasury

International Comparison
of Debt Burden

*Fact #1   The U.S. national debt, relative to the size of the
economy, is larger than that of most other industrial nations.*

- In recent years, the national debt in the U.S. was between 40 and 50 percent of the GNP, while in Japan it
  was 40 percent, in Canada it was 26 percent, and in West
  Germany it was 20 percent.

Interpretation
of the Facts

1. The Threat of the National Debt

Virtually every economic ill has in some way been tied to
the national debt: inflation, high interest rates, cutbacks in
investment, the decline in U.S. competitiveness, the highly
skewed income distribution, and ultimately a decline in the
standard of living. Beyond these economic impacts, there
are those who raise more comprehensive concerns such as
the way a growing national debt affects the way that citizens
view their government. Even so, about one in ten economists
says, "Don't worry."

It Is a Serious Threat

Most observers who see the national debt as a threat emphasize one of the following areas as the focal point of adverse impacts:

Inflation   Monetarists, in particular, maintain that it is not
budget deficits per se that cause inflation but whether they
are financed by printing more money. Debt that cannot be
sold to the public must be bought by the Federal Reserve,

a prospect that terrifies monetarists since Fed purchases pump up money growth, planting the seeds for another bout of inflation.

Interest Rates   Injecting such a huge sum of additional credit demand into the markets (financing the deficit) inevitably drives up interest rates. Proponents refer to various studies such as one done in 1985 by the International Monetary Fund which concluded: "A balanced budget would have reduced interest rates on one-year U.S. Treasury bills by more than 2 percentage points in 1984." Additional concern is expressed over the large present stream of foreign capital that has helped significantly in financing the large federal deficits of the 1980s. If the flow of foreign capital is reduced or withdrawn, interest rates would shoot up and threaten what the Congressional Budget Office terms an explosion of federal debt—a vicious circle in which high interest rates begin to compound a rapidly rising debt.

Investment   In the 1960s, 90 percent of the nation's net savings was available for investment and capital formation while from 1981 to 1984, only one-third was available. In short, federal deficits consumed two-thirds of net savings. A comparison of the U.S. government's share of all the funds available to domestic nonfinancial borrowers in the last two business cycles shows that in the deepest recession years, 1975 and 1982, the percentages absorbed by the federal government were 41 and 40 percent respectively. In 1977 and 1984, strong recovery years, the percentages had dropped to 16.7 and 26.2 percent respectively. The difference of 10 percentage points was equal to nearly $70 billion worth of credit that would have been available to the private sector but instead was absorbed by the Treasury. That, in a nutshell, is the "crowding-out" thesis. Lawrence Kudlow, the Office of Management and Budget's chief economist early in the Reagan adminstration, captured this perspective succinctly: "The heavier Federal debt burden now means the government is absorbing real resources from the economy. And without capital you can't grow." (*The New York Times*, September 15, 1985, p. 34). From the other end of the political spectrum, Walter Heller, chairman of the Council of Economic Advisers under President Kennedy, agreed: "Federal deficits absorb the saving that could otherwise finance the private sector capital investment that is vital to growth in productivity and GNP potential." (*The Wall Street Journal*, October 26, 1984.)

International Competitiveness   America's business community is perhaps the strongest proponent of the view that the large budget deficits hurt U.S. competitiveness. Many business leaders during the mid-1980s felt that the large budget deficits were behind the very strong dollar, which was the "biggest single head wind" they faced in the international trade arena. According to Ruben Mettler, chairman and CEO of TRW and head of the Business Roundtable from 1981 to 1983: "Reducing the budget deficit will change, over time, the relationship between the dollar and the other world currencies. It has a very direct effect on being competitive." A number of observers see a close link between the budget deficit and the trade deficit. Martin S. Feldstein of Harvard, President Reagan's former chief economic adviser, observed: "The primary reason that the United States has become a capital importer and an international debtor is our vast Federal budget deficit."

Increase Taxes   Those who foresee increased taxes always link them to the rising interest burden. The House Budget Committee stated categorically in a 1985 report that the rising interest burden "will eventually lead to higher taxes which may affect economic efficiency." Barry Bosworth of The Brookings Institution looked at the rising national-debt-to-GNP ratio and concluded: "In the future we'll have to increase taxes every year not to pay for new programs but to pay interest on the national debt."

Income Distribution   The House Budget Committee in its 1985 report stated flat out: "The rising interest burden makes the distribution of income more unequal." Specifically, the winners are lenders and importers, while the losers are borrowers and export industries. Income redistribution could also be the result of taxes having to be raised or government services reduced to meet the rising interest burden.

Standard of Living   The Congressional Budget Office acknowledges it could be a long time before even very large deficits begin to result in stagnating standards of living. Although it happens slowly, it will happen, and as the damage accumulates, it will be increasingly difficult to reverse. Two senior economists at the Congressional Research Service are a bit more circumspect:

> The effect of today's debt financing on future generations will be exerted by slowing the modernization and expansion of the capital stock, which will reduce future productivity and hence living standards. This would be true if government borrows funds (uses resources) that would otherwise be invested in productive capital (including human capital) and if government spends the money in ways that do not enhance productive capacity. . . . The effect of government deficits on future living standards depends then on whether investment or consumption-enhancing programs would be cut if government spent less. (William A. Cox and David Grinnell, "The Federal Debt: Who Bears Its Burdens?" *Issues Brief*, Congressional Research Service, The Library of Congress, April 15, 1986, p. 7.)

Citizen Confidence in Government   The House Budget Committee argues that the ultimate cost of chronic deficits has been "the way citizens view their government":

> In the short term, Americans may find it an attractive "bargain" to receive $100 in national defense and government services for only $80 in taxes, as at present. In the longer

term they will react in anger and disappointment when they find the deficit must be paid for, after all, with higher taxes and inflation. As this process proceeds, confidence in government and the competence of fiscal management will erode, further weakening the political institutions of our society. That may be the final and most costly burden placed on future generations. (Cited in James Fallows, "The Three Fiscal Crises," *The Atlantic*, September 1985, p. 28.)

Recent Deficits Are Different   All previous large national deficits occurred either during wars or economic recessions. The deficits of the 1980s are much less cyclical. Indeed they seem to defy economic growth. Despite the fact that 1983 and 1984 were strong growth years, the deficit in 1985 was $4.5 billion higher than the recession-bloated deficit of 1983.

The chairman of the House Budget Committee, William Gray III, argues that we now have "a structural deficit." It is not related to economic performance and rises too rapidly to be submerged by rising revenues from economic growth. Many economists are distressed not only by the national debt itself but also because it has recently been growing faster than the economy. They see the debt sopping up an ever-rising share of the funds that either the government could use for depressed farmers or battleships, or which the nation's businesses could use for investment in the factories and housing that generate economic growth.

It Is Not a Serious Threat

Just a generation ago, most economists subscribed to the view that a rising national debt imposes no burden on the economy at large "because we owe it to ourselves." In other words, the claims of bondholders and the obligations of taxpayers offset each other.

Today, a number of economists still feel either that deficits do not matter or that their alleged "evil" influence on the economy has been blown all out of proportion.

Consider the question of their impact on inflation. Some economists, such as Gar Alperovitz and Jeff Faux, call the "deficits cause inflation" thesis a "myth" that is clearly refuted by the evidence. They cite the following:

1. For eight of the eleven years between 1971 and 1981, federal deficits as a percentage of the GNP moved in the opposite direction from changes in the price level.
2. In only one of the eleven years (1977) was there an acceleration of inflation the year after the relative deficit increased.
3. In 1981–1983, the budget deficit tripled while the inflation rate *dropped* from 14 percent to 4 percent.

It has also been pointed out that the deficits issue goes beyond the federal government. State and local governments also help determine the shape of the American economy. These governments (in all but one year since 1965) have sometimes run surpluses large enough to offset the deficit of the federal government. It is especially instructive that throughout the 1970s, the consolidated deficit declined from a 1972 deficit of 0.3 of the GNP to a 1979 surplus of 0.5 percent of the GNP as inflation was climbing steadily from 3.4 percent in 1972 to a 13.3 percent rate in 1979.

Albert Wojnilower, chief economist for First Boston Corporation, feels the deficit issue has been blown out of proportion:

> With a world in which there is double-digit unemployment virtually everywhere outside the U.S. and the Far East, the case for reducing the deficit is questionable. When the U.S. and the rest of the world have lots of excess capacity in both industry and labor, we can have large deficits without inflationary consequences. This will not always be true.
>
> I have taken the position consistently and, on the whole, correctly that changes in the budget deficit have only a minor consequence for interest rates, if any. ("What Happens If Budget Deficit Isn't Slashed?" *U.S. News & World Report*, July 22, 1985, p. 24.)

The True Danger May Be a Budget Surplus
Robert Eisner

If we begin to measure the federal budget accurately to take account of the effects of inflation, we will realize a disturbing fact: The balanced budget contemplated by the Gramm-Rudman-Hollings deficit-reduction act will, with a 4 percent annual rate of inflation, produce sizable real budget surpluses during the 1990s. These surpluses will sap purchasing power and plunge the economy into a depression. . . .

Consider the case of the Carter Administration. Faced with seemingly explosive inflation, Carter reacted sharply to the then supposedly large federal deficits believed responsible. He allowed taxes to rise, limited spending and encouraged tight money. Carter thus weakened a sluggish economy and contributed to his own demise.

Those Carter policies were based on false intelligence, misread by friend and foe alike. They were unnecessary and misguided. The official numbers showed a total deficit of $153 billion over the Carter years. In fact, we did not have any real federal budget deficits from 1977 to 1980. If we measure the effect of inflation in shrinking the real value of the federal debt, the Carter budgets added up to a real budget surplus of $72 billion.

Despite all the talk about new deficits, the general trend of real federal debt—the debt adjusted for inflation—has been downward. Subtracting financial assets from liabilities and adjusting for inflation, we find that from 1945 to 1980, the real net debt of the federal government fell by 58 percent. The real net debt per capita declined from $4,017 in 1972 dollars at the end of 1945 to $1,032 at the end of 1980, a drop of almost three quarters. By the end of 1984, it was up to $2,183 and is now several thousand dollars higher. But it remains far below its post-World War II peak.

And that's important because the significance of deficits, after all, is that they add to debt. But with inflation, that is simply not necessarily so. You can run a "deficit" while the real value of its debt declines.

This should properly lead to a quite revised view of recent history. We did not have large deficits contributing to inflation during the Carter years, 1977 to 1980. We rather had inflation—propelled chiefly by huge increases in prices of oil and agriculture products—converting presumably large deficits into real surpluses. (Robert Eisner, "Deficit: The True Danger May Be a Budget Surplus," *Washington Post*, February 2, 1986.)

2. The Balanced Budget Bill

In December 1985, President Reagan signed the Balanced Budget and Emergency Deficit Control Act of 1985 (known as the Gramm-Rudman-Hollings bill after its chief sponsors). This fulfilled a long-standing goal of conservatives and a variety of others to have as the law of the land achievement of a balanced budget, by force if necessary.

Gramm-Rudman-Hollings works as follows.

The Gramm-Rudman-Hollings Act prescribes that Federal Budget deficits cannot exceed targets that are gradually reduced until the budget is balanced in 1991. The President may not propose and the Congress may not consider budget resolutions that do not conform to these targets. If the Congress and the President fail to agree on a budget consistent with the deficit targets, a Presidential sequestering order will mandate across-the-board spending reductions in accordance with procedures specified by the act. Under sequestering, deficit targets are attained by reducing the growth of defense and nonexempt, non-defense government spending by an equal amount. Several programs or types of domestic spending are exempt, or partially exempt, from such reductions, including social security and medicaid. (*Economic Report of the President*, 1986, Washington, D.C.: U.S. Government Printing Office, p. 64.)

To its proponents, Gramm-Rudman-Hollings was the necessary shock-treatment to stop hemorrhaging deficits. Neither Congress nor the President was willing to slash government spending or increase taxes enough to significantly reduce the deficit. A law was the only way to force a serious nonpartisan consideration of this issue when drawing up the country's budget.

The Reagan adminstration, in its 1986 *Economic Report of the President*, responds to the argument that Gramm-Rudman may cause a contraction of aggregate demand, inducing a slowdown in economic activity:

> As long as the monetary authority maintains steady, predictable monetary growth, no serious or protracted economic disturbances are expected from reducing the deficit. Moreover, the legislation allows for delays in implementing the deficit reduction should real economic growth fall below 1 percent for two consecutive quarters, or a recession be forecast by the Congressional Budget Office or the Office of Management and Budget.

The administration argues that long-term macroeconomic effects depend on the extent to which deficits are reduced by spending cuts or tax increases. Quite simply, the spending cuts would contribute to long-term economic growth while tax increases would be detrimental to long-term economic growth.

A very vocal chorus says, no, Gramm-Rudman-Hollings is not the answer. One criticism is that the act side-steps the Constitution's requirement that "no money shall be drawn from the Treasury but in consequence of appropriations made by law." Thus, it undercuts one of the basic roles of government: choosing wisely among a host of competing demands for federal spending.

Others feel it makes hash of congressional budget and appropriations processes. It effects a tremendous shift of power to the House and Senate Budget Committees and away from committees with policy expertise.

Finally, it holds serious risks for presidents. It dictates the size of the budget they can propose and it can sharply reduce their flexibility in deciding how the government's finite resources are allocated.

In general, liberal economists and politicians do not see the need for a wrenching, painful bout of fiscal belt-tightening over the next five years. Two liberal academic economists, Barry Bluestone and John Havens, prescribe a different deficit reduction process:

Step 1. Redistribute federal spending priorities toward infrastructure development.

Step 2. Reduce interest rates through continued monetary expansion, particularly in a period of low core rates of inflation.

Step 3. Enact temporary tax boosts before further cuts in non-defense spending.

Step 4. Enact additional cuts in non-defense programs but only as a last resort.

(B. Bluestone and J. Havens, "Reducing the Deficit Fair and Square," paper prepared for Joint Economic Committee Symposium, January 16–17, 1985.)

3. The Future

The latest official government projection by the Congressional Budget Office (August 1987) is quite pessimistic. It shows the deficit rising again to a level of $192 billion in 1989 (from $156 billion in fiscal 1987). The administration also projects a rising deficit, but only to $166 billion in fiscal 1989 before falling again.

Many dismiss the projection of the Congressional Budget Office because it is built on the assumption of five more years of uninterrupted healthy economic growth. It is highly unlikely that such an historically unprecedented period of uninterrupted growth would occur.

The pessimists maintain that although interest rates have fallen, the mathematical base on which the interest is figured and paid keeps expanding. Since this phenomenon will not correct itself, they see a continuing growing deficit.

Even Robert Eisner becomes more pessimistic about deficits when he looks into the future. There he sees that even after adjusting for inflation, prospective deficits are still large and should be reduced.

Finally, today's huge and rapidly expanding national debt raises a fundamental moral question for some critics. They ask whether one generation of taxpayers has the right to bequeath to the next the burden of its borrowing, much of it for the current generation's historically high standard of living.

CHAPTER
★ 6 ★
Taxes

The Issues

"Nothing is certain but death and taxes." Taxes may be certain, but they change yearly; and there is no agreement on what they should look like. Indeed, taxes are one of the most controversial economic topics. There is considerable disagreement among economists about two specific issues: What should be done about corporate income taxes? What are the economic impacts of major tax reform? The opposing, and somewhat emotional, positions will be highlighted in the Interpretation section.

In addition to these issues, the American people often wonder about such questions as:

- How much have taxes gone up since World War II?
- Which taxes have increased the most?

- Which income groups are bearing the greatest burden of increased taxes?
- What's been happening to the corporate income tax?
- How do the various federal, state, and local taxes compare in terms of their overall amount and rate of growth?
- Have taxes really come down in the 1980s?

Federal taxes have escalated dramatically in the past two decades. They totaled a modest $41 billion in 1946, a still modest $143 billion in 1966, and a not at all modest $826 billion in 1986. The tax increase champion by far is the Social Security tax, which shot up 848 percent between 1966 and 1986.

Still, federal tax increases pale in comparison to state and local increases. The figures for 1946, 1966, and 1986 respectively are: $13 billion, $85 billion, and $619 billion.

Definition: **Tax rate.** There is a rate specified in tax law (the statutory rate) such as the 14 percent and 28 percent rates for the federal personal income tax established in the 1986 Tax Reform Act. Then there is the rate that people and corporations actually pay—the effective tax rate—after they have taken all their tax deductions, exemptions, and credits. Many of these subtractions leading to a lower tax bill are referred to as tax loopholes or, more formally, tax expenditures.

The Facts

All Taxes: Federal, State, and Local

Fact #1   From 1946 to 1966, federal taxes increased by just over three and one-half times and state and local taxes increased by just under seven times; in the 1966–1986 period, federal taxes increased just under six times and state and local taxes increased by over seven times.

Fact #2   *In 1987, the average American had to work from January 1 through May 3 just to pay off his or her share of federal, state, and local taxes.*

Fact #3   *The combined effective tax rates—for federal, state, and local taxes—go from 17 percent for the bottom tenth of the population to 26.4 percent for the top tenth (under the most progressive assumptions) and from 24 percent to 25 percent for the bottom tenth and top tenth (under the least progressive assumptions).*

- In 1946, state and local taxes were equal to 31 percent of federal taxes but by 1986 this figure had reached 75 percent.

Fact #4   *Taxes have grown from 29.7 percent of the national income in 1946 to 42.7 percent in 1986.*

- Between 1946 and 1986, federal taxes only rose from 22.5 percent to 24.4 percent while state and local taxes rose from 7.2 percent to 18.3 percent.
- Of the total 13 percentage-point increase, nearly 9 percentage points were added in two five-year periods: 1955–60 (3.5) and 1965–70 (5.4).
- Of the total 13 percentage-point increase, over 11 percentage points came from state and local tax increases and only 2 points from federal tax increases.

All Federal Taxes

Fact #1   *In the twenty-year period 1966–1986, total federal taxes increased by 476 percent. Personal taxes increased by 486 percent, corporate taxes by 165 percent, and Social Security taxes by 848 percent.*

- In 1950, the corporate income tax raised 34 percent of federal tax revenues, while the payroll tax raised only 11 percent; by 1986, these percentages were 10 percent for the corporate tax and 39 percent for the payroll tax.

Table 1
Federal Taxes, 1966–1986
(Billions of $)

Year or Quarter	Total	Personal income tax	Corporate income tax	Indirect business tax & nontax accruals	Social Security taxes
1966	143.5	61.7	31.4	15.5	34.9
1967	152.6	67.5	30.0	16.2	38.9
1968	176.9	79.7	36.1	17.9	43.2
1969	199.7	95.1	36.1	18.9	49.6
1970	195.4	92.6	30.6	19.2	52.9
1971	202.7	90.3	33.5	20.3	58.7
1972	232.2	108.2	36.6	19.9	67.5
1973	263.7	114.7	43.3	21.1	84.6
1974	293.9	131.3	45.1	21.6	95.9
1975	294.9	125.9	43.6	23.8	101.6
1976	340.1	147.3	54.6	23.3	115.0
1977	384.1	169.8	61.6	25.0	127.7
1978	441.4	194.9	71.4	28.0	147.0
1979	505.0	231.0	74.4	29.3	170.3
1980	553.8	257.9	70.3	38.8	186.8
1981	639.5	298.9	65.7	56.2	218.8
1982	635.3	304.5	49.0	48.1	233.7
1983	659.9	294.5	61.3	51.6	252.5
1984	726.5	309.3	75.9	55.7	285.5
1985	786.8	345.6	73.6	56.1	311.5
1986	826.2	361.8	83.2	52.3	328.9

Source: Economic Report of the President, 1987, Washington, D.C.: U.S. Goverment Printing Office, Table B-78, p. 337.

Fact #2 *Revenues as a share of GNP rose from 17.6 percent in 1976 to a peak of 20.1 percent in 1981, then fell to 18.1 percent in 1983; they are projected to be 19.3 percent in 1987.*

The Personal Income Tax

Fact #1   *Marginal tax rates rose steadily to a peak in 1980; since then, the decline has been significant, particularly for higher income levels.*

Fact #2   *Despite all the loopholes, the present income tax is progressive—that is, the average tax burden rises with income—though the distribution of total federal taxes became less progressive between 1977 and 1984.*

Fact #3   *In 1948, more than three-fourths of family income was exempt from federal taxation; today, less than one-third is.*

Fact #4   *In 1948, the individual exemption was worth $600; had that exemption kept pace with inflation it would have been $5,560 in 1986 instead of $1,080 (the Tax Reform Act of 1986 raised it to $1,900 in 1987).*

Fact #5   *Over the past thirty years, the average effective tax rate on middle-income married couples with two children nearly tripled, while that for single people and married couples increased by only one-sixth.*

- In 1954, typical married couples with two children paid about 4 percent of their income in taxes; by 1980, they paid 14 percent.

Fact #6   *Among the very wealthy—those making more than $200,000 a year—nearly half pay an average tax rate of only 11 percent and 10 to 15 percent pay virtually nothing, due principally to numerous tax shelters and favorable capital gains treatment prior to 1987.*

Fact #7   *In 1985, those officially defined as poor paid an average tax rate on income and payroll taxes of 10.5 percent for a family of four and 11.1 percent for a family of six, up from 4.0 and 6.1 percent respectively in 1978.*

Fact #8   Federal taxes for the vast majority of Americans increased in the early 1980s despite the Reagan tax cut of 1981.

- Because of inflation and increases in Social Security taxes, only families earning more than $30,000 in 1981 enjoyed a net decrease in taxes between 1982 and 1984, leaving 80 percent of taxpayers as net losers.

- The 0.2 percent of families with incomes above $200,000 experienced a $60,000 (15 percent) reduction; and 35 percent of the total tax savings from the cut went to the richest 5.6 percent of taxpayers.

Fact #9   The richest Americans will pay relatively less in taxes in 1988 than they did in 1977 while the poor will pay more.

- The top 1 percent of taxpayers will pay 29.3 percent of their income in taxes in 1988 vs. 31.8 percent in 1977 while the bottom tenth will pay 9.7 percent in 1988 vs. 8.2 percent in 1977.

Social Security Taxes

Fact #1   More than half of today's young and low-income wage earners pay more in Social Security payroll tax than they do in federal income tax.

Fact #2   In 1988, social security taxes on all but the richest 10 percent of taxpayers will be at a higher rate than income tax rates on the same taxpayers (assuming that employer's share is actually paid by the worker).

Fact #3   In 1949, the maximum Social Security tax payment was $60 (Social Security benefits accounted for 1 percent of the federal budget); in 1987, the maximum was $3,387 (and the benefits in 1986 accounted for 21 percent of the budget).

Fact #4 *The typical young worker entering the workforce in the mid-1980s will not get back even $1 for every $1 he or she and the employer put in.*

Fact #5 *In order for today's young to receive retirement benefits at current real levels, it is estimated that the workforce in 2050 will have to surrender 41 percent of its total payroll in Social Security taxes.*

Corporate Income Taxes

Fact #1 *The effective tax rate on the total income of corporations exceeded 40 percent in the early 1950s but declined almost continuously during the next thirty years until it reached 13 percent in 1982.*

Fact #2 *Effective corporate tax rates may vary widely from "negative" effective rates for the airlines and financial companies to rates in excess of 32 percent for leisure and personal care companies, textiles firms, and tobacco companies.*

Fact #3 *Within the same industry effective tax rates can vary dramatically, depending on a company's skill and timing in "mining" the tax code effectively.*

- The average 6 percent rate for chemical companies spanned a − 18.5 percent rate for Dow Chemical and a 38.5 percent rate for Nalco Chemical.
- In computers, while Digital Equipment Corporation, IBM, and NCR Corporation paid effective tax rates of more than 25 percent, Wang Laboratories, Sperry, and Prime Computer paid 2 percent or less.

Fact #4 *In a 1982–1985 survey (Citizens for Tax Justice,*

Table 2

Effective Tax Rates by Industry
For 275 Major Companies
(1981–1984)

	Profit (Millions of $)	Tax (Millions of $)	Rate (Percent)
Airline	$441.7	($33.1)	−7.5
Financial	4,826.2	(139.2)	−2.9
Railroads	13,308.4	236.0	1.8
Telecommunications	41,035.8	927.5	2.3
Paper & Forest Products	7,158.8	258.3	3.6
Aerospace	13,354.0	587.8	4.4
Chemicals	13,810.8	827.7	6.0
Utilities (Electric & Gas)	53,956.1	3,788.6	7.0
Electrical, Electronics	21,735.3	2,539.5	11.7
Conglomerates	5,427.5	736.7	13.6
Services, Trade	12,720.6	1,994.2	15.6
Rubber	2,417.4	462.2	19.1
Oil & Gas, Coal, Mining	77,615.7	14,955.4	19.3
Building Materials, Glass	3,422.9	677.6	19.7
Drugs, Hospital Supplies	16,228.7	4,770.5	20.3
Food & Beverages	22,686.3	4,770.5	21.0
Automotive	15,952.4	3,805.9	23.9
Computers, Office Equipment	27,709.1	6,742.9	24.3
Miscellaneous Manufacturing	7,752.4	1,927.3	24.9
Publishing & Broadcasting	6,735.3	1,691.5	25.1
Instruments	8,306.5	2,099.4	25.3
Construction	2,434.3	708.9	29.1
Leisure, Personal Care	7,799.5	2,513.8	32.2
Textiles	2,390.2	801.0	33.5
Tobacco	11,300.2	4,096.1	36.2
ALL-INDUSTRY TOTALS	**$400,546.1**	**$60,265.7**	**15.0**

Source: Citizens for Tax Justice, "Corporate Taxpayers & Corporate Freeloaders," August 1985, p. 14.

"130 Reasons Why We Need Tax Reform," July 1986) of 250 corporations more than half paid no federal income taxes, or received outright tax rebates, in at least one of the five years.

- The two principal tax avoidance vehicles were accelerated depreciation and the investment tax credit.

- The 130 companies earned $72.9 billion in pretax domestic profits in the years they did not pay federal income taxes, which, at the 46 percent statutory rates, would have yielded $33.5 billion in income taxes; instead, they received $6.1 billion in tax rebates, for a negative tax rate of −8.3 percent.

- Forty-two of the 250 companies paid either nothing or received a net rebate over the entire four-year period from 1982 to 1985, for total net tax rebates of $2.1 billion on $59.1 billion in pretax domestic profits.

- AT&T, the company with the largest domestic profits in the 1982–1985 period—$25 billion—also had the largest (by far) tax rebate ($636 million).

Fact #5   Of the same 250 companies surveyed, fifty companies—or one out of five—paid more than 30 percent of their profits in federal income taxes and seven had effective tax rates in excess of 40 percent.

- The $4.8 billion in taxes paid by the seven highest taxed firms on their $10.9 billion in pretax profits was almost two and one-half times the amount paid by the 104 companies paying less than 10 percent on their $156 billion in pretax profits.

Fact #6   For all 250 companies, the overall 1982–1985 effective tax rate was 14.9 percent, less than one-third the 46 percent statutory tax rate.

- Had these companies paid the full rate on their $388 billion in 1982–1985 profits, their taxes would have totalled $178.5 billion, or $120.5 billion more than they actually paid.

Fact #7   There is no correlation between tax "incentives" or "breaks" and improved capital spending or job creation—indeed, the opposite holds true as the most highly taxed companies perform positively while the most lightly taxed perform negatively (according to a study of 259 companies in the 1981–1984 period—Citizens for Tax Justice, "Money for Nothing," February 1986).

- The forty-four companies that paid no taxes or received refunds reduced their aggregate capital spending by 4 percent and reduced their workforces by 6 percent.

- The forty-three highest taxed companies increased their capital spending 21 percent and expanded their payrolls by 4 percent.

Fact #8   Of the thirty-one top exporting companies, the seventeen companies that cut exports paid an effective tax rate of 6.3 percent while the fourteen companies that increased exports paid an effective tax rate of 23.1 percent.

Corporate Income Taxes—
International Comparison

Fact #1   Japanese companies paid (in 1983) a higher absolute amount in income taxes than American companies, despite a Japanese GNP only one-third the size of the U.S. GNP and significantly lower profitability rates than U.S. firms.

- While the U.S. provided companies with tax concessions totaling $62 billion in fiscal 1983—$1.67 for every dollar paid in corporate income taxes—Japan's "special taxation measures" for corporations amounted to only $1.1 billion, a mere 2.7 cents for every corporate tax dollar.

- The effective overall corporate income tax rate in Japan in 1983 was more than 50 percent compared to a 14 percent federal rate (in the 250-firm study) in the United States.

- The corporate income tax in Japan contributes close to 30 percent of national government revenues.

- The Japanese taxation of equipment and structures is quite even with a rate of 33.7 percent for equipment and 37.8 percent for structures while the rates in the U.S. are 5.7 percent and 37.8 percent respectively.

Tax Loopholes

Fact #1   *In 1986, tax loopholes for individuals and corporations totaled an estimated $424.5 billion, more than half the total federal taxes collected ($304.6 billion from individuals and $119.9 billion from corporations).*

The Tax Gap

Fact #1   *The revenue loss from unreported, legally earned income is significant and growing, amounting to $121 billion in 1987.*

- Unreported income from illegal sources, including drugs, gambling, and prostitution, cost an additional $9 billion in lost tax revenue in 1981.

- The amount of income reported by individual and corporate taxpayers declined from 91.2 percent in 1973 to 89.3 percent in 1981. (Joint Economic Committee, U.S. Congress, *Tax Reform*, November 29, 1984, p. 20.)

Tax Policy

Fact #1   *In the 1975–1986 period, eight major tax bills and dozens of minor tax bills were enacted.*

- Excluding the 1986 Tax Reform Act, 1,800 pages of new legislation was added to the basic 1954 tax code in the tax years from 1975 to 1984, plus more than 4,000 pages of accompanying legislative history issued by Congress.

Interpretation
of the Facts

---

1. The Corporate Income Tax

Despite volumes of writing, very little agreement has been reached on what to do about taxing corporations. The two basic positions are: (1) raise corporate taxes so corporations will once again pay their fair share and (2) abolish the corporate income tax.

These two positions are forcefully and succinctly conveyed in the following two passages. Arguing for higher corporate taxes is Robert McIntyre, director of federal tax policy at Citizens for Tax Justice. As might be expected, he is a liberal since one would be hard pressed to find a conservative leading the charge for higher corporate taxes. But the second speaker calling for the abolition of the corporation income tax is also a liberal, Lester Thurow of the Massachusetts Institute of Technology. These two liberals are at opposing ends of the same issue.

The Corporate Income Tax

Increase It
Robert McIntyre

The data are clear. Corporate tax avoidance continues unabated. While some corporations pay effective tax rates close to the statutory rate, many pay no income tax whatsoever. This fuels the deficit, distorts economic choices, and shifts the tax burden to those wage-earners and businesses which are unable to exploit tax shelter opportunities.

The existing corporate tax system is a mess. It fails to pro-

Abolish It
Lester Thurow

The corporate income tax should be abolished regardless of whether you are a conservative or a liberal. Based on our principles of taxation, the corporate income tax is both unfair and inefficient. In a country with a progressive personal income tax, every taxpayer with the same income should pay the same tax (horizontal equity), and the effective tax rate should rise in accordance with whatever degree

duce adequate revenue, and does so at great cost to economic efficiency. What we need is a corporate tax system that produces adequate revenues with minimal economic distortion.

To achieve this, we need a corporate tax system that taxes companies on what they really earn—not on some figment of their tax accountants' imagination. This means an end to special credits and deductions. It means a depreciation system which is neutral among different types of assets and which is based on the way buildings and machines actually wear out or become obsolete.

We need a tough minimum corporate tax of at least 25 percent of "book" income—a rate equal to the marginal rate the President has proposed for middle-class families—as a symbol of the minimal contribution expected from large, profitable corporations to support the nation's government.

But what we need most of all is the political will power to get the job done. (Robert McIntyre, "Corporate Tax-payers & Corporate Freeloaders," Citizens for Tax Justice, Washington, D.C., August 1985, p. 19.)

of progressivity has been established by the political process (vertical equity). The corporate income tax violates both of these canons of equity.

When you review the arguments, there isn't any case for the retention of the corporate income tax. It is both unfair and inefficient. It ought to be eliminated. And all corporate incomes—retained or paid out as dividends—ought to be taxed at personal income tax rates appropriate to the shareholders who own them. In doing so we will increase the fairness of the tax system, improve the allocation of investment funds, and create a powerful incentive for more investment.

While corporations are legal entities that write checks to government, they do not pay taxes. They simply collect money from someone—their shareholders, their customers, or their employees—and transfer it to government. There is no such thing as taxing corporations as opposed to individuals. This immediately raises the issue of who ultimately pays the corporate income tax. The incidence of the corporate income tax is an area of economics with a large literature and little or no agreement. Depending upon the ex-

act assumptions used, the definition of incidence, and the
time periods under consideration, it could be a tax on
shareholders, a sales tax on
consumers, or a tax on employees. While there may be a
certain perverse political virtue in collecting a tax where
no one is sure whether he pays
it, simple economic efficiency
and equity would seem to call
for the elimination of taxes
where incidence is uncertain.
(Lester Thurow, *The Zero Sum
Society: Distribution and the
Possibilities for Economic
Change.* Copyright © 1980 by
Basic Books, Inc. Reprinted
by permission of the publisher,
pp. 97–8).

2. The Economic Impact of the Tax Reform Act of 1986

When it became clear in 1985 and early 1986 that major tax
reform had a good chance of becoming law, everyone was
asking: What will this do to the economy? Economists were
called to testify and their answers, often based on comprehensive, detailed analysis, varied considerably.

Take just one set of hearings, in mid-September 1986, just
before final votes on the bill's passage. Testimony was given
that:

• Increases in perceived equity and efficiency of the tax
code would boost economic growth (Joseph Minarik of
the Urban Institute and Robert McIntyre of Citizens for
Tax Justice).

- The legislation "will have at least a modest depressing effect on the economy in the short-term" because of sharply curtailed tax incentives for business investment and construction (Lawrence Chimerine of Chase Econometrics).

- It is just barely, marginally desirable, solely on the basis of the long term; for the short term, it is negative (Alan Greenspan of Townsend-Greenspan, now chairman of the Federal Reserve Board).

- The bill would slow growth in both the short and long terms and would lead to a less productive, more labor intensive economy (Roger Brinner of Data Resources).

- The increase in business taxes would cut investment and retard technological progress enough to produce a 5 percent shortfall in potential economic growth over the next decade (Lawrence Summers of Harvard University).

- The bill would go "in the opposite direction from what you would do if you wanted to address the problem of international competitiveness" (Jerry Jasinowski of the National Association of Manufacturers).

There was general agreement on one point: by putting an additional $25 billion a year in individuals' pockets, the legislation would encourage more consumption, further depressing the country's already low savings rate.

The President's Council of Economic Advisers stated in the summer of 1986 that the new tax system, by raising economic growth 0.25 percent a year, could add $100 billion to the economy's annual output. On the other hand, John D. Paulus, managing director and chief economist of Morgan Stanley, had this to say about tax reform:

> . . . any tax proposal that redistributes income away from business toward consumers in the United States invites disaster. By magnifying the twin problems of U.S. overcon-

sumption and declining global competitiveness while simultaneously increasing the nation's dependence on foreign capital and the global investor's perception of U.S. economic weakness, the tax reform proposal threatens to have cataclysmic consequences for the world financial system. (John Paulus, "Tax Reform: Good Idea, Wrong Country," *Washington Post*, November 26, 1985, p. A-17.)

CHAPTER
★ 7 ★

Productivity

The Issues

When productivity stops rising, people's standard of living stops rising. Thus, productivity growth is at the heart of the question: Will future generations enjoy a higher standard of living?

In general, productivity saves in the use of scarce resources per unit of output; holds down inflation by offsetting rising wage rates and other input prices; and increases the international competitiveness of domestic production. At the same time, productivity advances stemming from technological change may cause major job losses in specific occupations, firms, industries, or geographical areas.

In short, it is a powerful contributor to economic growth, inflation, unemployment rates, international competitiveness, and people's standard of living. No other economic variable can claim such power.

Definition: **Productivity** is the basic measure of how efficiently the nation's businesses produce goods and services. The most common measure of productivity—labor productivity—is the output of goods and services per hour worked. As productivity increases, jobs are lost unless demand for the goods or services increases accordingly.

The Facts

The Record Since World War II

Fact #1   Productivity growth in the U.S. was very strong from 1950 to 1968 and very weak from 1969 to 1986.

- The average annual productivity growth rate from 1950 to 1968 was exactly three times the average for 1969 to 1986: 2.7 percent to 0.9 percent.

- Between 1950 to 1968, only three years had productivity growth below the healthy rate of 2 percent; in the years from 1969 to 1986, only 4 years had productivity growth above 2 percent.

- The earliest period had seven years of strong productivity growth (3 percent or better) and the later period had three such years.

- The earlier period had one year of weak productivity (less than 1 percent) and the later period had nine years, including five that were negative.

Fact #2   In the eight years from 1979 to 1986, productivity growth was at a very feeble 0.4 percent average.

Fact #3   From the 1850s to the 1960s, there was a steadily rising rate of productivity growth: 1850–1889, 1.3 percent; 1889–1919, 2 percent; 1920–1939, 2.5 percent; 1947–1960, 3.3 percent; 1961–1965, 3.6 percent.

Fact #4   If the productivity rate increases of the 1960s had continued to the present day, the nation's output would be about a third higher than it is.

Fact #5   Nonfarm productivity in the 1980s expansion (1983 to 1986) is the worst since World War II—inching up at a 1.3 percent annual rate, compared with an average of 2.7 percent in all recoveries since 1946.

Manufacturing versus Services Productivity

Fact #1   The manufacturing versus services productivity record is mixed: from 1929 to 1965, the annual average productivity growth rate in manufacturing was only 0.2 percent greater than in services. Since then, the gap has generally widened, becoming greater than 4 percentage points in the 1982–1985 period.

- From 1946 to 1965, the annual average productivity growth rates for manufacturing and services were 2.9 percent and 2.5 percent respectively while the rates in the 1982–1985 period were 4.7 percent and 0.4 percent respectively.

Fact #2   Manufacturing productivity increased by 3.5 percent in 1986, marking the first time since the government begin keeping this statistic in 1950 that the U.S. outpaced all its major competitors.

- Gains were 2.9 percent in Britain, 2.8 percent in Japan, and 1.9 percent in West Germany and France.

Fact #3   The average growth rate of nonmanufacturing productivity has shifted down from 2.8 percent a year from 1948–1967, to 0.9 percent from 1967–1973, to a scant 0.1 percent from 1979–1986.

Fact #4   Throughout the 1980s, manufacturing productivity in the U.S. has been growing at its fastest rate since the mid-1950s.

- The average 4.4 percent annual rate through mid-1986, in the expansion begun in 1982, compares with an average of 3.6 percent for the equivalent period in five previous postwar business cycles.

Fact #5   Overall service productivity was no higher in mid-1987 than in 1979.

- The productivity of the 18.8 million people in such industries as health care and in law and accounting firms declined an average of two-tenths of 1 percent annually in 1980–1987.

Fact #6   There have been a number of stellar productivity performers among individual service industries since 1965.

- From 1965 to 1980, there was high productivity growth (5 to 8 percent over a seven-year period) in petroleum pipelines, air transportation, drug and proprietary services, telephone communication, and gasoline service stations.
- Since 1979, productivity has risen 20 to 40 percent in such deregulated industries as airlines, railroads, and telecommunications.

Fact #7   Manufacturing productivity suffered no setback in the 1970s and indeed had a greater advance (28.6 percent) than in the highly acclaimed 1950s (23.3 percent).

Fact #8   Most of the recent industrial productivity champions are manufacturers most exposed to foreign competition, who have been automating, cutting overhead, closing plants, and reorganizing operations on the factory floor.

- Since 1970, productivity growth for tiremakers has been 40 percent; for automakers and parts producers 20 percent; and for steelmakers 18 percent.

- Manufacturers of TV and radio components increased productivity by 75 percent.

U.S. versus Foreign Competitors

Fact #1   For the first time since World War II, the United States is essentially competing as a peer among equals because the gap in productivity levels has shrunk to the point where U.S. output per hour in manufacturing is now just 10 percent higher than in Japan and 15 percent higher than in continental Europe.

Fact #2   While American manufacturers increased their rate of productivity growth from near zero to about 3 percent per year in 1983–1985, Japan has registered 8 percent annual gains over a far longer period; thus its productivity increased 45 percent more than that of the U.S. in the 1978–1985 period.

Fact #3   The U.S. manufacturing productivity growth rate, which lagged far behind that of its major competitors for many years, has recently been closing the gap.

- In 1973–1979, the U.S. rate was well under 2.9 percent while West Germany's rate was over 4 percent and Japan's was nearly 6 percent; in 1979–1985 the U.S. rate was over 3 percent while West Germany's was just slightly higher and Japan's was under 6 percent.

Interpretation
of the Facts

1. Productivity Growth Sources

The chief long-term factor driving up productivity growth is technological advancement, largely through research and development. A host of other factors contribute, the major ones being: advances in knowledge, economies of scale, im-

proved resource allocation, growth in the labor force, capital
per worker, and the basic values of society.

Given the numerous studies of productivity and the lengthy
and detailed list of major contributing factors, one would
assume that the productivity slowdown of the 1970s is well
understood. It is not.

There is general agreement that the leading factors drag-
ging down productivity growth in the 1970s were: the great
influx of inexperienced workers (especially teens and women),
a host of social regulations, the decline in R&D spending,
the oil shocks, inflation, and interest rate fluctuations that
jolted the economy. According to John Kendrick, a widely
recognized productivity expert among economists, most of
these negative impact factors have been reversed in the 1980s.

The explanatory strength of one factor—investment—is
in particular dispute. Numerous analysts concluded that investments in machines and equipment had begun to falter
badly and were no longer profitable. However, by three
major measures—gross private investment, nonresidential
investment, and investment in producers' durable equipment—investment was actually higher as a percent of GNP
in the 1970s than in the 1950s. In addition, America's investment in manufacturing did not falter in the 1970s in
comparison to that of other Western nations. What did decline was the amount of investment per worker; but the
number of workers grew very rapidly. In the early 1980s,
the rate of tangible capital formation per worker in the U.S.
was less than one-third of that in Japan. This was largely
due to the vast disparity in the real (inflation-adjusted) cost
of capital, which was 7.5 percent in the U.S. and 2.5 percent
in Japan.

2. Is Productivity Growth
Always Good?

To the vast majority, productivity growth is good. It is, among
other benefits, the source of higher wages, higher profits,

and lower prices. For theoreticians, productivity growth is an absolute necessity if America is to compete effectively in the international arena.

However, organized labor, among others, feels productivity is increasing too fast and robots are putting too many people out of work. They believe that technology making something possible, or the market making it attractive, is not a good enough reason to rend irrevocably our social fabric.

3. Productivity in the Future

Most experts predict gains in long-run productivity. The basic underlying factors all look good.

- Labor force. The overall growth rate is slowing substantially and the young and inexperienced workers of the 1970s are becoming the mature, experienced workers of the 1980s.

- Capital per worker. A higher rate of investment will expand capacity rapidly and speed the spread of new technology.

- Research and development. Private and public R&D spending has rebounded sharply to 2.7 percent of the GNP, close to its 1968 peak.

Perhaps the major source of further gains is one that cannot even be measured by economists' traditional tools—the behavior of management shocked into action by tough new competition. Abundant evidence exists that management is taking productivity seriously. Robert Hayes, co-author of the 1980 *Harvard Business Review* article "Managing Our Way to Economic Decline," observed: "I've been astonished at the speed with which some American companies that I have watched closely have been able to make just a remarkable turnaround." Jerome Mark, associate commissioner of the Bureau of Labor Statistics, also noted in 1984 that "there's no question that there has been a productivity drive. We have been in business since 1884—I've been here for the last 33 years—and I've never seen anything like it."

Finally, there is the sheer drive of technological advance. The biggest problem here may well be the inability of management rapidly to assmilate new technologies. This has been true throughout American history in regard to major new technologies. Productivity did not grow much for nearly twenty years after the introduction of the assembly line in 1901, and there were similar lags after the building of railroads. The spread of computers, robots, automated handling systems, computer-aided manufacturing—all the information technologies—may not translate into immediate or even short-run productivity gains. But based on the history of new technologies, long-term gains seem assured.

Consider what has happened at one of America's basic business institutions, General Electric. From 1981 to 1985, GE was pushed by its new chairman, John Welch, through a costly, painful struggle to improve its productivity. Investments in machinery, automation, and other capital expenditures averaged $2 billion to $3 billion more than GE's profits, and GE's workforce was cut by one-quarter. The result was an average gain in productivity of about 4 percent a year, four times the rate for U.S. business as a whole.

CHAPTER ★ 8 ★

Consumer Debt and Personal Savings

The Issues

The proliferation of credit cards and extended maturities on loans in the 1980s have made borrowing and consuming ever easier. Between 1977 and 1984, consumers added to their credit bill $370 billion—a staggering 60 percent more than they had added in the previous twenty-seven years.

Is this too much? Many observers feel that consumer debt is at a dangerously high level. This in turn raises the even more important issue of whether consumers can continue to take on an even greater debt load or must retrench.

The flip side of the consumption/borrowing coin is savings. The record of the American public is not encouraging. The savings rate in recent years has fallen to very low levels.

Economists disagree about the threat to the nation's economic health from the very low savings rate and, relatedly, the impact of tax policies and other public policies on saving and borrowing by individuals.

Definitions: **Consumer credit:** The sum total owed for loans on cars, home improvements, college education, appliances, and other items.

Installment credit: The sum total owed on revolving lines of credit, principally credit cards.

Personal savings rate: The percentage saved out of personal disposable (after-tax) income.

The Facts

Consumer Debt

Fact #1 *Personal debt—especially consumer credit and mortgage debt—took off in 1976; the net increase in debt in the 1976–1985 period averaged 350 percent to 380 percent more than the levels in the previous decade.*

- Comparing the period 1976–1984 to the previous decade (1966–1975), the respective average yearly level for mortgage debt was $95 billion compared to $26.8 billion and for consumer credit was $40 billion compared to $11.8 billion.

- For consumer credit, only one year prior to 1976 had exceeded $20 billion; starting in 1976, only one year fell below $20 billion.

Fact #2 *The aggregate level for both consumer loans and mortgage debt has nearly tripled in the past decade.*

- In the 1976–1985 period, mortgage debt increased from $483 billion to $1,400 billion while consumer credit went from $242 billion to $668 billion.

Fact #3   *Consumer debt has accelerated its rate of expansion in recent years.*

- Since the recession ended in late 1982, consumer debt has risen more than twice as fast as either total consumption or disposable income; it grew 25 percent more rapidly than in either of the last two major recoveries.

- By the end of 1986, consumers owed $2.5 trillion, almost ten months of after-tax earnings.

- In just three years (1983–1985), home mortgage debt increased by 37 percent to $1.5 trillion and installment debt surged by 67 percent to $548.7 billion.

- The greatest growth in consumer credit has come in the use of bank cards as bank credit card debt rose from $44.2 billion at the end of 1983 to $73.7 billion by October 31, 1985—a hefty 67 percent increase in less than two years.

Fact #4   *Since 1982 the household debt burden as a percentage of disposable income has risen from about one-quarter to nearly one-third of disposable income. In 1987, 15 million households were using at least 50 percent of disposable income to service debt.*

Fact #5   *The installment debt burden also rose dramatically beginning in 1983, reaching a record 19.2 percent of disposable personal income in mid-1986, compared with only 14 percent in early 1983.*

- It totaled $605 billion in September 1987.

Fact #6   *Millions of families are financially overextended and the toll as measured in personal bankruptcies is rising.*

- It is estimated that 20 to 25 million households are financially overextended or "entangled" in debt.

- An increasing number of debtors are deciding that the

only way out is to declare personal bankruptcy; the number rising from 179,112 in 1978, to 341,189 in 1985.

Savings

Fact #1   *The personal savings rate has shown a remarkable stability over the past thirty-five years—in the seven five-year periods from 1951 to 1985, the average for each period ranged from just under 6 percent to just over 8 percent.*

Fact #2   *Personal savings as a percent of personal disposable income has been on the decline for the past twelve years.*

- The savings rate fell from 8.6 percent in 1973 to 3.8 percent in 1986, with a particularly sharp 28 percent drop between 1981 and 1983.
- The twelve-year decline is more extraordinary because it occurred during a period when real per-capita disposable personal income rose 15 percent.

Fact #3   *The savings rate in 1985 plunged to an all-time low.*

- In September 1985, the savings rate fell to a record low 1.9 percent.
- In a number of months in mid-1985, interest payments on consumer debt actually exceeded savings.

Fact #4   *For 1986, the annual personal savings rate was still only 3.8 percent—the lowest yearly rate since 1949.*

Fact #5   *The U.S. personal savings rate is the lowest of any major industrial country.*

- In 1984, personal savings rates in the seven leading industrial countries ranged from a low of 12.2 percent in the United Kingdom to a high of 23 percent in Italy.

Interpretation
of the Facts

1. High Borrowing and Low Savings

Most economists believe that America's tax system has encouraged present consumption patterns. The system heavily rewards borrowers and punishes savers.

The other major reason given for the decline in the savings rate is demographic shifts. The savings rate of the baby boomers contrasts sharply with that of the preceding generation. The former are dissavers, the latter are savers. From 1965 to 1974, when the savings rate was relatively high, both groups grew about 12 percent to 13 percent, with the younger group adding only about 1.5 million more people than the older. But from 1974 to 1980, when the savings rate declined, the younger group increased by nearly 20 percent, or 10.4 million people, while the older group grew by less than 2 million. And, from 1980 to 1985, as the savings rate fell even more, the younger group soared by an additional 10.3 million, while the older group actually shrank by about 75,000.

In short, older households may well have boosted their savings in recent years, but many more younger Americans have been at the point in their life cycles when they are most likely to borrow and spend the money their elders are squirreling away.

2. The Threat of High Borrowing
and Low Savings

Many experts have become alarmed about the high level of consumer debt. They believe debt problems have the potential to slow economic growth and lead to a recession. They also feel many debt-laden families could sink into insolvency when the slump arrives.

The low personal savings rate has not been around long enough for judgments to have been formed. While it was in the 5 to 8 percent range during the past two decades there was little concern. If it remains in the recent 2 to 4 percent range, concern is likely to mount.

Generally, most economists do not believe current high levels of consumer debt pose an economic threat. First, they note that what consumers are doing to their balance sheet is less than what government and businesses are doing. Second, they point to the fact that households are in better shape to repay their debt than in the past. While debt has been growing fast, liquid assets (checking and savings accounts, stocks, money market funds, bonds, and other financial instruments that can be converted readily into cash) have been growing faster. For instance, in 1980, installment debt was 10.9 percent of consumer liquid assets while in 1985 it was 9.9 percent. Also, the ratio of overall household debt to liquid assets fell from a postwar peak of 69 percent in 1979 to 65 percent in late 1985.

Finally, it has been argued that consumers today can bear a given level of debt more easily because of extended maturities on loans. These lengthier loans have much lower monthly payments—an important effect of the low inflation rate—making it possible for consumers to maintain spending, since it is the size of monthly payments in relation to income that counts most.

3. Future Savings and Debt

The consensus is that consumer debt is likely to continue increasing. Indeed, although consumer credit reached a record high 19.2 percent in relation to personal income, many economists predict it will continue to grow rapidly: 25 percent of disposable income by 1990 is the figure some suggest.

The eagerness of lenders to offer credit cards and to create new types of loans encourages consumers to borrow. A prime example is home equity loans. From a base of nonexistence ten years ago, they have grown to where they now account for nearly $35 billion in consumer borrowing.

Pessimism about future savings stems from the savings' experience of the past decade. Since 1979, the incentive to save has increased dramatically, led by IRAs but including lower tax rates and deregulated interest rates on savings and checking accounts. Equally important, inflation has come way down. Thus, a saver in the Carter years would have gotten a meager 5 percent return on a passbook savings account. This "savings" was eroded by double-digit inflation and the interest taxed by the IRS up to 50 percent. Today, those savings can be earning at least 7 to 8 percent in a wide variety of accounts and financial instruments with inflation claiming only 3 to 4 percent of the return and the IRS tax burden down to a maximum of 28 percent.

Yet Americans today are saving less of their income than in 1979, despite government attempts to encourage savings in the 1980s with All-Savers Certificates, expanded IRAs, improved Keogh plans, lower tax rates, and deregulated interest rates on savings and checking accounts. Lawmakers have also done little to discourage borrowing and net savings have stayed low. Recent experience may be proving those economists right who have argued for years that government-provided savings incentives do little to increase thrift.

Another powerful force working against any sustained upward move in savings is demographics. The adverse trend cited earlier—the low-saving younger age group—will continue. Indeed, by 1990 there will be around 35 million more people in the prime spending group than in the savings group.

Possibly the most fundamental reason for the low rate of savings and the likelihood that it will continue in this way is the spectacular increase in the value of basic underlying assets: housing and stocks. From 1977 to 1983, the value of the nation's housing stock increased by nearly $2.5 trillion. Because they are amassing wealth in the form of housing, homeowners do not have to put away as much money for retirement. Instead of saving from their paychecks, they are "saving in their houses."

There's also little doubt that the wealth effect from the booming stock market is dampening the need to save. The over 200 percent rise in stock averages between the fall of 1982 and the spring of 1987 increased consumer wealth by hundreds of billions of dollars. Those fortunate enough to share in that bonanza would feel little need to add to their savings. Thus, the basic projection seems to be more of the same for at least the next five years—consumers hot on borrowing and cool on saving.

CHAPTER
★ 9 ★
Income and Wealth
of Americans

The Issues

The statistics on income and wealth, which come chiefly from the U.S. Census Bureau and the Federal Reserve, speak for themselves. They reveal how financially well-off many Americans currently are, the differences among subgroups, and trends over time.

The most controversial issue is whether the hallmark of American society—the middle class—is "shrinking," "dying," or "disappearing," all of which have been suggested in recent years. Generally, organized labor and liberal economists say it is, because of the loss of so many good-paying manufacturing jobs. Mainstream economists say it is not diminishing at all or only slightly. In fact, the definition of the middle class is a subject of great dispute.

Definitions: **Middle class:** Although most Americans who are neither millionaires nor living in poverty think of themselves as middle class, economists primarily rely on two definitions: (1) those who make between $15,000 and $35,000 a year; and (2) households with incomes between 75 percent and 125 percent of the median, putting the middle class between $18,675 and $31,000 in 1986.

The distribution of income: This is usually defined as the share of total income going to each of the 20 percent "quintiles" of the population.

Net worth: The difference between gross assets and liabilities (also commonly used as a measure of wealth).

The Facts

Household and Family Income Levels

Fact #1   *Median family income in 1986 was $29,458 while median household income was $24,897.*

Fact #2   *There is a wide range of family incomes—from $13,660 to $36,653 in 1985—depending on age, race, and marital status.*

- Married couples did far better than single-parent families, with two-earner couples at the high end of the range and female-head families at the low end of the range.

- The income of whites was 74 percent greater than that of blacks.

- By age, the under 25 and over 65 had the two lowest income levels, while families in the 45–54 age bracket had the highest overall median family income.

Fact #3   *Family incomes (adjusted for inflation) rose steadily with few interruptions until 1973; since then, they have come*

Table 1

Family Incomes in 1985
(Median income in 1985 dollars)

Family Category	Income Level
All families	$27,735
Married couple, wife working	36,431
Married couple, wife not working	24,556
Single parent, male head	22,622
Single parent, female head	13,660
all white	29,152
all black	16,786
all Hispanic	19,027
Family head under 25	15,089
Family head 25–34	26,023
Family head 35–44	32,669
Family head 44–54	36,653
Family head 55–64	30,605
Family head over 65	19,162

Source: Economic Policy Institute, "Family Incomes in Trouble," Washington, D.C., October 1986, pp. 2–3.

down for all family structures, ages, and races (with the exception of over-65 families).

- The median family income of $27,735 in 1985 was actually 5 percent lower than the median family income of $29,169 in 1973 (compared with a 23 percent gain from 1965 to 1973).

- The hardest hit have been the category of young families (with household head) whose income has dropped 22 percent since 1973.

- For the past fifteen years, the income level of whites has consistently been 70 to 80 percent greater than the income level of blacks.

Figure 1

Median Family and Household Income, 1960–1985
(In 1985 dollars)

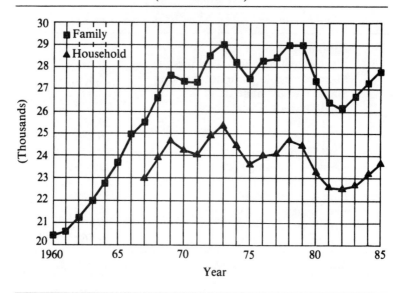

Source: Economic Policy Institute, "Family Incomes in Trouble,"
Washington, D.C., October 1986, p. 2

---

*Fact #4 In the 1980–86 period, the bottom 40 percent of
the population had an increase in income of just $199 while
the top 40 percent had an increase of $4418 and the richest
10 percent had an increase of $10,339.*

- Female-headed households actually had a $550 drop in
  real income (after taxes) from 1980 to 1985.

*Fact #5 Since 1973, young couples have done very poorly
compared to older couples in terms of income increases.*

- From 1973 to 1984, the Consumer Price Index and the
  average income of all married couples went up 134 per

cent, with the following income increases for different aged couples:

—65 and over, up 172 percent
—55–64, up 142 percent
—45–54, up 133 percent
—35–44, up 130 percent
—25–34, up 120 percent

Fact #6   *From 1960 to 1986, real average incomes increased by 38 percent while real earnings per worker rose by only 12 percent in services and 24 percent in manufacturing; the main reason for the difference is the sharp rise in the real value per employed worker of interest payments (up 209 percent) and net transfer payments made through the social-security and welfare systems (up 182 percent).*

Fact #7   *The median income of households headed by college graduates was $37,500 in 1985 or 54 percent greater than that of high school graduates.*

  • While the median income of all households rose just 2.2 percent from 1980 to 1985, householders with five or more years of college had solid gains of 15 percent.

Fact #8   *A twenty-five-year-old male who in 1953 and 1963 could expect to increase his income over the next two years by 118 percent and 108 percent respectively could expect a mere 16 percent increase in income in 1973.*

Fact #9   *A thirty-year-old male earned (in 1986 dollars) an average of $25,253 in 1973 while ten years later, the average thirty-year-old man earned only $18,763 (after adjustment for inflation)—one-fourth less.*

The Distribution of Income

Fact #1   *Income inequality was at an all-time high in 1986, with the top fifth of all households receiving 46.1 percent of total income while the bottom fifth received 3.8 percent; also the richest fifth of all families had 43.7 percent of family income, the highest ever, while the poorest fifth had 4.6 percent.*

Fact #2   In 1985, the top 5 percent received more income than the bottom 40 percent.

Fact #3   The distribution of income at the extremes has been remarkably constant over forty years.

- In 1947, the poorest 20 percent received 5 percent of income, a share that never went below 4.5 percent and never above 5.6 percent during the next forty years.

- At the other end, the richest 40 percent have received between 64.2 and 67.3 percent of total income for the past forty years.

Family Wealth

Fact #1   In 1984, the median net worth of the nation's 86.8 million households was $32,667.

- The net worth of the typical white household was $39,135, or twelve times as great as the figure for the typical black household ($3,397) and eight times as great as the typical net worth of Hispanics ($4,913).

Fact #2   Eleven percent of all Americans (over 9 million households) had no net assets or were in debt in 1984. Nearly one-third of all black households and one-quarter of Hispanics had no net assets or were in debt, while fewer than one in ten whites had no assets or were in debt.

- Another 21 percent of households hold assets worth less than $10,000, and nearly one-third of all households have a net worth of less than $10,000.

Table 2

Net Worth by Race and Spanish Origin

	Total	White	Black	Spanish
Households (thousands)	86,790	75,343	9,509	4,162
NET WORTH		(percent)		
Zero or negative	11.0	8.4	30.5	23.9
$1 to $4,999	15.3	14.0	23.9	26.3
$5,000 to $9,999	6.4	6.3	6.8	7.6
$10,000 to $24,999	12.4	12.2	14.0	11.4
$25,000 to $49,999	14.5	15.0	11.7	9.5
$50,000 to $99,999	19.3	20.7	9.3	13.1
$100,000 to $249,999	15.3	16.9	3.3	5.1
$250,000 and over	5.9	6.5	0.6	3.1
Median Net Worth	$32,667	$39,135	$3,397	$4,913

Source: Census Bureau, reported in "Wealth Disparity Surveyed," *Washington Post*, July 19, 1986, p. A10.

Fact #3   There is a huge disparity in wealth between younger and older households. The average net worth for households under thirty-five was only $5,764. The figure was $73,664 for households headed by a person aged 55–64.

- Though the elderly account for just one-sixth of the population, they hold title to one-third of all household net worth and 40 percent of all financial assets.

Fact #4   Net worth for married couple households ($50,116) is three and one-half to five times as great as for single households ($13,885 for female householders and $9,883 for male householders).

Fact #5   The percentage of families with net worth—in con-

stant (1983) dollars—exceeding $25,000 rose slightly from 1970 to 1983.

- The percentage of all families having a net worth exceeding $25,000 was 43 percent in 1970, 45 percent in 1977, and 50 percent in 1983.

Wealth in the Stock Market

Fact #1 *A relatively small proportion of Americans (mostly wealthy) own much stock, but of those who do, many have a sizable percentage of their personal wealth tied up in it.*

- In mid-1986, only 20.5 percent of all households directly owned any stock at all (the same percentage as in 1983).
- The median holding in 1986 was $5,000, while the average holding was $75,000.
- Households with incomes of more than $100,000 (only 3 percent of all households) have 71 percent of all stock.
- More than half of all stock (54 percent) is owned by the tiny percentage of households with a net worth of more than $2.5 million.
- Only 1.6 percent of those whose net worth is less than $100,000 own any stock.
- Only 2.9 percent of households have more than 25 percent of their net worth in stock.

Fact #2 *"Black Monday" (October 19, 1987) dramatically demonstrated that a great deal of personal wealth can be lost very quickly as on that one day, wealth held in the form of stock declined by over $500 billion.*

- In the bull market that lasted from August 1982 to August 1987, the Dow Jones Industrial Average rose by 250 percent.

The Rich

Fact #1   Wealth became much more concentrated in the two decades between 1963 and 1983 as the share owned by the top 0.5 percent of households rose from 25 percent to 35 percent.

Fact #2   The average net wealth per household varies greatly between the vast majority of Americans and the very rich.

Table 3
Average Wealth Per Household, 1983

Wealth Category	Number of Households	Average Wealth per Household
Top 0.5%	419,590	$8,851,736
Next 0.5%	419,590	1,702,376
Next 9.0%	7,552,620	419,616
Remaining 90%	75,526,200	39,584

Source: Federal Reserve and Joint Economic Committee

Fact #3   An extraordinary amount of national wealth—more than 45 percent—is held by the top half of 1 percent of families.

 • This same group owned 58 percent of unincorporated businesses, 46 percent of all personally owned corporate stock, 77 percent of the value of trusts, and 62 percent of state and local bonds.

Fact #4   The most affluent 10 percent of families own nearly 72 percent of the nation's wealth.

Fact #5   The vast majority of the rich are white: 2.1 percent of all the households in America are white with an income over $500,000, while only .1 percent of all the households are black with that same income.

Fact #6   Entrepreneurs, who head about 2 percent of all families, head nearly 33 percent of the wealthiest families, those with incomes greater than $280,000.

- After entrepreneurs come families headed by lawyers and accountants and then those headed by health professionals.

Fact #7   The combined net worth of the 482 wealthiest individuals and families is at least $166 billion in business investment assets. This gives them control over an estimated $2,000 billion in business assets, or about 90 percent of all fixed nonresidential private capital in the U.S. in 1984.

The Middle Class

Fact #1   The middle class is not necessarily "dying."

- Among full-time year-round workers, the middle third actually increased its share of total earnings from 1970 to 1982, from 26.2 percent to 29.4 percent.
- The proportion of workers with middle-income jobs (those paying $17,200 to $20,000 in 1982) was almost exactly the same in 1982 as in 1973.
- A ranking of 416 occupations by 1982 pay shows the share of workers in middle-income jobs to be stable— 34 percent in 1973 and 33.4 percent in 1982.
- In 1969, 50 percent of full-time workers were middle income, while in 1983, 46 percent were middle income.

Fact #2   But the middle class is shrinking.

- Statistics from the U.S. Census Bureau show families with annual earnings of between $15,000 and $35,000 made up 53 percent of all families in 1970 and 44 percent in 1982.

- The Congressional Research Service concludes that there has been a small decline of the middle class in recent years, noting that the share of total income received by the middle fifth of the population declined from 17.9 percent in 1967 to 17.0 percent in 1984.

- If the middle class is defined as those families with incomes between $20,000 and $50,000 (in 1984 dollars), then the fraction of middle-class families has declined from 53 percent in 1973 to 48 percent in 1984.

Interpretation of the Facts

---

1. The Future: Is the Middle Class Disappearing?

America, long and widely known for its huge middle class, has heard unprecedented charges in recent years that its middle class is dramatically shrinking. Organized labor, as embodied in the AFL-CIO, has been the loudest voice propounding this thesis, as in the excerpt below "Yes."

A chorus of other voices, principally coming from mainstream economists, has been raised, saying in essence that the evidence points to no such shrinkage. Robert Samuelson, an economic columnist for *Newsweek*, captures the thrust of these economists' argument in the excerpt "No."

Is the Middle Class Disappearing?

Yes	No
Industrial Union Department, AFL-CIO	Robert Samuelson
At the same time that the number of poor families has been swelling, the number of middle class families has been shrinking. As poll after poll	Somehow the notion of a declining middle has struck a responsive chord. The middle class' impending shrinkage has been proclaimed by several

shows, most people in this country consider themselves middle class. Unfortunately, in recent years it has become more difficult for many families to sustain or for young families to achieve a middle class standard of living. . . .

The expansion at the top and bottom, of course, is related to a decline in the proportion of middle class families (with income from $15,000 to $50,000) in this country from 1974 to 1978, a loss of 1.2 million families.

The same trends appear in the later period, 1979 to 1985, but at a faster rate. By 1985, compared to the distribution of families in 1979, there were 3.7 percent fewer families in the middle class, with most of the shift creating more lower income families—an additional 2.1 percent or 1.33 million lower income families— and an increase in the proportion of upper income families. . . .

Harvard economists Blackburn and Bloom have also identified a shrinkage of the middle class, in a study which finds, "The decline of the middle class appeared in every measure we examined. Whether we used our concept of family or the Census Bureau's definition, middle class

major magazines and economists. Even when it hasn't been announced explicitly, the idea has subtly flavored popular economic commentary. Ordinary middle-income jobs are seen to be vanishing, replaced only by high-paying and low-paying work. There's a reinforcing media imagery of shut-down factories, booming fast-food restaurants and affluent young professionals.

But this sweeping notion of a declining middle never has rested on hard evidence; it has been a pure case of social theorizing by stereotype. Yet it's flourished. Why?

Most popular notions about job polarization dissolve on close examination. Some workers have lost, but others have gained. True, many well-paying steel and auto jobs have vanished, but the loss equals only a small part of total employment (0.5 percent). Contrary to popular belief, production jobs in most high technology industries pay above-average wages. Many service jobs are low-paying, but many also pay well. Likewise, many of the low-paying service jobs simply replace other low-paying jobs (farmhands, laborers) whose growth is now small. When all these changes—and many more—are

families fell as a share of all families. . . .

No one has yet been able to determine which of the causes of the shrinking middle class are most important. Yet, the factors discussed [earlier] create an environment in which it will be tremendously difficult to forestall a further erosion of the middle class. These pressures include high unemployment, falling real wages and income, an increased share of profit and non-labor income in the economy, an increased maldistribution of wealth, persistent racial and gender gaps, and a loss of good jobs due to deindustrialization and the employment shift towards a "service economy." (AFL-CIO, *The Polarization of America*, Washington, D.C., 1986, pp. 75–77.)

considered, there's no pronounced trend for jobs to cluster at the top and bottom of the pay scale.

So our middle-income jobs remain, but our middle-class security is shaken. There are two realities here—what actually is happening and what we think is happening—and I'm not sure which is more significant. It's important to separate economic fact and fiction. Believing something that isn't true contributes to a false (and, in this case, unduly pessimistic) view of our own well-being. ("The Myth of the Missing Middle," *Newsweek*, July 1, 1985, p. 50.)

CHAPTER
★ 10 ★
Poverty

The Issues

Scarcely any economic issue stirs the passions of Americans
to the degree that poverty does. At one extreme are those
who feel that most people in poverty are welfare chiselers
and that the government should get out of the poverty business altogether. At the other extreme are those who feel
that the government should establish a cradle-to-grave welfare state.

The beliefs of the vast majority of Americans lie somewhere between these extremes. Conservatives feel the government is doing too much and should pare back its programs
significantly. Liberals want to keep the successful programs
in place, perhaps expand them, and even add a few new
wrinkles. These arguments, and the new common ground
solution for many conservatives and liberals—workfare—are

explored in the Interpretation section. To understand and judge these arguments, a thorough understanding of all the basic facts is essential to judge the poverty question.

Definition: **Poverty** has been defined officially in America for only a little over two decades. In 1964, the Johnson administration created the poverty line by looking to a 1955 survey that had found that the average family of three or more spent about one-third of its income on food. The poverty line was then set at three times the cost of the cheapest nutritionally sound diet the Department of Agriculture could devise.

Beginning in 1968, the poverty line was adjusted upward annually to reflect inflation. Since the real income of average U.S. families has risen since then, the 1986 poverty line equals about 33 percent of median family income compared to 44 percent in 1964. In 1986, the poverty lines were:

$ 5,701, one person under age 65
  7,370, two persons, head of household under 65
  8,738, three persons
11,203, four persons

Some experts argue that the poverty lines are set too low since the government picked an "economy" diet of admittedly inadequate nutritional value as the basis for the standard. A healthy "low cost" diet would cost about 20 percent more. If that higher standard had been in effect in 1984, the number in poverty would not have been the official 35.5 million, but 45 million, or nearly one-fifth of all Americans.

The Facts

National Poverty Statistics

Fact #1 *Since 1959, the number of Americans living in poverty has never gone below 24 million and the poverty rate has never gone below 11 percent.*

Fact #2 *The poverty rate was cut in half between 1960 and 1973 (22.2 to 11.1 percent), held quite steady until 1979, rose sharply to a peak of 15.2 percent in 1983, and declined to 13.6 percent in 1986.*

Fact #3 *In the 1960s, the poverty rate dropped 10.3 percentage points; in the 1970s it dropped 0.4 percentage points; from 1980 through 1986 it increased 1.9 percentage points.*

Fact #4 *The poverty rate in 1986—13.6 percent—was just below the rate in 1967, three years after the War on Poverty was launched.*

- About 32.4 million people were in poverty, 13 million in married couple families.
- Two-thirds were white.
- The poverty rate was 11 percent for whites, 31.1 percent for blacks, and 27.3 percent for Hispanics.
- Nearly 40 percent of the poor (12.7 million) lived in households that had incomes 50 percent less than the poverty line.

Fact #5 *The poverty rate varies dramatically for different age groups.*

- In 1986, the poverty rates were: 21.2 percent for under 15, 16 percent for 15–24, 16.2 percent for 25–44, 8.2 percent for 45–54, 10 percent for 55–59, 9.9 percent for 60–64, and 12.4 percent for 65 and older.

Black Poverty and
the Black Underclass

Fact #1 *The poverty rate for black Americans has never fallen below 30 percent since these statistics first began to be kept. Its peak was 55.1 percent in 1959, the first year poverty statistics for blacks alone became available.*

Fact #2   *The poverty rate for blacks has been, since 1959, consistently triple (or more) that for whites until 1984 when it dropped slightly below its historical ratio of 3:1.*

Fact #3   *In 1985, blacks had their largest decrease in poverty since 1968 and were the only group that showed a substantial decrease in poverty, from 33.8 to 31.3 percent. The rate for people of Hispanic origin actually rose from 28.4 to 29.0 percent in 1985 but fell sharply in 1986 to 27.3 percent.*

Fact #4   *In recent years, a seemingly permanent black underclass has emerged that is largely isolated from mainstream America and numbers 2 to 3.5 million (about one-third of all poor blacks).*

- Blacks compose only 12 percent of the population, but make up 62 percent of those who stay poor for a long time and 58 percent of the "latent" poor (those who would be poor but for welfare).

- In 1950, 16 percent of children born to blacks and other minorities were born to unwed mothers; by 1983, 58 percent of black infants were born to unwed mothers, compared to 12.8 percent of white newborns.

- In 1960, about 21 percent of black families with children were headed by a woman with no husband present. By 1985, half of such families were headed by women, compared to 15 percent for whites.

- In December 1955, blacks and other minorities had an unemployment rate of 8.2 percent, compared to 3.7 percent for whites. In December 1985, black unemployment was 14.9 percent, compared to 5.9 percent for whites. For black teenagers the rate was 41.6 percent, versus 15.9 percent for white teenagers.

- In 1960, about three out of every four black children under eighteen lived with two parents; by 1984, only 41 percent did (contrasted with 81 percent for white children).

- Of black children today, one in two lives in poverty and one in two grows up without a father.

(Most statistics above cited in "While Most Gain, Millions Suffer," *Washington Post*, January 20, 1986, pp. A1 and A11.)

Children

Fact #1   *The poverty rate for children in 1986 (19.8 percent) was nearly the same as in 1965, the year after the War on Poverty was launched, and it was one-third higher than in 1973.*

- For children in female-headed families the rate was 54.4 percent vs. only 10.8 percent in all other families.

Fact #2   *A child in America is six times more likely to be poor than an elderly person.*

Fact #3   *More than one out of every two children under age eighteen being raised by a mother alone was in poverty in 1985.*

- At 53.6 percent, their poverty rate was more than quadruple that of children in two-parent families.
- Approximately two-thirds of black children (67.1 percent) and Hispanic children (66.7 percent) living in female-headed families were poor in 1986.

Fact #4   *In 1986, the poverty rate for children under eighteen living in families was 17.7 percent for whites, 45.6 percent for blacks, and 40.7 percent for Hispanics.*

Fact #5   *Of the 33.7 million poor people in 1984, 12.9 million—35 percent—were children.*

The Elderly

Fact #1   *Poverty rates among the aged have declined by nearly two-thirds since 1959, from 35.2 percent to 12.4 percent in 1986.*

- For elderly married couples in 1985, the rate was only 6 percent while for elderly female-headed families it was 23 percent.

Fact #2   *From 1959 to 1972, the poverty rate for the aged was always double or more that of non-aged adults; since then, it has shrunk to a ratio as low as 1.1:1 in 1983.*

Fact #3   *The first year in which the aged poverty rate was less than that of children was 1974, and it has remained substantially below the children's rate ever since.*

Fact #4   *Between 1959 and 1984, the elderly went from being 30.5 percent of the poor to comprising only 9.8 percent of the poor.*

Fact #5   *In 1985, the poverty rate among the elderly was lower than for any other age group; when one accounts for noncash benefits, the adjusted poverty rate of the elderly is less than half the rate for prime working-age adults.*

Fact #6   *Elderly women are much worse off than elderly men.*

- Of the 3.3 million people aged 65 and over living in poverty in 1984, 2.7 million of them, or about 70 percent, were women.
- Fifteen percent of elderly women and 8.7 percent of elderly men live in poverty.
- Forty-three percent of elderly men and 20 percent of elderly women were receiving pensions to supplement their Social Security benefits.

- Of 8 million elderly who lived alone in 1984, 6.4 million, about 80 percent, were women.

Female-Headed Families

Fact #1 *The feminization of poverty occurred two decades ago: in the 1960s the percentage of women among the adult poor grew significantly. It remained relatively stable in the 1970s but declined from 1979 to 1984.*

Fact #2 *The greatest differences in poverty rates are between two-parent and female-headed families.*

- In 1986, the poverty rate for female-headed households, with and without children, was 34.6 percent, compared to 6.1 percent for married-couple families.

Fact #3 *Families headed by a female under age 65 accounted for 45 percent of the poor households in 1984, more than two and one-half times the proportion in this category in 1959.*

- Less than half (48 percent) of poor families in 1984 were married-couple families.

Fact #4 *In recent years (1979–1985), poverty grew substantially faster among married-couple families (up 32 percent) than among families headed by women (up 23 percent).*

Poverty While Working

Fact #1 *In 1986, 41 percent of all poor people 15 years old and older worked and about 2 million worked full-time, year-round (about 14 percent of the adult poor).*

- Overall, 8.9 million people who worked in 1986 remained in poverty, compared to 6.6 million a decade earlier.

Fact #2   In 1985, nearly one out of five married couples was below the poverty line, despite the heads of those households being employed year-round (in 1973 and 1979 the figures were 12.7 percent and 14.1 percent, respectively).

Duration of Poverty

Fact #1   Many people move in and out of poverty each year.

- In the period 1969–1978, about 25 percent of people surveyed had lived in poverty or received welfare benefits at some time.

- Nearly half of the individuals living in poverty for one year had climbed out of poverty within a year or two.

- Only 2.6 percent of the survey sample could be classed as persistently poor (failing to meet the government's poverty living standard in eight or more of the ten years).

- Less than 0.9 percent of the households were poor during all ten years.

Fact #2   Research on Aid to Families with Dependent Children (AFDC) indicates that nearly half of AFDC recipient periods last less than one year, whereas only 16 to 18 percent last five years or more.

Poverty Programs—
Beneficiaries

Fact #1   Around one-half of federal transfer payments for the poor go to the elderly and disabled through Medicaid and Supplemental Social Security.

- When all noncash benefits such as food stamps and subsidized housing are counted, only one elderly person in thirty is poor.

Fact #2   About half the money spent on welfare at any one time goes to single mothers.

Fact #3 *The average poor rural American in 1983 received $635 in cash, food, and other income benefits from government programs based on need, compared with $1,406 for urban residents.*

Fact #4 *One of three American children lives in a household that receives some form of government welfare, including food stamps, Medicaid, or cash payments.*

- In 1984 one of four white children lived in households receiving one or more means-tested benefits, compared to 68 percent of black children and 52 percent of Hispanic children.

Fact #5 *Around one-quarter of all black families and 3 percent of all white families over the past fifteen years have received AFDC payments.*

Fact #6 *In 1987, around 11 million Americans in 3.7 million families received AFDC payments; the number of families was near the 1981 all-time high of 3.9 million.*

Fact #7 *The number of welfare recipients trained for jobs is minuscule.*

- The main program, the Work Incentive Program, moved 13,000 people off welfare in 1985 (about 1 percent of those on AFDC).
- Current "workfare" programs are estimated to cover about 1 percent of AFDC recipients.
- Funding for work and training programs was cut 50 percent in real dollars from 1981 to 1986.

Fact #8 *Without government support programs, one American in four would fall below the poverty level.*

Fact #9 *Most government transfer payments do not go to the poor.*

- Of the $300 billion in noncash benefits from all governments in 1985, four-fifths of the cases (totaling $250 billion) involved no required income test; thus, the money went mostly to the nonpoor.
- Of the $365 billion spent by the federal government in 1985 in cash and in-kind benefits, $299 billion went for non-means-tested programs while just $66 billion went for means-tested programs.

Fact #10   The number of people receiving benefits from means-tested programs in 1984 were: food stamps (7 million households), free or reduced price school meals (5.6 million), subsidized housing (3.6 million), and Medicaid (8.3 million households).

Poverty Programs—Costs

Fact #1   From 1965 to 1975, means-tested noncash transfers increased sevenfold from $5.7 billion to $38.2 billion (in constant 1984 dollars); total means-tested real transfers tripled, jumping from $24.0 billion in 1965 to $72.7 billion in 1975.

Fact #2   In the 1975–1984 period, expenditures on means-tested cash assistance actually declined, but this was more than offset by continued growth in noncash benefits; thus by 1984 total means-tested expenditures in real terms were nearly three and one-half times the 1965 level ($80.3 billion compared to $24.0 billion in 1965).

Fact #3   The two top poverty programs (in terms of federal spending) in 1986 were food stamps ($10.4 billion) and AFDC ($9.5 billion).

Fact #4   Federal cash welfare programs, after growing by 70 percent in real dollars from 1965 to 1976, have declined by 6 percent since then.

<u>Fact #5</u> *Non-cash welfare benefits accounted for about 10 percent of total federal welfare expenditures in 1965, about half in 1975, and two-thirds in 1986.*

Interpretation
of the Facts

---

1. Preventing Poverty in America

There is perhaps no other economic question for which the battle lines between the traditional old-fashioned camps of conservatives and liberals have been more clearly drawn. Each group views poverty with economic lenses that focus only on those facts they want to see—essentially those facts that would support their respective agendas to reduce the welfare state or expand it. By the mid-1980s, the lines were considerably fuzzier, particularly with regard to what should be done to combat poverty. The program known as "workfare" has forged some undreamed-of conservative-liberal alliances. Yet there is still a wide gulf of disagreement about how to view the poverty problem and the question of the success or nonsuccess of past welfare programs.

The Conservatives Charles Murray's 1984 book, *Losing Ground*, stirred sharp debate by insisting that government aid to the poor was not only ineffective but fundamentally pernicious because it destroyed individual initiative, undermined family life, and created an army of people dependent on the dole. In Murray's words: "We tried to provide more for the poor and produced more poor instead. We tried to remove the barriers to escape from poverty and inadvertently built a trap."

Take, for instance, the decline in the number of black poor. In 1970, this was taken as evidence of the Great Society's success. To Murray, it correlated with GNP growth, not with antipoverty spending. Most of the decline occurred before the boom in social programs.

The argument that the government is "rewarding" people for being poor has been made by many other leading conservatives including Nobel Prize-winning economist Milton Friedman; former Reagan White House domestic policy head Martin Anderson; black economists Thomas Sowell of the Hoover Institution and Walter Williams of George Mason University; and George Gilder, author of *Wealth and Poverty*, which was the first major conservative broadside against the welfare state.

A major critique of welfare is based on its impact on the erosion of the family. It is a chicken and egg situation. It is argued that increasing poverty funds contributes to the breakup of the family and the tremendous rise in female-headed households because AFDC funds only go to female-headed households. Changes in family structure were found by a University of Michigan study to be "by far the most important" cause for thrusting so many people into poverty in the decade (1969–1978) studied.

This feminization of poverty is also an integral part of the criticism conservatives direct at poverty programs. Their point is not that people have babies simply to exploit welfare. Rather, Murray thinks the welfare liberalization of the 1960s and early 1970s loosened the social controls against illegitimacy. Pressures on men to marry and to work dropped. Meanwhile births among unmarried women rose to account for half of all black births and one-tenth of white births.

Where Murray and many other conservative critics part company is about solutions. Murray calls for scrapping all the major welfare programs—AFDC, Medicaid, food stamps, subsidized housing, disability insurance, compensatory education, and affirmative action programs that give special breaks to minorities. Murray maintains that ending these programs would force many of the poor to get jobs, and most of the rest would depend on private charity. In Murray's view, the poor, on the whole, would be better off. Still, he is not particularly cheery about this new system: "I am proposing triage of a sort, triage by self-selection."

One solution most conservatives agree on is "self-help." Listen to Robert Woodson, chairman of the Council for a Black Economic Agenda and president of the National Center for Neighborhood Enterprise: "If Black America is to achieve its rightful place in American society, it will not be by virtue of what white America grants to black Americans but because of what black Americans do for themselves. We must end our preoccupation with what white America feels about or does to us." To paraphrase Harvard economist Glenn Loury, while all of our energy is directed to the struggle against the "enemy without," the "enemy within" goes relatively unchecked.

This self-help solution, however, does not belong to the conservatives alone. While it appeals to them in shifting the focus away from a "civil rights" strategy that relies on government intervention, it also appeals to many liberals who are hesitant to tell blacks how to behave or how to escape their poverty. Roger Wilkins, former head of the Urban League and a black liberal, accepts both the need for changing underclass culture and the assumption that "only black people can do this." "It's all up to blacks" appears to be a new left-right consensus.

The Liberals Murray's thesis has captured much of the attention in the poverty debate. Yet for every expert who lines up behind Murray in condemnation of the welfare system, there is another who argues that programs for the needy have indeed lifted millions out of want and that it is both callous and simplistic to call the War on Poverty a failure. After all, it cannot be denied that food stamps have largely eliminated hunger, Medicaid has provided health care unimagined thirty years ago, and Social Security has sharply cut poverty among the elderly.

Liberals also attack Murray's view that growth of the welfare state blocked the progress that economic growth had been making in reducing the poverty rate by an average of one percentage point a year until the late 1960s. "He ignores the fact that the unemployment rate in the 1980s is much higher than in the 1960s, and economic growth is slower, too," says Robert Greenstein, director of the Center on Budget and Policy Priorities in Washington, D.C. "When unemployment goes up, the poor and minorities are hurt more than most."

Liberals also charge that Murray and his fellow conservatives espouse a number of myths and like to hide from the facts:

- *Myth:* Government welfare programs do no good.
  Fact: One American in four would now fall below the poverty level without government support programs.

- *Myth:* Poor people refuse to work and just live off welfare.
  Fact: Of 7.3 million families living in poverty in 1984, more than half had at least one worker and more than 20 percent had two or more workers. Also, 1.4 million able-bodied poor sought work but were unable to find it.

- *Myth:* Most poor people are black, members of households headed by women, and reside in central cities.
  Fact: In 1984, more than two-thirds of the 34 million poor were white, only one-third of the poor lived in female-headed households, and two-thirds of all poor families resided in rural or suburban areas.

Although there is no one set liberal agenda, Peter Edelman (professor of law at Georgetown University and an assistant to both Robert and Ted Kennedy) encapsulates the basic program. His mix would include:

A. Prevention—Keeping Things That Have Worked:
- Head Start
- Prenatal and infant health care

- Federally financed help in reading and math for poor children in the early grades
- Help teenagers enter the job market:
  - more attention to basic skills in high schools
  - getting the schools to work more closely with local employers
  - expanding the Job Corps
  - improving vocational education

B. Motivation—New Initiatives
- Guarantee a part-time job to low-income students on condition that they stay in school and perform satisfactorily
- A federally funded job guarantee to young people, but only if they have completed their education or training and still cannot find work
- Find and seek to remove all the barriers to working:
  - establish day care centers
  - give families who pay no taxes their tax credit for day care in the form of a direct cash payment

(Peter B. Edelman, "What Shall We Do About America's Poor Now?" *Washington Post*, February 3, 1985, p. 61.)

2. Workfare: The Common Ground of Conservatives and Liberals?

"Workfare" is the new rallying cry in the field of welfare reform. *Time* magazine reported in 1986: "In statehouses across the country, Democrats and Republicans have joined forces to support legislation that combines the job programs traditionally favored by liberals with efforts to pare the welfare rolls advocated by conservatives."

By late 1986, thirty-nine states were running workfare experiments. Significantly, three of the five biggest states in the union—California, New York, and Illinois—plan to apply workfare ideas to their entire welfare caseloads. However, multi-component programs that emphasize education and training, though receiving the most publicity, are the exception.

Workfare Positives According to the one comprehensive study of it done to date, workfare is a success. The study, done by the Manpower Demonstration Research Corporation, focused on workfare programs in San Diego, Baltimore, and Arkansas. Persons in the experimental groups found more jobs, earned more money, and cost the government less than did welfare mothers in a control group. Specifically, employment rates for workfare graduates were 3 to 8 percentage points higher than for other welfare recipients. The study also found that most states came out ahead. The reduction in AFDC outlays ranged from almost none in Maryland to 11 percent in Arkansas; in most areas, they ranged from 5 to 8 percent.

Workfare can take many forms. Differences often lie in the degree of toughness involved. At one extreme—the soft, all-voluntary one—is Massachusett's Employment and Training Choices program, affectionately known as ET. This is the first major workfare-type program and its successes have been highly touted. In the first three years after its October 1983 inception, 30,000 welfare recipients were placed in unsubsidized jobs in the private sector. Massachusetts spent $71 million on ET during its first two years and estimates it saved $223 million during that time. ET's supporters point to two reasons for its success: first, its seems to have changed the perception that welfare mothers are unemployable; second, it is based on providing incentives for voluntary participation rather than mandatory requirements.

California enacted legislation in the fall of 1985 for a workfare program that would do "something that never has been done," according to its Health and Welfare Secretary David Swoap: bring all liberals and conservatives together and combine work requirements with training programs. GAIN (Greater Avenues for Independence) is big. It is an attempt to impose a mandatory program on the largest welfare caseload in the country. It provides for job counseling; supervised job searches; job training for the unskilled; classes for those who lack English or a high school diploma; and a contract listing the steps to be taken. For those who cannot find work elsewhere, public-service jobs will be found.

Workfare Negatives Workfare may have developed an unusual degree of bipartisan support but it also has its share of bipartisan critics. The objections raised are numerous and forceful:

- Much of the "success" of workfare is really a by-product of a robust economy between 1983 and 1985.
- It displaces people in the regular labor force.
- It excludes 60 percent of all adult AFDC recipients by exempting single parents with school-age children.
- A number of states have found welfare savings to be less than program cost—roughly 50 cents returned to the state treasury for every dollar spent on workfare.
- It places too much emphasis on getting clients into the job market quickly rather than enrolling them in education courses leading to more useful and lucrative lines of work.
- A survey of thirteen states with more than 2.5 million families on welfare found only 58,000 people enrolled in workfare.
- There may not be enough jobs to go around for the programs' undereducated participants.
- It is a sort of punishment for being poor, since the vast majority of welfare recipients are young, unwed mothers with few if any marketable skills who are forced to take demeaning low-paying jobs under workfare.
- Very few families leave welfare rolls through workfare.
- It does not address America's most serious unemployment problem—the jobless rate of black teenagers.
- It does not do much to employ those in the underclass who have few welfare benefits to "work off," namely, able-bodied men.

• Studies have shown that huge "gross" job placement gains turn out to be slim or nonexistent "net" improvements over the placements that would have happened anyway.

• The grandiose claims for ET do not stand up to close inspection:
  – One-third of those placed in jobs are only in part-time jobs.
  – Half of its full-time job placements paid less than $4.50 an hour.
  – Half of the part-time placements paid less than $3.75 an hour.
  – A year after they leave the program, about half of ET's success stories still are not earning enough to go off welfare completely.
  – Most fundamentally, only 6.8 percent of the welfare cases in 1985 got full-time jobs through ET, and thus it does not come close to "solving the problem" of the culture of poverty.
  – The numbers distort the program's success, since only 31 percent of welfare recipients participated in ET.
  – ET, like most workfare programs, has placed the most easily employable in jobs first.

3. The Future of Poverty in America

The experts are in general agreement regarding the future of poverty in America: it is not going to change significantly. As highlighted in the opening chapter, it is one of America's stubborn "constants"—the poverty rate in the twenty-three years since the War on Poverty was launched in 1964 has fluctuated between 11.4 and 19 percent. After spending hundreds of billions of dollars in the past two decades "attacking" poverty, 32.4 million Americans were living in poverty in 1986.

Workfare, the latest warrior to combat poverty, has been generally found to be only a partial remedy. It will likely help alleviate the problem in certain states and cities, but it is not likely to lead to a substantial reduction in the number of the nation's poor.

In short, the experts echo Matthew: "Ye have the poor always with you."

CHAPTER
★ 11 ★

The Trade
Deficit

The Issues

Inflation is out. Unemployment is out. Poverty is out. Trade
is the IN economic topic of the 1980s.

Everyone is talking about it and virtually everyone has a
solution to the sizeable U.S. trade deficit. Few know what
they are talking about.

Here we are entering an economic arena filled with emotions. It's often an "Us vs Them" mentality and thus the
simple solution is "let's get them." So the U.S. Congress in
1985 and 1986 was besieged with literally hundreds of trade
initiatives—most of them protectionist. Finally, action was
taken in 1987 as a major omnibus trade bill, the first in over
a decade, worked its way through the House and Senate
despite vigorous Administration opposition to many of its
provisions.

This keen interest has arisen in recent years because like the budget deficit in the 1980s, the trade deficit has exploded. The deficit went from tolerable levels of under $40 billion a year before 1983 to deficits that averaged $120 billion in the 1983–1986 period. This was rightly perceived as a heavy mortgage on our future. Others raised cries of alarm about the massive loss of U.S. jobs.

In such an emotion-laden arena, facts are needed more than ever as the U.S. faces the major issue of whether to erect protectionist walls around its industries or let international market forces assert themselves.

The Facts

Merchandise Trade Balance

Fact #1   The U.S. had either a trade surplus or a very small deficit (less than $10 billion) up to 1977; since then, the trade deficit has not gone below $25 billion and has gone as high as $156.1 billion in 1986.

Fact #2   The 1986 trade deficit of $156.1 billion was about four times as large as the record high deficit up to 1983.

Fact #3   The trade deficit is projected to increase to around $170 billion in 1987 despite the steep three-year fall in the value of the dollar.

Fact #4   U.S. trade in the 1982–1986 period deteriorated both in terms of product groups and trading partners.

- The U.S. merchandise trade balance worsened in nine of the ten major product groups used to classify trade, including such disparate sectors as chemicals, food, and live animals, and machinery and transport equipment. It improved only in the mineral fuels and lubricants sector.

Table 1
Merchandise Trade Balance, 1970–1986
(billions of $)

Calendar Year	Merchandise Trade Balance	Exports	Imports
1970	.2	42.7	42.4
1971	−4.8	43.5	48.3
1972	−9.7	49.2	58.9
1973	2.8	70.8	73.6
1974	−12.8	98.1	110.9
1975	1.8	107.6	105.9
1976	−17.3	115.2	132.5
1977	−39.2	121.2	160.4
1978	−42.4	143.7	186.0
1979	−40.4	181.9	222.2
1980	−36.4	220.6	257.0
1981	−39.7	233.7	273.4
1982	−42.7	212.2	254.9
1983	−69.4	200.5	269.9
1984	−123.3	217.9	341.2
1985	−148.5	213.1	361.6
1986	−156.1	226.8	382.9

- The U.S. bilateral trade position worsened against all of the top ten trading partners and nineteen of the top twenty.

Fact #5   From 1983 to 1986, American exports rose about 21 percent in real terms (about 15 percent slower than average export growth over past expansions); imports surged 80 percent in real terms (about twice as rapidly as in past expansions).

Fact #6   Since 1950, the only period of real strength in U.S. trade was the 1970s, when the growth in exports was greater than the growth in imports and when average yearly increases

<u>*Figure 1*</u>

Growth in Exports and Imports
(average yearly rates)

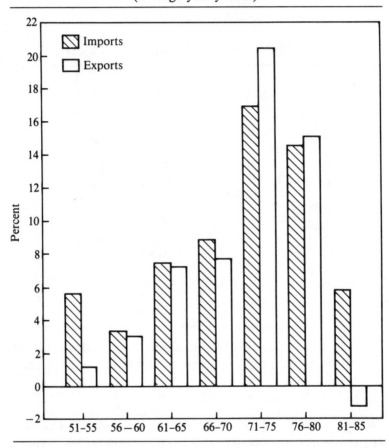

for both exports and imports shot way above 10 percent to
increases ranging from 14 to 21 percent.

<u>*Fact #7*</u> *The monthly trade deficit went above $10 billion
in June 1985 for the first time. In October 1987, a record
$17.6 billion monthly trade deficit was recorded.*

Changes in Trade Balance
for Key Industries

Fact #1 *The following industries went from a trade surplus in 1980 to a trade deficit by 1984: semiconductors, electronic components, photographic equipment, general aviation aircraft, shipbuilding and repair, confectionery products, textiles, leather goods, household appliances, telephone equipment, musical instruments, tool and die machine tools, and computer-controlled machining centers.*

Fact #2 *In a few short years agriculture went from being one of America's strongest trade surplus sectors to a small surplus in 1986.*

- The U.S. agricultural trade surplus peaked at $26.6 billion in 1981, declining steadily to $7.5 billion in 1986.

- The deterioration of the trade balance is due to a slow but steady increase in imports from $17.2 billion in 1981 to $20.5 billion in 1987 and to a sharp decrease in exports from $44 billion in 1981 to $28 billion in 1987.

- In May 1986, U.S. farm trade ran in the red for the first time in twenty-seven years (and went on in the following two months to record deficits).

Fact #3 *The manufacturers' trade balance had a swing of $158.8 billion in just six years, from a surplus of $13.7 billion in 1980 to a $145.1 billion deficit in 1986.*

- Foreign manufacturers now supply 26 percent of the U.S. market for all goods except farm and petroleum products, a share double their 13 percent of a decade ago.

- The monthly trade deficit in manufactured goods hit $16.1 billion in July 1986.

Fact #4 *The U.S., which once dominated world markets in*

capital goods, saw import's share of the U.S. market rise from 8 percent in 1970 to 26 percent in 1984.

- In 1984, 50 cents of every dollar spent on capital equipment went overseas.

Fact #5   Although the U.S. remains the leading exporter of high technology products ($65 billion in 1984), its trade balance has steadily declined from a peak surplus of $26.7 billion in 1981 to a $2 billion deficit in 1986.

- Although the trade surplus did not begin to fall until 1982, the U.S. export share of high technology products declined in the 1970s, peaking at 29.7 percent in 1968 and hitting its low of 23.1 percent in 1978.

Fact #6   Electronics trade slipped into the red for the first time in 1984, posting a $6.8 billion deficit.

- The deficit reflected a flood of imports, a 13 percent decline in exports of computers, and a $2.9 billion trade deficit in semiconductors.

Fact #7   The U.S. trade deficit for energy, having peaked at $75 billion in 1980, fell to $29 billion in 1986.

Export Trends

Fact #1   For the first time since World War II, the U.S. slipped to second place in total exports in 1986, behind West Germany and only slightly ahead of Japan: West Germany sold $245 billion, the U.S. $217 billion, and Japan $209 billion.

Fact #2   The U.S. share of world exports slipped from 12 percent in 1980 to 11 percent in 1986.

Fact #3   Nearly one-fifth of everything manufactured in the United States is exported.

- Leading the wide variety of exported products in 1984 were machinery ($40.6 billion), grain and cereal ($16.1 billion), and office equipment ($14.6 billion).

Fact #4 *In 1986, the U.S. had a world-high $48 billion of service exports; the Office of Technology Assessment says that the true value may be twice as high.*

- The previous record trade surplus in services—$10.7 billion in 1982—is expected to be topped in 1987.

Fact #5 *In the 1960s and 1970s, real exports increased about 7.5 percent a year. From 1980 to mid-1985, they actually fell by 12 percent.*

Fact #6 *The high tech share of exports rose from 34 percent to 42 percent during the 1980s.*

- U.S. exports have become increasingly concentrated in areas where American producers have a comparative advantage and where world demand promises to grow quickly: aircraft instruments, specialty chemicals, telecommunications equipment, computers, semiconductors, drugs, and biological products.

Fact #7 *Over one-third of total exports come from the top fifty exporting companies—$73.4 billion out of a 1986 total of $217.3 billion.*

- The top five export companies for both 1985 and 1986 were (1986 amount in parentheses): General Motors ($8.4 billion), Boeing ($7.3 billion), Ford Motor ($7.2 billion), General Electric ($4.3 billion), IBM ($3.1 billion).

Fact #8 *Almost 60 percent of the $8 billion in export loans from the Export-Import Bank from 1978 to 1987 went to two industries: aircraft and nuclear power.*

Fact #9 *Eighty-eight countries in 1984 required some form of countertrade in which the U.S. exporter, to complete the deal, promises to buy or market products from the partner nation; only fifteen countries had such requirements in 1982.*

Import Trends

Fact #1 *Imported goods accounted for 19 percent of all products sold in 1986, up from 13.4 percent in 1980; in the summer of 1987, they reached 25 percent, their highest share ever.*

- Imports grew by 65 percent from 1980 to 1986 to a record 27 percent of the U.S. market for goods other than oil and farm products.

Fact #2 *Seventy percent of the goods U.S. firms produce face fierce competition from abroad.*

Fact #3 *In nearly every major manufacturing industry from 1960 to 1985, imports substantially increased their percentage share of the U.S. market.*

Fact #4 *The U.S. has been the world's strongest importing nation in recent years. In 1986, it bought 55 percent of the manufactured goods exported by developing countries while Western Europe took half that much and Japan only 9 percent.*

Fact #5 *In 1985 and 1986 there was a sharp deceleration in U.S. import growth, down to growth rates of 6 percent and 7 percent respectively from a 25 percent rate in 1984, due primarily to the falling value of the dollar.*

Cost of Protectionist (Import-Restricting) Trade Policies

Fact #1 *In recent years, at least one-third of the U.S. market for manufactured goods has been protected by voluntary quotas and other quantitative trade restrictions.*

Figure 2
Increase in Import Share
1960–1985

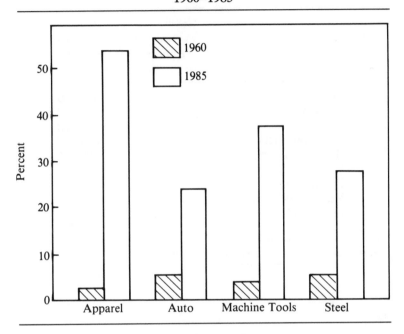

Fact #2   Import controls to protect nineteen industries from foreign competition cost American consumers (directly through increased import prices and indirectly through increased domestic prices) a staggering $66 billion in 1986.

Trade Deficit by Country

Fact #1   The U.S. in 1986 had a trade deficit of more than $3.5 billion with ten other countries whereas its largest individual surplus was $3.5 billion.

Table 2

The High Price of
Protectionism, 1984

Industry	Total cost to consumers (Billions of dollars)	Cost per job saved (Dollars)
Textiles and apparel	$27.0	$42,000
Carbon steel	6.8	750,000
Automobiles	5.8	105,000
Dairy products	5.5	220,000
Benzenoid chemicals	2.7	1,000,000
Orange juice	0.5	240,000
Specialty steel	0.5	1,000,000
Rubber footwear	0.2	30,000
Motorcycles	0.1	150,000
Canned tuna	0.1	76,000

Source: Institute for International Economics

Table 3

U.S. Trade Balances in 1986
(Billions of dollars)

U.S. Surplus Positions		U.S. Deficit Positions	
1. Netherlands	+3.5	1. Japan	−58.6
2. Australia	+2.7	2. Canada	−23.3
3. Egypt	+1.9	3. Taiwan	−15.7
4. Belgium & Luxembourg	+1.2	4. West Germany	−15.6
5. U.S.S.R.	+0.6	5. South Korea	−7.1
6. Pakistan	+0.5	6. Italy	−6.5
7. Turkey	+0.5	7. Hong Kong	−6.4
8. Ireland	+0.4	8. Mexico	−5.2
9. Morocco	+0.4	9. United Kingdom	−4.6
10. Kuwait	+0.3	10. Brazil	−3.5

Source: 1986 U.S. Foreign Trade Highlights, U.S. Dept. of Commerce,
International Trade Administration

Fact #2 *Japan and Canada supplied around 40 percent of all imports in 1986 and three of America's top ten suppliers were Southeast Asian countries.*

Fact #3 *The newly industrialized countries (NICs) of East Asia are the fastest growing contributor to the U.S. trade deficit and also are becoming one of the largest contributors.*

- From 1980 to 1986, the U.S. trade deficit with the Asian NICs increased 651 percent compared with an increase of 380 percent with Japan.
- Between 1980 and 1986, exports to the U.S. from Hong Kong increased 88 percent, from Taiwan 188 percent, from Korea 207 percent, and from Singapore 145 percent.
- The aggregate U.S. trade deficit in 1986 with these four nations was $30.9 billion, more than with Europe's four largest deficit contributors: West Germany, Italy, the United Kingdom, and France.
- From August 1986 to August 1987, the U.S. trade deficit with the Asian NICs soared by $7.2 billion while it shrank by $4.7 billion with W. Europe and widened by only $1.2 billion with Japan.

Fact #4 *With all developing countries, the U.S. ran a $54 billion trade deficit in 1986, nearly one-half of the $113 billion deficit with developed countries.*

Fact #5 *When the trade surpluses of other countries with the U.S. are ranked according to the percentage of the total trade between the two nations, Japan is only fifth, behind Romania, Taiwan, Brazil, and Hong Kong.*

The Dollar as Contributor
to the Trade Deficit

Fact #1 *The U.S. dollar appreciated in value by 65 to 70 percent from 1980 to February 1985.*

- This means that the dollar in February 1985 bought 70 percent more foreign-made goods in comparison to American-made goods than it did at its low point in 1980.

Fact #2   The dollar then fell dramatically, and by May 1987 it had plunged 40 percent against the currencies of the other group of ten countries and by November 1987 it was down about 50 percent against both the yen and the mark.

Fact #3   Despite the steep drop in the dollar's value, import prices increased by just 14.5 percent from the fall of 1986 to the fall of 1987, and much of that was due to a sharp 62 percent rise in the price of oil.

- Despite an appreciation of 70 percent in the yen, the dollar price of car imports—dominated by Japan—increased only 13 percent from June 1985 to June 1986.

- For depressed industries, like steel, import prices actually dropped two percent in this period.

Fact #4   More than half of all U.S. imports come from Canada, Latin America, and Pacific basin countries other than Japan, countries where the dollar in 1985 and 1986 and early 1987 actually appreciated against their currencies.

- By late 1987, the dollar was down only 6 percent against both the Canadian dollar and the Singapore dollar, only 4 percent against the S. Korean won, and was unchanged against the Hong Kong dollar.

- Steel firms are hit especially hard by competition from weak-currency countries.

- For textile and apparel firms the dollar in 1985 and 1986 grew stronger against fourteen of the top twenty-five exporters.

The Current Account and Capital Flows

Fact #1   The current account (which measures not only goods but services and investment income as well) deteriorated from *a surplus of $7 billion in 1981 to a deficit of $141 billion in 1986.*

- The current account balance was mostly positive in other major industrialized countries in 1986: Japan, $85.8 billion, W. Germany, $35.4 billion, Italy, $4.1 billion, France, $3.4 billion, U.K., − $0.2 billion, and Canada, − $6.7 billion.

Fact #2   *As recently as 1982, the U.S. lent or invested abroad $119 billion, reflecting the traditional U.S. postwar role as a supplier of capital to the world; by 1984, the outflow had been reduced to $9 billion.*

Fact #3   *While the U.S. remains the premier international investor, with $270 billion in total holdings around the world in 1985, the rate of growth of U.S. foreign investment has dropped precipitously.*

- In the late 1970s, investment grew by 14.4 percent a year while in the early 1980s, it grew by only 4.5 percent a year.
- The rate of return on overseas investment also slipped from 18.2 percent in 1980 to 10.5 percent in 1984.

Fact #4   *U.S. investment has not been flowing in the most profitable direction—to developing countries—where the rate of return on investment was 17.2 percent in the early 1980s compared with 10.9 percent in the industrial world.*

- In 1966, 26.8 percent of total U.S. foreign investment was in the Third World. By 1984, that had shrunk to 23.1 percent with a practically zero growth rate.

Fact #5   *Capital inflows have been very strong in the 1980s— e.g., foreign private assets in the U.S. more than quadrupled from 1978 through 1985, increasing by over $650 billion.*

Fact #6   *The net capital inflow in 1986 hit a record 5.1 percent of GNP.*

Interpretation
of the Facts

1. The Trade Deficit—Causes

Mention the tremendous rise in the trade deficit in the 1983–85 period to a mainstream economist and three causes will quickly be cited: the overvalued dollar, high real interest rates, and the large U.S. budget deficit. C. Fred Bergsten, head of the Institute for International Economics, explains the interrelationship:

> The mechanism is straight forward: the budget deficit pushes real interest rates to unprecedented levels, attracting capital from abroad and keeping US funds at home, and the dollar rises so high in the exchange markets that large trade deficits quickly ensue. Indeed, we may now understand the "miracle" of supply-side economics: foreigners supply most of the goods and most of the money. (C. Fred Bergsten, "The Trade Deficit Could Be Ruinous," *Fortune*, August 5, 1985, p. 106, © 1985, Time Inc. All rights reserved.)

Since the process begins with the large and rising budget deficit, many economists blame Reaganomics. To Professor Alan Blinder of Princeton University, the numbers tell the following brief story about Reaganomics:

> From 1981 to 1984 the Reagan tax cuts raised the combined budget deficit of all levels of government by nearly $100 billion. Since the gap between domestic savings and domestic investment hardly changed, the laws of arithmetic required that our trade deficit in goods and services rise by nearly $100 billion. And so it did. (Alan S. Blinder, "Reaganomics Made the Trade Gap Inevitable," *Business Week*, May 20, 1985, p. 42.)

The impact of the strong dollar is a matter of some dispute. Most estimates put it as the leading cause for the dramatic jump in the trade deficit. U.S. special trade representative Clayton Yeutter has estimated the dollar impact as "more than half," while his predecessor, William Brock, put the figure at two-thirds. A study by Wharton Econometric Forecasting Associates puts the impact at "more than 60 percent," while Stephen Marris of the Institute for International Economics says the impact was 72 percent. Thus, most major analyses have concluded that between one-half to three-fourths of the early 1980s increase in the trade deficit was attributable to the strong, and most say overvalued, dollar.

Most economists feel this climb (and overvaluation) was due to a combination of factors beginning with the large federal budget deficits. By producing a sharp rise in real interest rates, these deficits attracted a large inflow of foreign capital to the United States. Thus, foreigners' purchase of dollars to invest here drove up the value of the dollar. Other reasons cited are: a faster recovery from recession here than in most other industrial nations, a desire on the part of foreign investors to put their money into a "safe haven," and Latin American countries curtailing their buying here because of their burdens in paying off their international debts.

2. The Trade Deficit—Cures

Since the major cause is felt to be the huge dollar run-up, the major cure that is prescribed calls for a substantial weakening of the dollar. To accomplish this, the U.S. must cut its budget deficit significantly. Also, other countries—particularly Japan and West Germany—must adopt more stimulative policies to strengthen their currencies.

This prescription was increasingly challenged as the trade deficit stubbornly persisted at high levels throughout 1986 and into 1987. More and more economists began to say that even if the dollar continues to decline, the trade deficit will persist because of other factors that economists have not generally considered. These include: the loyalty of consumers and businesses to foreign brands and their quality;

the use of long-term contracts by U.S. customers and foreign firms; and the willingness of foreign companies to accept lower profit margins to maintain market share.

For a number of economists, this all leads to a harsh fact of life: even if everything goes right—the dollar drops substantially, the European and Japanese economies surge, import barriers abroad come down, and U.S. firms get increased assistance on the export front—American industry still will be hard-pressed to hold its own against foreign competition.

Two further problems with the "falling dollar" solution are cited by many experts, including Alan Greenspan. First, there is a high cost to be paid in higher prices and thus higher inflation rates. This shrinks the wealth of the U.S. since a depreciated dollar makes it cheaper for foreigners to buy U.S. real estate and U.S. corporations. It also means U.S. citizens will have to sacrifice more of their labor or more of their savings or both to buy foreign goods.

The second problem is the terrible difficulties in knowing how far the dollar must fall to right the trade imbalance. In the fall of 1985, Rimmer de Vries, senior vice president of the Morgan Guaranty Trust Company, figured the dollar's exchange rate should be reduced to roughly 200 yen and 2.4 Deutsche marks (from 221 yen and 2.7 marks), with comparable drops against other major currencies. Then the U.S. trade deficit would come down to $50 billion. Nearly two years later, the dollar had fallen to around 140 yen and 1.8 Deutsche marks with a trade deficit still operating in the $160 to $170 billion range. The question of exchange rates is clearly a mine field for predictions.

Another often-prescribed cure is to reduce foreign trade barriers. The U.S. Department of Commerce contends that if the Japanese abandoned all their trade restrictions, American exports would increase by as much as $17 billion. The Institute for International Economics suggests a more realistic figure is in the $6 to $8 billion range and notes that much of this is offset by U.S. restrictions in steel, textiles, food, and other imports. Finally, a University of Michigan study concludes that if Japan removed all restrictions against U.S. imports, it could absorb only $2 to $3 billion in new imports.

Going beyond all these more technical considerations is a deeper, ethical question: If the United States must bring its external transactions back toward balance, some other nations' trade surpluses must shrink. Ideally, Japan's trade surplus, the world's largest, would drop. But this would account for probably no more than $50 billion of the $150 to $200 billion adjustment the United States must make. The surpluses of other industrial nations, and many of the world's developing nations, also will have to diminish.

3. The Trade Deficit's Impact on the Economy

Before turning to the deficit's effect on U.S. jobs, two other economic forces need to be explored. First, it is maintained by many that the trade deficit in 1985 and 1986 had become the main roadblock to resumed economic growth. They drew on evidence such as *Time* magazine's Board of Economists' estimate that the trade deficit cut U.S. growth in half during the first half of 1985, and to Data Resources' estimate that between one and two percentage points were shaved off GNP growth in 1983–1985 by the trade deficit.

Some observers have also pointed to an impact on productivity. They argue that the trade deficit is at least partly responsible for the fact that productivity in the 1983–1985 recovery years grew at an average annual rate of 2.6 percent in contrast to an average pace of 3.4 percent in earlier postwar upturns. They base this argument on the observation that in a number of industries, the import surge has kept capacity utilization below its most efficient level and has depressed capital spending.

The estimates of the number of jobs lost due to the trade deficit vary but a number of them do cluster in the 2 to 2.5

million range. The Commerce Department has a 2 million figure since Reagan took office in 1981; Data Resources has the same 2 million figure, with 1.5 million of them in manufacturing jobs. Bergsten of the Institute for International Economics puts the loss at 2.5 million. The highest figure comes from using a standard Commerce Department measure that each billion dollars in trade means 25,000 jobs, implying a job loss of 3.9 million with 1986's $156 billion deficit.

Some leading economists, however, argue that there has been little, if any, job loss due to the trade deficit:

> One of the most durable and widespread myths about the economy these days is that the US has "lost" many jobs as a result of the trade deficit. . . . The basic fact is that the level of the trade deficit or the rate of increase of the trade deficit, if the increase is steady, has nothing to do with the total amount of employment or unemployment. (Herbert Stein, Senior Fellow, American Enterprise Institute, in "Best Selling Fiction: 3 Million Lost Jobs," *Wall Street Journal*, July 29, 1985.)

> The heavy demand for United States dollars has also left interest rates lower than they otherwise would have been and has clearly contributed to a lower rate of inflation. These in turn have reduced the sense of instability and risk associated with capital investment. It is unclear on balance how much of a job loss, if any, the strong dollar has produced. (Alan Greenspan, then with Townsend & Greenspan, now chairman, Federal Reserve Board, cited in "Economic Scene," *The New York Times*, September 11, 1985, p. D2.)

> It is difficult to conclude that overall United States employment and output have been unduly restrained by the trade deficit and the rising dollar. In the absence of the policies that have led to the capital inflow and the strong dollar, while losses of jobs from these sources would have been less, so probably would have been the creation of new jobs. (Henry C. Wallich, former member of Federal Reserve Board, cited in "Economic Scene," *The New York Times*, September 11, 1985, p. D2.)

4. Protectionism

For more than 100 years the one issue that distinguished the two major parties more consistently than any other was trade. The Democratic Party from the time of Andrew Jackson tended to favor low tariffs and to oppose trade barriers. The Republican Party from the time of Abraham Lincoln favored high tariffs and protective barriers for American producers.

Today, the positions are reversed. The leading proponent of free trade is the Republican president, Ronald Reagan, while the leading fighters for trade barriers are congressional Democrats. Both parties, despite their rhetoric, have practiced protectionism over the past decade. William Cline of the Institute for International Economics notes:

> Open trade reached its postwar peak in 1974–76 as concern about inflation temporarily peeled away some important quotas (steel, sugar, petroleum, meat). But by 1977 trade protection had begun a relentless upward creep, and major new non-tariff barriers emerged even as tariffs themselves sank to modest levels in the range of 5%–10%. The Carter administration adopted new quantitative restrictions on imports of shoes and color-TV sets, and implemented a "trigger price mechanism" for policing entry of foreign steel at below cost (although this mechanism's harassment effect meant it went beyond enforcement of "fair trade"). Then the Reagan administration forced "voluntary" quotas on Japanese cars, imposed new quotas on sugar, and successively tightened longstanding protection of textiles and apparel. It agreed to a tight regime of quotas against the European Community restricting subsidized as well as fairly traded steel. (William R. Cline, "Protectionism: An Ill Trade Wind Rises," *Wall Street Journal*, November 6, 1984.)

This same trend toward protective policies has become standard practice in virtually every industrialized country. Stephen Marris, formerly a top-ranking economist with the Organization for Economic Cooperation and Development and now senior fellow at Washington's Institute for International Economics, states:

What we have seen since the (1978) Bonn summit is a complete breakdown in the Keynesian consensus and a radical change in the industrial powers' philosophy away from coordinated economic policies to a belief that if every nation looks after itself, the world will look after itself. The result is the most dramatic divergence of economic polices experienced in the postwar era. (Lawrence Minard, "Noah's Ark, Anyone?," adapted by permission of *Forbes* magazine, August 12, 1985, © Forbes Inc., 1985.)

Pros In the mid-1980s, a group of mainly younger economists began challenging the conventional economic wisdom that the cost to the nation as a whole from protectionism almost always exceeds benefits received from the sheltered industries. Their argument centers on high tech industries. Their analysis shows that predatory trade practices may sometimes increase the national income of the country that adopts them and reduce the incomes of trading partners. This is true for high tech industries because their sources of comparative advantage lie in R&D spending, learning by doing, and economies of scale. Thus comparative advantages are not fixed but can be temporary, and most importantly, can be created by government.

The other "pro" protectionist line of argument is quite simple: others are doing it, so the U.S. must do it also. This is the point made by some liberal Democrats in backing protectionist trade measures. Robert Kuttner, a leading liberal economist and correspondent for the *New Republic*, writes:

In sum: The US is no longer powerful enough to be the world's largest free-trade zone while other nations, rich and poor, commit economic planning. Other nations must share the burden of defining—and upholding—whatever trade regime all of us can agree on. If everybody wants free trade fine. But I suspect that what everybody really wants is a delicate mix of some open trade and some development economics. The trick is to make that mix equitable. (Robert

Kuttner, "Blind Faith in Free Trade Doesn't Pay," *Business Week*, October 14, 1985, p. 22.)

Cons One of the leading opponents of protectionism in Congress is Senator Phil Gramm:

> Tariffs and quotas, by lowering the demand for foreign goods, lower the supply of US dollars on the world currency market, raise the value of the dollar, and make American exports less attractive, thus, lowering employment in industries where the US is most efficient and most competitive. The net result is that protectionism does not create jobs, the nation is made poorer as prices rise, and the American economy becomes less competitive as jobs are transferred from our least efficient, least competitive sectors. (Phil Gramm, "New Protectionism = Old Sophistry," *Wall Street Journal*, October 4, 1985.)

As for slapping a tariff on imports, opponents counter with an array of charges. The tariff, they argue, is nothing more than a good old-fashioned tax hike in disguise. And its a bad tax because it imposes a high tax rate on a narrow class of people, those who buy imports from certain countries. Besides paying the tax, American consumers would pay higher prices for American-made goods since the protected domestic industries would be free to raise prices. Finally, exporters get hurt by the dollar-strengthening effect of a tariff and also because the price increases triggered by a tariff would raise many of U.S. exporters' costs.

The desire to restrict imports from developing countries creates at least two major threats to U.S. interests. Massive debts are owed to U.S. banks. If the U.S. makes it impossible for debtor nations steadily to increase such exports as garments, shoes, and steel, it will also make it impossible for these countries to repay their debt or even to make scheduled interest payments.

Then there is the broader issue of the U.S. role in the basic development strategy pursued by developing countries. For a number of decades, the U.S. has been encouraging developing countries to follow an export-led, market approach to economic development. Those following this approach have generally done quite well. These success stories, however, have only been possible because the U.S. and its allies have been willing to purchase growing volumes of their exports. Without these markets, developing countries will suffer economic loss. It will become impossible for such nations as China and India to follow these successful strategies.

Those who oppose protectionism believe it will restrict world trade and hurt economic growth and jobs. One estimate is that world exports would be 40 percent higher if the General Agreement on Tariffs and Trade—GATT—treaty (essentially espousing free trade principles) were followed to the letter. The final result would be big global gains in jobs, standards of living, and wealth.

5. The Future of the Trade Deficit

There is virtually unanimous agreement that the trade deficit is headed down, but not by enough. Most trade experts see the deficit dropping to $100 billion or slightly less because of the much lower dollar, but then a plateau is reached.

If these predictions are correct, then we reach the dangerous position of solidifying our status as a debtor nation and watching our debt to the rest of the world grow. Estimates of the magnitude of that debt with the rest of the world are examined in the following chapter.

CHAPTER ★ 12 ★

The United States as a Debtor Nation

The Issues

Early in 1985, the United States become a debtor nation for the first time since 1914. In and of itself, this would not have provoked many fears. Coming as it did on top of record-level budget deficits and trade deficits, it immediately inspired rumors that the U.S. was going the way of Third World debtor nations that have been caught in a global debt crisis since the early 1980s.

The key issue is whether or not debtor nation status—with prospects of a rising debt over the next few years, which is all but inevitable—poses a serious threat to the U.S. economy. There is considerable disagreement on how the U.S. and the other debtor nations got to this point and also on what can or should be done about it. The long-run health and stability of the global economy rides on the answer.

Definition: **Debtor nation:** A nation whose assets owned abroad are less than foreign assets held in its borders.

The Facts

U.S. Transition from
Creditor to Debtor

Fact #1 *When the United States in 1985 became a debtor nation for the first year since 1914, foreign interests owned $107.4 billion more in the United States than Americans owned overseas.*

- The U.S. accumulated more foreign debt in 1985 than any other country in its total recorded history.

Fact #2 *In 1986, the total foreign debt rose to $263.6 billion, a 13.5 percent increase over 1985.*

Table 1

Net Investment Position of U.S., 1978–1986
(Billions of dollars)

Year	U.S. Assets Abroad	Foreign Assets in U.S.	Net Investment Position
1978	$448	$372	$76
1979	511	416	95
1980	607	501	106
1981	720	579	141
1982	839	692	147
1983	894	788	106
1984	915	886	28
1985	953	1,060	− 107
1986	1,068	1,331	− 264

- More than three-fourths of the $400 billion swing from 1982 to 1986 was due to the increase of foreign holdings of debt instruments such as government bonds (from $100 billion in 1982 to −$209 billion in 1986). The corporate equity swing was only $58 billion (−$58 billion to −$116 billion) while the direct investment swing was only $32 billion ($583 billion to $551 billion).

Fact #3   *Foreigners are essentially bankrolling most U.S. investment; in 1986, nearly two-thirds of our net investment in housing and in business plant and equipment would not have occurred without dollars saved by foreigners.*

Fact #4   *Paying back the huge foreign debt will be very costly; in 1986, the U.S. sent overseas a net $10 billion in interest and dividends, a figure that is expected to grow to $50 billion by 1990.*

Fact #5   *The United States transition to debtor nation status was precedent shattering: there was no previous case in history of a country reversing so dramatically from creditor to debtor. In three years the U.S. went from the world's largest creditor to its largest debtor.*

Fact #6   *The projected debt for the end of 1987 is around $400 billion.*

Foreign Ownership of U.S. Assets

Fact #1   *Foreigners in 1987 owned $1.3 trillion of American assets—almost one-sixth of those holdings in real estate, industry, and banks and the rest ($1.1 trillion) in stocks, bonds, and savings (up from only $233 billion in 1976).*

Fact #2   *The largest increases in foreign direct investment (buildings, plant, and equipment) have been by Britain and* *the Netherlands, up $37 billion and $24 billion respectively in the 1980–1986 period (to levels of $51 and 43 billion); Japan's increase was only $18 billion (from $5 billion to $23 billion).*

Fact #3   In 1986, 260 American corporations were taken over by foreign interests.

- The Carnation Company is Swiss and Celanese, Doubleday & Co., and RCA Records are West German, and Brooks Brothers clothiers is Canadian.

- Four hundred and thirty-five U.S. manufacturers are wholly or partly owned by the Japanese.

The Global Debt Crisis in the Third World

Fact #1   The Third World's total debt in 1986 reached $1100 billion, nearly 80 percent greater than 1980's figure of $634 billion.

- Approximately 80 percent of the debt of 131 less developed nations is long-term, and of that, 60 percent is owed to private lenders.

- Net new long-term loans have fallen every year since 1981, from a peak of $75 billion in 1981 to $30 billion in 1985.

- Interest paid rose from $40 billion in 1981 to $50 billion in 1985.

Fact #2   In 1986, the top three debtor nations (besides the U.S.) were Brazil ($109.2 billion), Mexico ($100.4 billion), and Argentina ($33 billion).

Fact #3   Seventeen big debtor countries account for nearly half of the total money owed. Nine of these countries had

Table 2

Seventeen Heavily Indebted Countries

| Country | Debt Outstanding, 1985[1] | | Average Annual Growth Rates, 1980–1984[2] (Percent) | | | | |
	Total (billions)	Of which private source (percent)	Gross Domestic Product	Exports	Imports	Investment	Per capita consumption
Argentina	$50.8	86.8	-1.6	3.6	-14.7	-16.8	-2.7
Bolivia	4.6	39.3	-4.7	-1.7	-15.8	-22.1	-7.8
Brazil	107.3	84.2	0.1	10.8	-7.3	-8.6	-1.2
Chile	21.0	87.2	-1.4	0.7	-4.2	-11.6	-2.1
Colombia	11.3	57.5	1.8	0.8	2.8	2.4	-0.1
Costa Rica	4.2	59.7	-0.4	1.1	-9.1	-9.4	-4.8
Ecuador[3]	8.5	73.8	1.1	2.6	-13.7	-16.9	-2.3
Ivory Coast	8.0	64.1	-2.3	1.3	-8.8	-19.5	-6.6
Jamaica	3.4	24.0	1.3	-2.5	-2.1	9.5	-1.4
Mexico	99.0	24.0	1.3	10.5	-14.5	-10.1	-1.4
Morocco	14.0	39.1	2.5	4.1	-1.0	-2.7	-0.2
Nigeria	19.3	88.2	-4.7	-13.3	-12.1	-19.3	-4.3
Peru	13.4	60.7	-0.7	-0.6	-10.8	-5.3	-3.7
Philippines	24.8	67.8	0.8	3.6	-4.8	-12.4	0.0
Uruguay	3.6	82.1	-3.7	2.2	-11.3	-20.2	-4.7
Venezuela[3]	33.6	99.5	-1.8	-3.8	-19.3	-15.6	-6.4
Yugoslavia[4]	19.6	64.0	0.6	-0.6	-8.1	-2.9	-0.5
TOTALS	445.9	80.8	-0.3	1.8	-9.2	9.7	-1.8

Source: World Bank, Washington, D.C., 1986.

[1] Estimated total external liabilities, including the use of IMF credit.

[2] Latest year for which data is available. Growth rates are computed from time series in constant prices.

[3] The merchandise trade balance for 1984 is not available; the value shown is for 1983.

[4] Average annual growth rates are for 1980–1983, except for Gross Domestic Product which is for 1980–1984.

negative economic growth rates in 1980–1984 and the other eight had slow growth.

- For these seventeen countries, 81 percent of the combined debt is owed to banks.
- In all but two countries (Columbia and Jamaica) investment declined and in ten of them it declined by more than 10 percent a year.
- All of the countries experienced zero or negative per capita consumption growth rates.

Fact #4   From 1975 to 1985, the debts of eighteen countries in Latin America, Asia, and Africa increased by $451 billion, of which $198 billion represented capital flight.

Fact #5   A number of countries—particularly Argentina, Mexico, and Venezuela—would have virtually no debt if massive capital flight had not occurred and the money was invested at home.

Fact #6   The Latin American debt situation is particularly serious as in each year since 1982, interest payments alone have absorbed $35 billion of Latin American nations' $90 to $100 billion annual export earnings.

- The ratio of debt to gross domestic product (with 20 to 25 percent being sound) was 40 percent in Brazil, 60 percent in Mexico, 70 percent in Argentina, and 120 percent in Chile in 1986.

Fact #7   The debt situation in Latin America has cost the United States 1 million jobs.

- As a consequence of diminishing markets for agricultural products, 400,000 jobs were lost.
- In 1986, there was approximately $400 billion in outstanding Latin debts.

Interpretation
of the Facts

1. The United States as a Debtor Nation

The United States, which was the world's largest creditor in 1982, became its largest debtor in 1985 because of the huge current account deficit. The deterioration in the current account, in turn, was the result primarily of the tremendous increase in the trade deficit. In addition, net receipts from services, particularly investment income, also fell considerably.

Some observers feel that the enormous federal budget deficit was a key contributor to the conversion of the United States from creditor to debtor status. They argue that high interest rates triggered by the budget deficit attracted a huge inflow of capital from abroad. This, in turn, led to a buildup of foreign assets here that by early 1985 became greater than the assets that Americans own abroad.

2. The Problems of Debtor Nation Status

President Reagan has generally brushed off the significance of growing foreign debt as a problem for the economy. He asserts it shows the strength of America because so many foreigners want to invest their money here. He has support from some respected international economists, among them Edward Bernstein, who served as the executive secretary and chief technical adviser of the U.S. delegation to the Bretton Woods conference and as director of research at the International Monetary Fund. Bernstein largely dismisses any adverse economic effects:

- The payment of investment income to foreigners "will not hinder the growth of domestic output and employment."

- The fear that a loss of confidence in the U.S. economy could lead to the flight of foreign capital, precipitating a financial crisis, "seems exaggerated when one considers the composition of foreign assets in this country."
- The feeling that the inflow of capital is depriving other industrial countries of the savings they need for recovery and depriving low-income countries of the resources they need for development cannot be supported from the empirical evidence. (Edward M. Bernstein, "The United States as an International Debtor Country," *The Brookings Review*, Fall 1985, pp. 34, 36.)

Those who see the trade deficit as a threat begin with the simple observation that as the debt grows, more and more exports of goods and services will be required to earn the income with which to pay each year's interest bill. According to William A. Cox, a senior specialist for the Congressional Research Service of the Library of Congress, the heavy imports of capital ultimately will require higher taxes to retire the enlarged national debt and will lower the average American's standard of living. The large and growing debtor status of the United States has been called "unsustainable and undesirable" by C. Fred Bergsten, director of the Institute for International Economics, and "a very unhealthy development" by Larry Chimerine, chairman and chief economist of Chase Econometrics.

Finally, there is a point of international morality: The United States has ceased to generate capital for the use of less fortunate or developed areas and is instead the greatest devourer of surplus capital.

3. The Global Debt Crisis' Impact on Americans

Regarding the negative effect, Treasury Secretary Baker went so far as to state that the debt crisis is fundamentally an American problem since the principal debtors are Latin and the chief lenders are U.S. banks. According to a series of witnesses appearing before a congressional subcommittee in 1986, the global debt crisis has torn through the U.S. economy, hurting sales to countries that previously were major markets, causing the loss of as many as 1.6 million domestic jobs. Alan Wolff, a trade lawyer and former deputy U.S. trade representative, summarized the prevailing sentiment: "Their debt crisis was our trade crisis." The witnesses' evidence? U.S. exports to six of the largest debtor nations—Brazil, Mexico, Venezuela, the Philippines, Chile, and Nigeria—dropped from $34 billion in 1981 to $18 billion in 1983, accounting for nearly one-half of the total decline in U.S. exports during this period. Furthermore, in 1984 and 1985, the U.S. trade deficit with Third World nations was about $50 billion—approximately one-third of the total $148.5 billion trade deficit in 1985.

4. Solving the Global Debt Crisis

IMF Austerity Measures   The front line attack continues to be the International Monetary Fund imposing strict economic austerity measures on debt-laden nations on a country-by-country basis. When a country is in crisis, the IMF makes a short-term loan. In return it requires a change in economic policies to enable the country to pay its foreign bills. The IMF insists that debtor countries gear their policies toward tighter budgets, focus less on consumer-oriented policies and more on exports, and generate more local saving. Often the domestic changes involve major currency devaluations—to encourage exports and discourage imports—big cuts in government spending, and tighter monetary policies to reduce inflation. Nearly all such policies trigger recessions in countries that have been living beyond their means, and often encourage domestic social unrest.

The Baker Plan   In October 1985, the Reagan administration departed from its longstanding hands-off policy on the global debt crisis by unveiling the Baker Plan. The major philosophical shift announced by Treasury Secretary Baker was that economic growth, not IMF-imposed austerity, offers the only genuine hope of an improvement in the fortunes of debtor nations. The only way this growth can come about is for U.S. banks, in concert with foreign lenders and multi-lateral institutions such as the World Bank, to step up their involvement with massive infusions of cash.

Everyone had a part to play. Debtor nations were to re-duce the state's role in their economies, adopt tax policies geared toward investment, allow the market to set foreign exchange rates, and encourage direct foreign investment. Baker and then Federal Reserve Board Chairman Paul Volcker were to pressure U.S. banks to increase their lending to these nations. European governments and Japan were expected to do the same with an overall goal of boosting lending by some $20 billion by 1988. The World Bank was also to in-crease the pace of its lending, making an additional $9 billion available over the same period. Also, the bank (along with the IMF) would take on the added job of watchdog, trying to make sure recipients followed sound economic policies and eventually repaid their commercial debts.

The reaction to the Baker Plan from the financial com-munity and economists was mixed but contained a heavy dose of skepticism. Art Pine, an economic columnist for the *Wall Street Journal*, noted a "potentially fatal flaw" in the plan: none of the major debtors had been willing to under-take a drastic economic overhaul yet and it was not clear that the prospect of new bank lending suddenly would be an effective persuader. Other judgments were quite harsh: "The Baker proposals have to be viewed not as a solution to the debt crisis but as another stopgap measure in the ongoing balancing act to keep the borrowing countries afloat. The underlying problem is untouched." (Shearson-Lehman Brothers, Bulletin Series, November 1, 1985, p. 4.) And "the new policy will fail because philosophically and institution-ally the international bankers are overwhelmingly geared to support 'investments' that have virtually no impact on the broader processes of growth and development." (Roy Posterman and Jeffrey Riedinger, "Seoul Offered No Solution to the LDC Riddle," *Wall Street Journal*, October 15, 1985.)

The Bradley Plan   Senator Bill Bradley agreed with critics of the Baker Plan. He felt that more than a debt program was required. In the summer of 1986 he proposed his own plan founded on the idea that a partnership is needed to help Latin nations fight poverty and increase their living standards. Believing that a program must be as bold as the problem is serious, Bradley proposed cutting interest rates on all commercial and official bilateral debts of fifteen Latin debtors by 3 percentage points for a three-year period and forgiving 3 percent of the loan principal a year for the same three-year period. This would provide $42 billion in debt relief from commercial banks and $15 billion in debt relief from bilateral loans by governments. Rather than imposing economic changes, the plan asks Latin countries to devise their own programs for liberalizing trade and promoting growth through proven strategies.

5. America's Foreign Debt in the Future

There is virtually unanimous agreement that the foreign debt will grow over the next five years. E. Gerald Corrigan, president of the New York Federal Reserve Bank, warned in 1985 that the U.S. debt owed to foreigners because of mounting trade deficits will reach $500 billion by the end of the 1980s. This figure, as large as it seems, quickly became surpassed. In 1987, three leading institutions cited much higher figures: the Joint Economic Committee of Congress expects the debt to peak in 1993 at roughly $700 billion; Allen Sinai, chief economist at Shearson-Lehman Brothers, sees $725–$775 billion by 1990; while Data Resources foresees a debt of $900 billion by the end of 1992.

PART II

American Business

Domestic Restructuring and Foreign Competition

CHAPTER ★ 13 ★

Big Business

The Issues

In the late 1960s and early 1970s, Americans heard all sorts of warnings about big business and the concentration of economic power. More and more of America's productive assets seemed to be owned by fewer and fewer people. In the last decade, however, one hears much less of such talk.

The fact is that big business is very much around—it's just not as healthy and as dominant as it was in the 1980s. This is particularly true of the industrial companies. Corporate profits overall in 1986 were down nearly $20 billion from their 1980 level and, for the largest industrial companies, total employment was down and sales were barely up in the first half of the 1980s. The one bright spot in big business has been in services, where commercial banks, diversified financial companies, retailers, and transportation companies have done very well in the past fifteen years.

The Facts

Corporate Profits

Fact #1   Corporate profits, after tax and after adjusting for inflation and the cost of replacing facilities as they wear out, rose a robust 22 percent a year from 1982–86 (from $86.9 billion in 1982 to $196.9 billion in 1986).

Fact #2   The profits of companies in wholesale and retail trade rose 150 percent from 1980 to 1986 (from $21.6 billion to $50.3 billion), but the profits of manufacturing companies fell (from $77.1 billion to $73.4 billion).

The "*Fortune* 500" Industrials

Fact #1   Big business is very big, as the top ten corporations in America in 1986 had sales in the $24-billion-to-$103-billion range.

- Only two companies, General Motors and Exxon, have ranked first on the *Fortune* 500 list in the thirty-three years since the list has been compiled (GM in 1954–1973, 1977–1978, 1985–1986; Exxon in 1974–1976; 1979–1984).

- Of the top ten, all but IBM were among the top 40 (ranked by assets) in 1917.

Fact #2   In nearly all important performance categories, big business fared worse in 1986 than in 1985 (just as 1985 had been worse than 1984).

- The total revenues of the *Fortune* 500 declined by 5 percent in 1986, as fully one-third of the companies reported lower sales than in 1985.

- Profits fell by 6.7 percent.

Table 1

The 10 Largest U.S. Industrial
Corporations (Ranked by sales) 1986

Rank 1986	Rank 1985	Company	Sales $ Thousands	Sales Percent Change	Net Income $ Thousands	Net Income Rank	Net Income Percent Change	Assets $ Thousands	Assets Rank	Rank in 1917
1	1	General Motors (Detroit)	102,813,700	6.7	2,944,700	4	(26.4)	72,593,000	1	34
2	2	Exxon (New York)	69,888,000	(19.4)	5,360,000	1	10.1	69,484,000	2	3
3	4	Ford Motor (Dearborn, Mich.)	62,715,800	18.8	3,285,100	3	30.6	37,933,000	6	21
4	5	International Business Machines (Armonk, N.Y.)	51,250,000	2.4	4,789,000	2	(26.9)	57,814,000	3	—
5	3	Mobil (New York)	44,866,000	(19.8)	1,407,000	8	35.3	39,412,000	4	15
6	10	General Electric (Fairfield, Conn.)	35,211,000	24.5	2,492,000	5	6.7	34,591,000	8	11
7	8	American Tel. & Tel. (New York)	34,087,000	(2.4)	139,000	115	(91.1)	38,883,000	5	2
8	6	Texaco (White Plains, N.Y.)	31,613,000	(31.7)	725,000	17	(41.2)	34,940,000	7	37
9	9	E.I. du Pont de Nemours (Wilmington, Del.)	27,148,000	(7.9)	1,538,000	6	37.6	26,733,000	10	8
10	7	Chevron (San Francisco)	24,351,000	(41.7)	715,000	18	(53.8)	34,583,000	9	39

Source: Fortune, April 27, 1987, p. 364.

- The seventy money losers tied the record established in 1985 but they lost more money.

- The bright spots in 1986 were in pharmaceuticals (first in return on sales) and tobacco (first in median sales increase).

Table 2
Fortune 500 Performance—1985 and 1986

	1985	1986
Sales	$1,807.1	$1,723.4
Change in Sales	2.75%	−4.63%
Profits (billions)	$69.6	$65.0
Change in profits	−19.1%	−6.7%
Assets (billions)	$1,519.5	$1,560.8
Number of sales increases	332	326
Number of profit increases	242	250
Number of money losers	70	70
Median return on sales	3.9%	4.1%
Median return on equity	11.5%	11.6%
Median total return to investors	24.13%	15.50%
Number of employees (millions)	14	13.4

Source: Fortune, April 27, 1987, p. 360.

Fact #3 *The 1980s have been lean years for the 500 largest industrials—sales actually declined 2 percent and profits slid 22 percent from 1981 to 1986. Total employment actually declined from 1979 to 1986.*

Fact #4 *The* Fortune *500 industrials accounted for around three-fourths of total manufacturing sales and 90 percent of total manufacturing profits in the mid-1980s.*

"The Service 500"

Fact #1 Big is also very big in services, as the top ten in 1986 had assets ranging from $74 billion to $196 billion. Of the top ten, five are banks, three are diversified financial companies (like American Express), and two are life insurance companies.

Fact #2 Profits of the 500 largest service companies in 1986 were 8 percent higher than in 1985, considerably better than the 500 industrials whose profits fell by 6.7 percent.

Table 3

The Ten Largest Diversified
Service Companies—1986

Rank		Company	Sales	Assets	
1986	1985		$ Thousands	$ Thousands	Rank
1	6	Super Valu Stores (Eden Prairie, Minn)	7,905,016	1,555,451	33
2	5	Fleming Cos. (Oklahoma City)	7,652,624	1,242,289	38
3	7	McKesson (San Francisco)	6,285,000	2,176,000	29
4	8	CBS (New York)	4,900,400	3,370,300	9
5	10	Fluor (Irvine, Calif.)	4,678,661	2,565,393	21
6	11	Hospital Corp. of America (Nashville)	4,665,592	6,793,372	1
7	13	Alco Standard (Wayne, Pa.)	4,334,022	1,229,711	39
8	15	Electronic Data Systems (Dallas)	4,321,000	2,409,600	22
9	•	American Can (Greenwich, Conn.)	4,292,800	5,350,100	2
10	28	National Intergroup (Pittsburgh)	4,166,294	2,270,904	26

Source: Fortune, June 8, 1987, p. 196.

• Not on last year's list.

Table 4

The Ten Largest Commercial
Banking Companies—1986

Rank		Company	Assets	Deposits	
1986	1985		$ Thousands	$ Thousands	Rank
1	1	Citicorp (New York)	196,124,000	114,689,000	1
2	2	BankAmerica Corp. (San Francisco)	104,189,000	82,205,000	2
3	3	Chase Manhattan Corp. (New York)	94,765,815	66,002,844	3
4	5	J.P. Morgan & Co. (New York)	76,039,000	42,960,000	5
5	4	Manufacturers Hanover Corp. (New York)	74,397,389	45,544,277	4
6	7	Security Pacific Corp. (Los Angeles)	62,606,000	38,408,000	8
7	6	Chemical New York Corp.	60,564,123	39,054,910	7
8	8	Bankers Trust New York Corp.	56,419,945	29,535,520	10
9	9	First Interstate Bancorp (Los Angeles)	55,421,736	39,457,006	6
10	13	Wells Fargo & Co. (San Francisco)	44,577,100	32,992,800	9

Source: Fortune, June 8, 1987, p. 200.

Table 5

The Ten Largest Diversified
Financial Companies—1986

Rank		Company	Assets	Revenues	
1986	1985		$ Thousands	$ Thousands	Rank
1	1	Federal Nat'l Mortgage Ass'n (Washington, D.C.)	100,406,000	10,540,000	5
2	2	American Express (New York)	99,476,000	14,652,000	4
3	•	Salomon (New York)	78,164,000	6,789,000	10
4	3	Aetna Life & Casualty (Hartford)	66,829,900	20,482,900	1
5	4	Merrill Lynch (New York)	53,013,471	9,606,349	7
6	6	CIGNA (Philadelphia)	50,015,800	17,064,100	2
7	5	First Boston (New York)	48,618,206	1,309,765	33
8	7	Travelers Corp. (Hartford)	46,299,600	16,046,600	3
9	•	Morgan Stanley Group (New York)	29,190,361	2,463,484	24
10	8	Bear Stearns Cos. (New York)	26,939,440	1,188,951	35

Source: Fortune, June 8, 1987, p. 204.

• Not on last year's list.

Table 6

The Ten Largest Savings
Institutions—1986

Rank		Company	Assets	Revenues	
1986	1985		$ Thousands	$ Thousands	Rank
1	1	Financial Corp. of America (Irvine, Calif.)	33,952,994	16,929,388	3
2	3	Great Western Financial Corp. (Beverly Hills, Calif.)	27,630,183	18,130,530	2
3	2	H. F. Ahmanson (Los Angeles)	27,592,294	21,687,190	1
4	4	CalFed (Los Angeles)	21,552,900	15,486,500	4
5	5	Meritor Financial Group (Philadelphia)	18,447,272	12,676,100	5
6	6	GLENFED (Glendale, Calif.)	16,387,444	11,660,817	6
7	12	Great American First Savings Bank (San Diego)	13,064,815	8,877,414	7
8	7	Golden West Financial Corp. (Oakland)	12,435,350	7,698,523	9
9	10	Gibraltar Financial Corp. (Beverly Hills, Calif.)	12,248,615	6,001,205	14
10	9	Home Federal Savings & Loan Ass'n (San Diego)	12,074,620	8,562,059	8

Source: Fortune, June 8, 1987, p. 206.

Table 7

The Ten Largest Life Insurance
Companies—1986

Rank		Company	Assets	Premium and Annuity Income	
1986	1985		$ Thousands	$ Thousands	Rank
1	1	Prudential of America (Newark)	103,317,115	17,380,277	1
2	2	Metropolitan Life (New York)	81,581,350	12,148,965	2
3	3	Equitable Life Assurance (New York)	48,577,698	5,500,913	4
4	4	Aetna Life (Hartford)	42,957,155	10,506,887	3
5	5	New York Life	29,793,627	3,477,186	7
6	8	Teachers Insurance & Annunity (New York)	27,887,103	2,654,607	13
7	6	John Hancock Mutual Life (Boston)	27,213,497	4,173,912	5
8	7	Travelers (Hartford)	27,210,137	4,023,926	6
9	9	Connecticut General Life (Bloomfield)	24,806,504	2,934,270	11
10	10	Northwestern Mutual Life (Milwaukee)	20,187,343	2,934,270	9

Source: _Fortune_, June 8, 1987, p. 208.

Table 8

The Ten Largest Retailing Companies—1986

Rank		Company	Sales	Assets	
1986	1985		$ Thousands	$ Thousands	Rank
1	1	Sears Roebuck (Chicago)	44,281,500	65,994,600	1
2	2	K mart (Troy, Mich.)	24,246,000	10,578,000	3
3	3	Safeway Stores (Oakland, Calif.)	20,311,480	7,443,877	4
4	4	Kroger (Cincinnati)	18,386,408	4,076,447	11
5	6	J.C. Penney (New York)	14,740,000	11,188,000	2
6	5	American Stores (Salt Lake City)	14,021,484	3,590,174	14
7	12	Wal-Mart Stores (Bentonville, Ark.)	11,909,076	4,049,092	12
8	7	Southland (Dallas)	11,081,835	3,421,088	15
9	8	Federated Department Stores (Cincinnati)	10,512,425	5,687,738	7
10	19	May Department Stores (St. Louis)	10,376,000	6,209,000	5

Source: Fortune, June 8, 1987, p. 210.

Table 9

The Ten Largest Transportation Companies—1986

Rank 1986	Rank 1985	Company	Operating Revenues $ Thousands	Assets $ Thousands	Rank
1	5	UAL (Elk Grove, Ill.)	9,196,233	8,716,517	6
2	2	United Parcel Service of America (Greenwich, Conn.)	8,619,703	4,801,133	9
3	1	Burlington Northern (Seattle)	6,941,413	10,650,956	4
4	•	Union Pacific (New York)	6,688,000	10,863,000	3
5	3	CSX (Richmond)	6,345,000	12,661,000	1
6	6	AMR (Fort Worth)	6,018,175	7,527,969	8
7	4	Santa Fe Southern Pacific (Chicago)	5,801,600	11,601,800	2
8	8	Delta Air Lines (Atlanta)	4,460,062	3,785,462	11
9	14	Texas Air (Houston)	4,406,897	8,194,611	7
10	9	Norfolk Southern (Norfolk, Va.)	4,076,407	9,752,445	5

Source: Fortune, June 8, 1987, p. 212.

• Not on last year's list.

Table 10

The Ten Largest Utilities—1986

Rank		Company	Assets	Operating Revenues	
1986	1985		$ Thousands	$ Thousands	Rank
1	1	GTE (Stamford, Conn.)	27,401,801	15,111,528	1
2	2	BellSouth (Atlanta)	26,218,100	11,444,100	2
3	3	NYNEX (New York)	21,804,600	11,341,500	3
4	4	Bell Atlantic (Philadelphia)	21,090,900	9,920,800	4
5	7	Pacific Gas & Electric (San Francisco)	21,002,253	7,816,661	10
6	5	Pacific Thesis Group (San Francisco)	20,320,500	8,977,300	6
7	6	Southwestern Bell (St. Louis)	20,299,800	7,902,400	9
8	9	U S West (Englewood, Colo.)	18,747,400	8,308,400	7
9	8	American Information Technologies (Chicago)	18,739,400	9,362,100	5
10	10	Southern (Atlanta)	18,141,116	6,846,591	11

Source: Fortune, June 8, 1987, p. 214.

Fact #3 The big winners in America's service economy in 1986 were the finance-oriented companies (those that get more than half their revenues from financial services) while the biggest losers were retailers and transportation companies.

- Diversified financial companies, including investment banks and property and casualty insurers, performed best of all with the earnings of the fifty biggest jumping 159 percent.

- The profits of the fifty biggest savings institutions rose 40 percent, a remarkable gain as net income had quadrupled the year before.

- The combined assets of the one hundred largest commercial banks and the fifty largest life insurers swelled by 17 percent.

- In contrast, the combined sales of the fifty biggest retailing, transportation, and utility companies and the one hundred largest diversified service companies fell 3 percent.

Fact #4 The Service 500 came through the 1973–1983 period of galloping inflation, deregulation, oil shocks, and steep recessions relatively unscathed.

- Four of the six service sectors tracked over this period— commercial banks, diversified financial companies, retailers, and transportation companies—boosted profits by more than the 124 percent rise in the CPI (Consumer Price Index) between 1973 and 1983; only the utilities and life insurance companies failed to have profit increases that exceeded the rate of inflation.

U.S. Multinational Corporations

Fact #1 U.S. multinational corporations in 1985 had total assets of $4,292 billion and employed 24,500,300 workers.

- Of these totals, parent companies had $3,454 billion in

assets and 18,074,700 workers, while foreign affiliates had $838 billion in assets and employed 6,425,600 workers.

Fact #2   In the eight-year period 1977–1985, total assets increased 111 percent while employment decreased 6 percent.

The "International 500"—The World's Largest Corporations

Fact #1   The dollar range for sales of the ten largest foreign corporations is just slightly less than the top ten American industrials—$20 to $82 billion.

Fact #2   Changes in the composition of the "International 500" list over the 1975–1984 decade show a drift toward more high tech and less smokestack companies.

- The industry with the greatest increase in sales (271 percent) was "measuring, scientific and photographic equipment," followed by office equipment and computers (235 percent).
- The two industries with the lowest increase in sales were industrial and farm equipment (56 percent) and metal products (50 percent).

Interpretation of the Facts

---

1. The Future of Big Business

One thing is certain. Big business is here to stay. Many observers are increasingly coming to the conclusion that it may even be on the rise because the newest technological breakthroughs require massive team efforts among scientists and engineers, as well as major capital outlays.

One cannot, however, look at the future of big business without at the same time considering the future of small business and the entrepreneur because they are the leaven of American business that helps to determine whether the business enterprise rises or falls. This is how Pat Choate, businessman, economist, and author puts it:

> What the Japanese and others realize is that the activities of big and small business are completely and complexly intertwined. In the United States, big business is the principal customer of small business. Small companies are major suppliers of components and services that would be too costly for big business to produce. In turn, the wages and dividends produced by big business underpin sales of all kinds from small business, but particularly services.
>
> In sum, if big business falters, so too will small business. If small business loses its vitality, big business will lose its principal outside supplier of goods and services and the American economy will lose its principal source of new jobs. (P. Choate and J. K. Linger, *The High-Flex Society*, New York: Knopf, 1986, p. 97.)

Small Business
and Entrepreneurs

The Issues

America rediscovered small business and the entrepreneurial spirit in the early 1980s. Articles began to appear everywhere with such titles as "The Entrepreneurial Mystique," "The Heart of Entrepreneurship," and "A New Heyday for Entrepreneurs." In 1984, a book was published with the subtitle *An Entrepreneur's Manifesto* (titled *Business Plan for America*). The book's author, business leader Don Gevirtz, captures the zeal that entrepreneurial enthusiasts possess:

> This new entrepreneurial configuration, dominated by small, equity-oriented firms, presents America's best hope for preserving its world economic leadership. As the pace of technological change hastens, small and medium-sized firms provide the American economy with a unique ability to adjust

229

to new market conditions. No other major industrialized country possesses such a storehouse of entrepreneurial energy. . . . To take full advantage of our entrepreneurial comparative advantage requires a major reordering of governmental and corporate priorities. To put into effect an entrepreneur-driven economic policy, however, will require a political transformation every bit as drastic as that now taking place on the economic battlefield. (D. Gevirtz, *Business Plan for America: An Entrepreneur's Manifesto*, © G. P. Putnam's Sons, New York, 1984, pp. 30–31.)

Along with the hopes for entrepreneurship, an image seemed to grow in the public mind that "small is beautiful." Statistics conveyed the sense that most, nearly all, or even all new jobs were being created by small business.

There was considerable hype but there was also a great deal of truth in the claims. New business start-ups were at record highs in the first half of the 1980s and the number of self-employed persons skyrocketed from 1970 to 1986, with women leading the entrepreneurial charge.

The Facts

New Business Startups

Fact #1   Nearly 3.7 million new businesses were started in the United States in the 1981–1986 period.

- For eight years straight (1979–86), an average of more than 10,000 new companies were being formed each week.
- In 1986, new business incorporations grew to a record level of nearly 700,000, more than double the number of 1975 and nearly four times the 180,000-per-year level of the early 1960s.

Fact #2   The number of self-employed persons, declining to a mere 9 percent of the working population in 1970 (from 80 percent in 1780), jumped dramatically from just over 5 million in 1970 to over 8 million in 1986.

Fact #3   *Women are the fastest growing group of entrepreneurs; they started businesses at more than twice the rate of men from 1977 to 1983.*

- However, if substantial entrepreneurial activity is defined as working full-time at a noncasual business that is not a side business, only 37 percent of female business owners are active entrepreneurs (vs. 65 percent of male owners).
- Thus, of all employed in nonagricultural industries, 9.5 percent of the men but only 3.2 percent of the women were substantially engaged in their own business.
- Self-employed women in 1983 had annual earnings of $3,767, approximately one-quarter of the $13,520 earned by self-employed men and one-third of the $12,079 earned by female paid employees.

Fact #4   *Four out of five new businesses fail within the first five years. There were 57,067 business failures in 1985, more than three times the record number up to 1982.*

Fact #5   *Business participation rates (startup percentage) vary greatly for whites and minorities: in 1982, it was sixty-three firms per 1,000 persons for whites, twenty-nine firms for Asians, twenty for Hispanics, and twelve for blacks.*

Fact #6   *Surveys of business colleges show that over 80 percent of the students list "starting my own business" as their long-range objective.*

Fact #7   *By the mid-1980s, the amount of capital pumped into new startups and young companies by venture capitalists, research and development partnerships, individual entrepreneurs, major corporations, and government agencies had grown to about $12 billion a year.*

Small Business

Fact #1   In the last half of 1983, 12.8 million persons owned businesses, 11.9 percent of persons working in nonagricultural industries.

- The 11.9 percent represents 7.4 percent who were self-employed, unincorporated business owners, 2.6 percent who were incorporated business owners, and 1.9 percent who were "paid employees and business owners."

Fact #2   Small companies strengthened their position relative to large companies in the 1970–1983 period: small companies held a higher proportion of assets in 1983 than in 1970 and companies with sales of less than $1 million doubled in number, accounting for virtually all the 1.3 million increase in the number of corporations.

Venture Capital

Fact #1   The venture capital industry, which was small and stagnant in the mid-1970s with less than $30 million invested annually, grew to a record $4.5 billion in 1983, dropped down to $3.3 billion in 1985, but sprang back to $4.5 billion in 1986.

- By 1985, venture capitalists had invested a total $19.6 billion, with $3 billion coming from abroad.

- An increasing proportion of venture capital funds—estimated at 71 percent in 1985—has been devoted to follow-up financing for companies that are already started.

Fact #2   About half of state governments (up from four in 1979) now engage directly in venture capital financing of companies within their borders—with funds worth an estimated $1 billion.

- The Massachusetts venture capital corporation invested a total of $57 million of public and private funds in twenty-seven young companies between 1979 and 1984.

Fact #3   More than 99 percent of all new businesses obtain their startup funds from personal savings and relatives.

Small Business and Jobs

Fact #1   Startup companies created over 14 million jobs in the 1981–85 period, 700,000 more jobs than were lost in company failures.

- Another 4.5 million jobs were generated by companies with fewer than 100 employees at the start of the period.

Fact #2   In terms of job creation, 29 percent of the 2.25 million jobs created in 1985 were in firms with less than twenty employees and more than half were in firms with fewer than one hundred.

- Between 1969 and 1976, small firms with less than twenty employees created as many as two-thirds of all the nation's new jobs.
- Half the jobs created each year come from self-employment or the formation of new businesses.
- During the 1981–1982 recession, an estimated 1 million new businesses were formed, creating a net gain of 1 million jobs in the economy.
- Less than 20 percent of the jobs created in 1985 were in firms of more than 1,000 employees.
- Eighty percent of the job growth is created by 12 percent of the firms, since most small businesses have three to five employees and stay at that level.

Fact #3   There has been an explosive growth in the number of high tech firms in the 1970–1985 period, but the total number of jobs created is not that large relative to other sectors.

- The number of firms in the office machine and computer sector went from 530 in 1965 to over 1,470 in 1980.

- While 120,000 jobs were created in computer and data processing from 1982 to 1984, nearly four times that many were added in bars and restaurants.

Small Business and Innovation

Fact #1   *A 1976 study by the National Science Foundation found that small companies produced twenty-four times as many major innovations as large firms and four times as many as medium-sized firms.*

Fact #2   *Small companies bring their new product innovations to market more quickly than larger firms, averaging 2.2 years to 3.1 years for large companies.*

Small Business and "Bottom-Line" Performance

Fact #1   *A dollar invested in a portfolio of companies with less than $5 million in capitalization in 1963 would have netted an investor $46 by 1980 while that same dollar invested in a portfolio with companies worth over $1 billion would have produced a mere $4.*

Fact #2   *From 1963 to 1981, publicly traded small- and medium-sized steel firms with capitalization under $60 million averaged an 18 percent return on equity—better than 2.5 times that of large steel companies (and even 50 percent above that of large computer firms).*

Interpretation of the Facts

---

1. What Is Entrepreneurship?

Entrepreneur—The Person Is Critical   There is a common image of the entrepreneur as a risk-taker, restless, hard-working, a maverick, a dreamer; in short, a modern day cowboy or cowgirl.

Perhaps the most revealing study on entrepreneurs was conducted by The Gallup Organization and *The Wall Street Journal* in early 1985 comparing business leaders in three sample groups: (1) 153 entrepreneurs who head young, rapidly growing companies; (2) 258 owners and managers of well-established companies with more modest growth rates; and (3) 207 top-level executives from *Fortune* 500 companies. Some common traits emerged but the differences were greater and more significant, indicating that a general set of personality traits is shared by most entrepreneurs.

The common traits were: an early inclination toward hard work and achievement; work experience before the age of fifteen; very long hours (sixty or more a week) spent on the job by two-thirds of each group.

The differences are most pronounced between entrepreneurs and big business executives. The entrepreneurs, as a group, tended to be less distinguished students, more likely to have been expelled from school, and less likely to have been student leaders or fraternity members than big business executives. The entrepreneurs ran businesses at an earlier age, but were fired more frequently and jumped from job to job.

A final arena of similarities and contrasts is family background. Both the entrepreneurs and corporate executives were more likely to have been first-born or only children. Significantly, the entrepreneurs show a strong tendency to name their fathers (38 percent) rather than their mothers (18 percent) as the more influential figure in their lives. By contrast, the corporate and small-business groups are more likely to say their mothers were more influential. One other common family background element discovered in a study of one hundred chief executives of the one hundred fastest-growing small firms is that nearly half came from families with entrepreneurial parents.

The fact that entrepreneurs share a common set of characteristics was confirmed in a 1983 study by McKinsey &

Company (a management consultant firm) of the members of the American Business Conference (ABC), a coalition of one hundred leaders of midsized, high-growth companies. The common characteristics of ABC leaders, relating primarily to their managing style, were:

- Enormous self-confidence, which wins respect and esteem from their employees.
- Stress open communications with their employees and go out of their way to impart their strong sense of mission to them.
- Stress fundamentals and are familiar with every facet of their firm's finances and operations.
- Allergic to bureaucracy.
- Have the ability to think as their customers do.
- Spend more than 20 percent of their time on employee development and motivation.
- Are eternally dissatisfied, as their search for improvement never ends.
- Invest heavily in the future and focus on the long-term growth of their firms.

Entrepreneurship—The Process Is Critical Perhaps the leading critic of the "personality" school of thought is Peter Drucker, the Clarke Professor of Social Science Management at the Claremont Graduate School and author of numerous books on American management:

Despite much discussion these days of the "entrepreneurial personality," few of the entrepreneurs with whom I have worked during the last 30 years had such personalities. But I have known many people—salespeople, surgeons, journalists, scholars, even musicians—who did have them without being the least bit "entrepreneurial." What all the successful entrepreneurs I have met have in common is not a certain kind of personality but a commitment to the systematic practice of innovation. Innovation is the specific function of entrepreneurship, whether in an existing business, a public service institution, or a new venture started by a lone individual in the family kitchen. (P. F. Drucker, "The Discipline of Innovation," *Harvard Business Review*, May–June, 1985, p. 67, © 1985 by the President and Fellows of Harvard College.)

Drucker offers his own definition of entrepreneurship. Debunking the popular idea that it refers to all small business or all new businesses, he stresses that the term entrepreneurship refers to a certain kind of activity. "At the heart of that activity is innovation: the effort to create purposeful, focused change in an enterprise's economic or social potential." He acknowledges that some innovations do spring from a flash of genius. But, he argues, most innovations, especially the successful ones, "result from a conscious, purposeful search for innovation opportunities, which are found only in a few situations." (Drucker, p. 67.)

Having turned aside personality or even risk-taking as major factors in entrepreneurship, Drucker argues that it is simply a matter of learning to practice "systematic innovation." This being the case, "management is the new technology that is making the American economy into an entrepreneurial economy."

Harvard Business School and the *Harvard Business Review* also downplay the personality factor and stress the process. To them, the key to entrepreneurship is in the manner in which entrepreneurs proceed with a very different order of questions than administrators:

They see entrepreneurship as a trait confined neither to certain types of individuals nor to organizations. It is found more in smaller and younger enterprises than in larger and older ones simply because the conditions favoring its development are more likely to be present.

Table 1

The Entrepreneurial Process

The Administrator's Questions	The Entrepreneur's Questions
What resources do I control?	Where is the opportunity?
What structure determines our organization's relationship to its market?	How do I capitalize on it?
	What resources do I need?
How can I minimize the impact of others on my ability to perform?	How do I gain control over them?
	What structure is best?
What opportunity is appropriate?	

2. Is Small Really Beautiful?

Part of the euphoria over entrepreneurship is the mystique that "small is beautiful" when it comes to corporate size. Greater jobs and greater innovations are the rallying cries of small business advocates. Just look at the facts, they say (many of which are presented in the first part of this chapter). Nevertheless, author Marc Levinson, among others, argues that the mythology about small business has far outdistanced the reality:

- Some small businesses are budding large businesses, but the reality is that the overwhelming majority will always be small.

- Levinson cites David Birch, guru to many small business advocates, who says most small businesses create no new jobs "after they have been in business for a year or two."

- Contrary to popular belief, corporations with more than 500 workers are still the major source of work in America, employing half the private sector workforce.

- Though small businesses have created the majority of new jobs in recent years, their relative performance owes less to the achievements of entrepreneurs than to the woes of large manufacturers.

- A job in a small company on average adds less to the GNP than a job in a large firm.

- Small firms are less capital intensive than large ones, so they usually produce less per worker.

- The two-employee corner laundromat or the self-employed bookkeeper is a far more typical small enterprise than the fast-growing high tech firm.

- The innovators are not necessarily small; among younger firms, the most innovative quickly outgrow the ranks of small business, while a firm that stays small is probably supplying few jobs or few innovations.

- Many small business jobs do not represent net employment growth, but are jobs that large corporations choose not to add. (M. Levinson, "Small Business: Myth and Reality," *Dun's Business Month*, September 1985, pp. 30–34.)

Many others note that small businesses do not have the corner on innovation, growth, or even entrepreneurship. The McKinsey study of the companies in the American Business Conference (cited earlier) concluded that many mature, medium-sized companies (annual sales $25 million to $1 billion) consistently develop new products and markets and grow at rates far exceeding national averages.

Further, it is argued, most Americans are fully aware that many of the country's largest corporations—IBM, 3M, and Hewlett-Packard are just a few of the best known—make a practice of innovation, taking risks, and showing creativity. Moreover, some of the largest companies have jumped on the entrepreneurial bandwagon by investing in new ventures. Among the most active is General Electric, which in the early 1980s invested $100 million in nearly thirty new firms and in 1982 started up an independent firm, Biological Energy Corporation, with $3 million in seed money. Control Data Corporation put up $40 million in cash, equipment, and supplies in the mid-1980s to launch a new venture, ETA Systems Inc., in order to speed up its supercomputer development.

3. The Future of Small Business and Entrepreneurs

Like big business, small business is here to stay. Indeed, by all measures and all accounts, entrepreneurs and small business have a very bright future.

But, it must also be stressed that some observers feel that there are some powerful forces working against that bright future. Don Gevirtz portrays the "powerful trend toward entrepreneurism" standing against "strong countervailing forces" of the cash-rich giant firms:

> Amid the chaos of an uncertain present, a new capitalism is fighting to be born. Although its origins are American, its influence can be felt from the aging boulevards of Europe to the congested backstreets of Tokyo. This new capitalism forged in the rapid technological changes of the past two decades expresses itself in the increasing demand by workers and managers for equity ownership, in the expanding multitude of small, successful innovative firms and in the ascendancy of entrepreneurial finance over the steady routines of conventional banking. . . . The future of this new "individualized" society, however, remains clouded in uncertainty—its ascendancy and its ultimate shape in doubt. Despite the powerful trend toward entrepreneurism, there also remain strong countervailing forces capable of eviscerating its progress. The very technology that has provided the gateway for a whole generation of entrepreneurs could, as they mature, play into the hands of cash-rich giant firms, including foreign companies with access to cheap capital. As automobiles and con-

sumer electronics fell under the sway of giantism in the early 20th century abroad, so microelectronics and biotechnology could also fall victim to future waves of mergers and acquisitions. Ultimately, the fate of the American economy will hinge upon its people. How people *choose* to invest, manage their careers, and live their lives will prove more important to entrepreneurism's future and that of the country than any technological imperative. (D. Gevirtz, pp. 218–219.)

CHAPTER
★ 15 ★
Deregulation

The Issues

The federal regulatory agencies and their primarily economic regulations, which are the focus of this chapter, came into being from 1887 to the mid-1930s, resulting in the familiar alphabet soup of government regulatory agencies: the ICC, CAB, FAA, FDIC, FCC, and of course, the Fed. The status of these agencies and their numerous regulations was not seriously challenged until the late 1960s and early 1970s. Somewhat ironically, the challenges to economic regulations arose and spread during the same period when numerous environmental and social regulations were being enacted.

There is only one basic question about regulations: Is an economic regulation good for the economy and the public

or is it harmful? In general, deregulation has been pushed
by conservatives (with notable exceptions in recent years)
and regulation has been supported by liberals.

The Facts

Major Steps of Deregulation

*Fact #1   Deregulation has taken place since 1968 in three
principal economic sectors: transportation, finance, and telecommunications.*

The major steps:

- 1968: The Supreme Court's Carterfone decision permits
  non-AT&T equipment to be connected to the AT&T
  system.

- 1969: The FCC gives MCI the right to hook its long-
  distance network into local phone systems.

- 1970: The Federal Reserve Board frees interest rates on
  bank deposits over $100,000 with maturities of less than
  six months.

- 1974: The Justice Department files antitrust suit against
  AT&T.

- 1975: The SEC orders brokers to cease fixing commissions on stock sales.

- 1977: Merrill Lynch offers the Cash Management Account, competing more closely with commercial banks.

- 1978: Congress deregulates the airlines.

- 1979: The FCC allows AT&T to sell nonregulated services, such as data processing.

- 1980: The Fed allows banks to pay interest on checking
  accounts.

- 1980: Congress deregulates trucking and railroads.

- 1981: Sears Roebuck becomes the first one-stop financial supermarket, offering insurance, banking, brokerage services.
- 1982: Congress deregulates city bus service.
- 1984: AT&T divests itself of its local phone companies.

Transportation Deregulation

Fact #1   _In the airlines industry, deregulation has brought many major benefits and numerous bankruptcies._

- Since Congress passed the Airline Deregulation Act in 1978, twenty-six new scheduled interstate carriers have entered the industry whereas during the regulatory period from 1938 to 1978, not a single new interstate trunk airline received permission to provide service.
- The number of city-pairs (service from one city to another) served by more than one airline increased by 55 percent from 1979 to 1984.
- Increased entry has led to lower average fares (13 percent lower since 1978, when adjusted for inflation) and a host of new types of fares, increasing consumer choice.
- The major cost was the numerous bankruptcies among smaller firms and a few major ones like Braniff.
- Of the 234 carriers certified since deregulation, only 74 were operating in 1987.
- Between 1978 and 1984, the number of communities reached by scheduled airlines fell to 541 from 632.

Fact #2   _In the trucking industry, there have been a number of key benefits and a number of major costs._

- With passage of the Motor Carrier Act of 1980, entry of new carriers into the trucking industry expanded dramatically, with the number of ICC-authorized carriers increasing from approximately 18,000 in 1980 to 33,548 in 1984.

- One survey found that average real truckload rates for large shippers declined by 25 percent between 1977 and 1982.

- Several surveys have found that service, as described by shippers, improved.

- By the end of 1983, more than 300 trucking companies, many of them sizable, had gone bankrupt.

- By the end of 1983, layoffs had left one-third of the Teamsters' trucking industry members without union jobs.

Fact #3   In the railroad industry, the principal benefits far outweigh any costs.

- The Staggers Rail Act of 1980 granted a greater degree of rate-making freedom to the railroads, with the result that railroads have been able to increase profits and substantially increase productivity (by 44 percent in the 1981–1984 period).

- Since passage of the Staggers Act, not a single Class 1 railroad has gone bankrupt.

- Average real freight rates for all commodity groups decreased slightly from 1980 to 1985.

- Railroads have been able to invest in and upgrade the quality of the track and equipment.

- The route miles over which train speeds were reduced because of the poor quality of the roadbed declined from 30,000 miles to fewer than 12,000 in 1984.

Fact #4   Deregulation has led to a striking increase in the power and control of the top half-dozen companies that dominate each transportation market.

- The six largest airlines controlled 84 percent of the market in 1986 versus 73 percent in 1978.

- Mergers reduced the ranks of large rail-freight carriers from thirteen in 1978 to six large regional systems in 1986 that carried 86 percent of the rail freight and earned 93 percent of the profits.
- The top ten less-than-truckload (LTL) companies accounted for nearly 60 percent of the LTL shipments in 1986 and 90 percent of the profits.

Banks and Financial Services Deregulation

Fact #1 *There has been a much greater variety of new services through competitive pricing and specialization.*
- The most visible "new service" is the automatic teller machines installed in banks, stores, and airports.
- Since the unfixing of brokerage commissions in 1975, discount brokers have emerged who can underprice their full service competitors by as much as 70 percent.

Fact #2 *Companies are trying to achieve economies of scale, both by merging with similar institutions and by taking on new services that are well-suited to distribution through existing facilities.*
- The most striking example is the Sears financial supermarket that (1) takes deposits through Allstate Savings and Loan, (2) writes insurance through Allstate Insurance, (3) sells and underwrites securities through Dean Witter Reynolds, (4) handles real estate through Coldwell Banker, and (5) is involved with consumer credit through both the Sears card and the Discover card, which it expects to compete with VISA and MasterCard.

Fact #3 *Services once provided at no charge are now being priced.*
- Banks now charge fees for checks, deposits, and other services that previously had no fee or only a token fee.

- The new fee structure entails a net transfer of benefits from small depositors to large depositors; a 1985 study found that a person maintaining an $8,000 average daily balance would, on average, earn $44 on the account over the year while someone with a $170 balance would pay $35 for the account and one with a $600 balance would pay $95 a year.

Fact #4   Within two years of the passage of the 1980 Depository Institutions Deregulation Act, bank failures began to increase sharply and the list of "problem banks" grew rapidly.

- In 1986, 136 banks failed, the greatest number of failures since 1938 (in 1984, 79 failed and in 1985, 120 failed).

- The Federal Deposit Insurance Corporation's list of "problem banks" reached 1,500 by the end of 1986, four times the 380 of 1976.

- In 1986, only one large bank holding company—J. P. Morgan & Co.—was rated AAA, down from fourteen in 1976.

Interpretation
of the Facts

---

1. Has Deregulation Been Good or Bad?

The 1986 *Economic Report of the President* and *The Economic Report of the People (1986)* offer very different perspectives on deregulation. The President's Council of Economic Advisers chose the transportation industry as its example, which clearly has had the greatest benefits relative to costs. The Center for Popular Economics chose the financial services industry, which may well have the least favorable ratio of benefits to costs.

Deregulation: Good or Bad?

Good
*President's Council
of Economic Advisers:*

Markets generate and use enormous quantities of specialized information that is extremely difficult and costly for government officials to obtain. When government substitutes for markets, either through regulation or government ownership, this information is usually lost and economic performance is sacrificed. Regulation often reduces the ability of firms to innovate and it frequently restrains competition, leading to higher costs and prices.

A great deal of economic research has shown that transport regulation served the interest of regulated companies and their unionized workers at the expense of the consuming public. Restrictions on the entry of trucking firms and airlines limited competition and kept prices high. Railroad regulation produced prices that were largely unrelated to demand and cost conditions and that were too rigid to allow railroads to compete with other transportation modes.

By the late 1970s a major deregulation effort was under-

Bad
*Center for
Popular Economics*

Like the free market orthodoxy as a whole, the theory of banking deregulation has been knocked around by the facts of economic life.

While bank deregulation is still new, it is possible to make some evaluation of its effects so far. These effects do not seem to agree with the promises of its promoters. Problems with bank performance have already appeared in four dimensions: stability; allocation of credit; provision of bank services; and concentration. . . .

But growing bank stability has high costs nevertheless. We are likely to see a growing number of failures among smaller banks and bailouts of large ones. And taxpayers will end up paying the cost of such bailouts.

The Fed's role as protector of the banking systems requires it to flood the system with more money when big banks run into trouble. This can raise havoc with other economic policies. . . .

Deregulation thus is likely to lead to a major transfor-

way. Under deregulation, firms have been able to set prices based on market demand, but constrained by competition. As a result, average passenger fares and many shipping rates have declined and the service variety has increased. Firms have responded to the pressure of competition by seeking wage concessions and improved productivity. . . .

To recapitulate, the experience in transportation demonstrates that prices usually decline when government-imposed limitations on competition are removed. It turns out that the market is a much more efficient processor of information than the regulatory system. Deregulation provides a much greater variety of services compared with the uniformity of service under regulation. The various wants of consumers are satisfied better when consumers are free to compare the costs and benefits of various product offerings and firms are free to respond to their demands. (Council of Economic Advisers, *Economic Report of the President*, Washington, D.C.: U.S. Government Printing Office, January 1987, pp. 159, 166.)

mation of the structure of American banking. One or two dozen giant financial conglomerates are likely to emerge in a dominant position in the financial sector, with a fringe of one or two thousand small, locally oriented institutions playing a marginal role. . . .

Partly as a result of its failure to deliver on its promises, the bank deregulation process sputtered and stalled in the mid-1980s. Consumer groups, small businesses, and smaller financial institutions have loudly pointed to the problems and have had an effect. In June of 1985, the US Supreme Court dealt a setback to interstate banking, when it upheld the right of states to form regional banking compacts which bar banks from certain states from entering. . . .

It is still possible, however, that the deregulationists will regain the momentum they had earlier. If this happens, it is likely that problems encountered so far will grow severe. And full success for the deregulation movement would lead us into a severely unstable world, similar in some respects to the 1920s.

It would be better to reform today's financial regulatory system. The reform should assure wide access to credit at a reasonable cost, while safe-guarding the stability of the financial system. Financial institutions should offer services in an efficient and equitable manner, and should contribute to the goals of full employment, productivity growth, the survival of stable neighborhood communities, technical and social innovation and other social objectives. (Center for Popular Economics, *Economic Report of the People*, Boston: South End Press, 1986, pp. 171, 173–174, 177, 180–187.)

2. The Future of Deregulation

Most observers feel that the major thrust of economic deregulation is behind us—that the degree of deregulation frenzy that took place in the late 1970s and early 1980s will not be seen again for some time. This is not to say that no further deregulation will take place. One likely area is utilities. But the consensus is that the major momentum is gone. In fact, some see a possible retrenchment—or "*re*regulation"—if various anticompetitive abuses and growing concentration become too severe.

CHAPTER
★ 16 ★

Corporate Marriages and Divorces: Mergers and Divestitures

The Issues

American industry in the late 1980s is not what it was as recently as 1980. Many observers argue that corporate America went through its most profound short-term restructuring ever in the 1980s due to merger mania and thousands of acquisitions, divestitures, stock buybacks, and leveraged buyouts.

It is not clear what difference this restructuring of American industry will make over the long term. Opinions vary from those who see it as a very healthy development, helping to get American companies in leaner, tougher shape to meet the foreign competition, to those who argue it's all just paper shuffling, a vast unproductive exercise in the redistribution of wealth rather than its generation.

253

The Facts

Mergers and Acquisitions

Fact #1   There were 3,336 corporate acquisitions in 1986 with a total value of $173 billion, off slightly from 1985's record $180 billion.

- In 1975, there were 981 mergers and acquisitions with a value of $11.8 billion.
- The high point for number of mergers was 6,107 in 1969.

Fact #2   While the number of transactions increased by about 20 percent during the period 1974–1986, the average reported value of merger transactions increased nearly tenfold (from $12.5 billion to $117.9 billion).

- The number of deals valued at over $100 million has grown from 15 in 1974 to 339 in 1986.

Fact #3   Many of the acquisitions have become enormous in scope; the top ten in 1985 had values ranging from $2.5 billion to $5.7 billion.

Fact #4   From 1968 to 1985, there were 60,000 mergers and acquisitions worth more than $800 billion. Early in the period, there were more mergers but they were relatively small, while in recent years the deals have averaged $86 million each.

- From 1968 to 1973, there was an annual average of 4,900 mergers and acquisitions with an average value (in 1982) of $30 million; the respective figures for the 1981–1986 period were 2,700 per year at an average of $86 million.

Fact #5   In the 1980s, 50 to 65 percent of all mergers and acquisitions activity took place in manufacturing and mining which account for only 25 percent of industrial output.

Fact #6   Mergers are taking place in all industries throughout the economy, particularly in those that have been recently deregulated.

- The banking industry had the most (234) mergers in 1984, due primarily to the Supreme Court's sanction of regional interstate banking.

- In communications, IBM in 1985 sold its portion of Satellite Business Systems to MCI Communications in exchange for up to a 30 percent stake in MCI.

- In transportation, United Airlines took a step toward becoming a broad transportation company in 1985 by acquiring the Hertz Corporation from RCA for $587.5 million. Texas Air became (in 1985) the nation's largest airline by absorbing TWA, Continental, and Peoples Express.

Fact #7 *The company most active in number of acquisitions and divestitures in the 1980s has been General Electric. From 1980 to 1986, it spent $11.1 billion to buy 338 businesses (including RCA for $6.3 billion) and shed 232 businesses worth $5.9 billion (while closing 73 plants and offices).*

Fact #8 *There was a great diversification of American firms between 1950–1975, mostly due to mergers, with the proportion of the top 200 manufacturing firms engaged in 10 or more "lines of business" jumping from 10 to 45 percent.*

Fact #9 *Somewhere between one-half and two-thirds of mergers simply do not work.*

- One out of three acquired companies get sold off within five years.

- Fifty-eight major acquisition programs undertaken from 1972 to 1983 were put to two financial tests to determine their success. Twenty-eight of the fifty-eight clearly failed both tests and six others failed one. Megamergers are the most likely to fail (study by McKinsey & Co. with the two tests being: Did the return on the total amount invested in the acquisitions exceed the cost of capital and did they help their parents outperform the competition in the stock market?).

- Among the biggest losers in the merger and acquisition game:
  — Mobil's purchase of Montgomery Ward.
  — Exxon's acquisition of Reliance Electric.
  — Baldwin-United's takeover of MGIC Investment.
  — Wickes purchase of Gamble-Skogmo.
  — Atlantic Richfield's purchase of Anaconda Minerals.
  — Fluor's purchase of St. Joe Mineral Corporation.

Fact #10   Hostile takeovers accounted for only 1.2 percent of the total mergers and acquisitions in 1982 and 1986; however, when the value of the deals is considered, they represent 18.4 percent of all transactions in 1982 and 19.7 percent in 1986.

Divestitures

Fact #1   In the period 1981–1984, the number of divestitures increased 40 percent to 900 and the dollar value of spin-offs nearly doubled to $29 billion.

- The three largest spin-offs were by General Electric ($2.4 billion), R. J. Reynolds Industries ($1.7 billion), and RCA ($1.5 billion).

Fact #2   Divestiture usually works well for the operation that is divested.

- According to a study (by economist Frederic Scherer, Swarthmore College) of fifteen operations that large companies divested from 1970–1982, all but one did better under their new owners.

Fact #3   Some major corporations have divested with a vengeance.

- Super-conglomerate ITT Corporation sold fifty-five subsidiaries in the first half of the 1980s.

- Gulf & Western Industries spun off some sixty-five diverse subsidiaries from 1983 through 1986 that were worth more than $4 billion.

- City Investing chose to liquidate its entire $8.5 billion in assets.

- Control Data Corporation in less than two years (1985–1986) discarded twenty businesses that were too far removed from its basic field.

Mergers/Acquisitions and Corporate Debt

Fact #1   _The surge of borrowing by companies to finance the recent tidal wave of mergers, stock buybacks, and leveraged buyouts was the major factor for the very high and growing level of corporate debt in the mid-1980s._

- Corporate debt in 1984 and 1985 grew 8.7 percent annually (after adjusting for inflation) compared to 2.7 percent from 1975 to 1983.

- U.S. corporations between 1980 and 1986 were replacing equity with debt to the tune of $500 billion.

Fact #2   _At the end of 1986, the debt of nonfinancial corporations stood at $1.71 trillion._

Fact #3   _Between 1974 and 1984, nearly all of the fifteen major industries increased their debt burden._

- Retailing, metals, and drugs all had double digit increases.

- Of the four industries reducing their debt, rubber and textiles rid themselves of the most, 5.2 percent and 4.6 percent, respectively.

Fact #4   The corporate debt burden has been very high in the 1980s compared to the 1960s and 1970s.

- One measure of the debt burden—the ratio of interest payments to cash flow plus interest—stayed below 20 percent in the 1960s, below 30 percent in the 1970s but rose from 36 percent to 43 percent in the first half of the 1980s.

- From 1983 to 1985, the cost of servicing debt absorbed 50 percent of the entire cash flow of corporations while in the 1976–1979 recovery it averaged only 27 percent of cash flow.

- The huge bull market in stocks steadily reduced the ratio of debt to the market value of equity from over 83 percent in 1984 to a 15-year low of 61 percent by mid-1987; the October stock crash drove the ratio back up to the 80 percent mark virtually overnight.

Fact #5   The quality of corporate debt, due primarily to a surge in junk bond financing, declined dramatically in the first half of the 1980s.

- The number of AAA-rated industrial and utility corporations dwindled to 27 from 56 in the 1975–1985 period.

- Corporate debt rated below investment grade rose from 11 percent of the total issued in 1982 to 24 percent in 1985.

- In 1986, Standard & Poor's downgraded debt totaling $188 billion of a record 347 companies.

- Of the $60 billion in below-investment-grade debt issued from 1977 to 1985, 3.2 percent was in default in 1986, which compares with an overall bond default rate of 0.13 percent from the late 1970s through 1985.

Interpretation
of the Facts

1. The Wave of Mergers
and The Economy

The basic argument in favor of the wave of mergers is that it is simply the market's way of strengthening America's economic muscle. Allen Sinai, chief economist for Shearson Lehman, explains: "We're in the midst of a metamorphosis. The outside layer of our economic skin is being replaced by a layer of tougher skin."

Supporters of mergers readily point to the many mergers that have worked successfully: Nabisco and Standard Brands, Allied and Bendix, Heinz and Weight Watchers. The success stories seem to share a common set of elements: (1) the companies involved are usually in closely related businesses; (2) they are often financed by stock swaps or cash, not borrowed money; (3) the price does not include a hefty premium; (4) the management of the acquired company usually remains.

Mergers are seen by their proponents as ways to acquire more sophisticated talent and technology, to gain new product lines, to benefit from expanding marketing capabilities and economies of scale, and to get out of old endeavors and into new ones.

Opponents of mergers begin with the fact that the majority of mergers simply do not work and thus the economy cannot be benefited. At times, their argument goes well beyond the pragmatic question: does it work? It gets into the much broader issue of wealth generation versus wealth redistribution. Robert Samuelson expressed this argument in an article focused on the broad theme of America as the "Spoils Society."

> In part, our society has become a vast spoils system. Enormous amounts of time and energy are spent not in creating

new wealth but in wrestling over the existing wealth. Adam Smith's idea was that societies prosper when everyone tries to get ahead, because profit-maximizing producers generate new wealth. But wealthy, complex societies injure Smith's invisible hand. You can advance just as easily by grabbing someone else's wealth. . . . The merger movement stems in part from management's misuse of shareholder wealth for unwise expansion. Although shareholders may suffer, executives often benefit in greater salaries or status. . . . But, in a larger sense, we all lose when distributional struggles get out of hand. No society has limitless amounts of talent or inventiveness. People playing distributional games cannot play creative games. Because these distributional struggles often involve immense stakes, they command some of our best minds, who are handsomely rewarded (Robert Samuelson, "And Now, the Spoils Society," *Newsweek*, December 30, 1985, p. 43).

2. Companies that Choose to "Grow Smaller"

In a nation and a society naturally attuned to growth, why are many American companies deliberately choosing to become smaller? Until they have done it, it's never clear if it makes sense for them to be lopping off divisions, selling assets and product lines, and narrowing their focus. At least one of the following reasons is used as justification for this "unnatural" course.

A. *Divestitures Are the Flip Side of the Merger Binge*
Mergers, especially those made in haste, often produce morning-after regrets. Even if they do not, the buyers often sell off pieces of the acquired company or of their own company to reduce the merger debt.

B. *Preempt Attacks by Corporate Raiders*   Many companies simply split up to help fend off corporate raiders who typically conquer in order to divide.

C. *Smokestack Companies Need to Finance Purchases*
Since many smokestack companies find their traditional business in a dead-end or downward spiral, they are trying to diversify by buying companies in more prosperous fields. This sometimes requires selling off some of their assets to finance the purchase.

D. *A Generation of Acquisition-Driven Executives is Passing Away* Many of the powerful conglomerate builders are no longer at the helm of their companies. They leave a new generation of corporate officers who can more easily divest operations than could the people who acquired them.

E. *The Decline or Death of Inflation in an Industry* The fact that inflation has been squeezed out of many industries has prompted asset juggling. A prime example is oil companies that led the diversification into mining and minerals and then began heavily selling what they could and writing off the rest.

F. *New Entrepreneurial Buyers* The ranks of buyers for corporate units has expanded with the flourishing of entrepreneurism in the 1980s. A particular spur to many entrepreneurial efforts has been the widespread use of leveraged buyout techniques.

G. *The Rise of the "Big Isn't Necessarily Better" Attitude* Simply put, more and more companies are concluding that bigger is not better, that a narrow base is better, and that professional managers cannot necessarily run whatever they put their mind to. As Martin S. Davis, the head of Gulf & Western, has put it: "Bigness is not a sign of strength. In fact, just the opposite is true."

3. The Future

The consensus is that merger mania is over. Merger activity will still continue at a healthy pace but it will be considerably more selective. One trend that is expected to continue: the buying of companies with well-established brand names. It is also anticipated that corporate divestitures will continue at a strong pace as companies sift through their recent acquisitions and sell off unwanted units.

The reason why major corporate restructuring is likely to continue is that the evidence overwhelmingly shows it to be a powerful force for improvement. Those industries and services that have had a disproportionate share of mergers, acquisitions, and leveraged buyouts have seen a corresponding jump in productivity.

CHAPTER
★ 17 ★
Automation

The Issues

In the 1960s, there were dire warnings about automation's impact on jobs. It was predicted that the jobs of millions of workers would disappear. It did not happen. There was neither a major loss of jobs, nor any major improvements in efficiency and productivity in the nation's offices and factories.

Now, in the 1980s, numerous headlines once again herald a major wave of automation in offices and factories. Is this the case? What impact will 1980s-style automation have? The focus now is not so much on how automation will impact jobs but how it will affect U.S. competitiveness. A great deal of hope for restoring U.S. competitiveness is being pinned on automation and its anticipated productivity improvements.

The Facts

Growth and Success—Overview

Fact #1   Purchases of factory automation systems rose from $7.4 billion in 1980 to $18.1 billion in 1985, a nearly 150 percent increase in just five years.

- The three components are computer-aided manufacturing, up 124 percent (from $6.8 to $15.4 billion); computer-aided design and engineering, up 531 percent (from $.4 to $2.5 billion), and communications links, up 146 percent (from $.1 to $.3 billion).

Fact #2   Computer-aided manufacturing consists of six major types of shop-floor automation, the two predominant ones being machine tools and controls and materials handling systems.

Table 1

Computer-Aided Manufacturing—Major Components

	(millions of dollars)		
	1980	1985	1990*
Factory computers and software	$935	$2,861	$6,500
Materials handling systems	2,000	4,500	9,000
Machine tools and controls	3,000	4,800	7,000
Programmable controllers	50	500	3,000
Robots and sensors	68	644	2,800
Automated test equipment	0,800	2,000	4,000
Total spending on CAM**	**$6,853**	**$15,375**	**$32,300**

Source: Dataquest, Inc.

* Estimates

** Computer-aided manufacturing

Fact #3 *Purchases of factory automation equipment accounted for at least half of business equipment outlays in 1983, in sharp contrast to only 17 percent of total equipment spending two decades ago.*

- In the 1975–1985 decade, corporate spending on information processing went up an average of 16 percent a year, and raw computer power for crunching data faster increased eighteenfold.

Growth and Success—
Company Examples

Fact #1 *Many companies from all industries, large and small, have had strongly positive performance results from automation.*

- Frost Inc., a family-run job shop, decided to automate totally: (1) it cut prices 30 percent while lifting gross margins to a respectable 35 percent; (2) sales per employee were up nearly 50 percent to $130,000; (3) only one part in 200 failed quality checks compared with one out of four before.

- IBM built one of the world's most fully automated plants in Charlotte, N. Carolina. In the first eighteen months of operation, direct labor content and the number of manufacturing steps was halved, output doubled, costs dropped 20 percent a year, and quality soared.

- Federal Kemper Life Insurance installed a new computer system in 1974 and regrouped employees into self-contained three-person teams; productivity increased fivefold from 1972 to 1985.

- Citicorp developed a sophisticated information system that allowed its North American Banking Group to pare its staff from 2,650 to 2,150 (from 1983 to 1986) and to transform it from 70 percent clerical to 60 percent professionals.

- IBM in 1986 introduced the PC Convertible, the first computer to be built entirely by robots.

Fact #2   Individual companies are spending huge sums to automate.

- From 1976 to 1986, pioneers such as Apple Computer, Boeing, Deere, General Dynamics, Hughes Aircraft, and Rexnord have invested billions of dollars, with much more budgeted for future automation.

- General Motors, by far the leader, is investing $40 billion in such futuristic projects as Buick City and the Saturn Project.

- IBM in 1985 plowed about $3 billion into strengthening its manufacturing capabilities and from 1986–1989, over $15 billion (one third of its total capital budget) is to be invested into turning its factories into showcases of sophisticated manufacturing technology.

- General Electric, to automate its Appliance Park complex in Louisville, Kentucky and other plants, is budgeting $1 billion over a five-year period in the late-1980s.

Disappointments—Overview

Fact #1   In 1986, only about two dozen U.S. companies had factories that even came close to the goal of total automation; less than 250 companies have made more than token investments in computer integration.

Fact #2   The computer revolution, involving the purchase of millions of computers by U.S. businesses, has not yet paid off in productivity growth.

- Despite the fact that most computers are in white-collar work, growth in white-collar productivity has been especially weak.

- White-collar productivity is about where it was in the late 1960s.

Fact #3 *Automation has reached a small percentage of the 14 million U.S. businesses with revenues of less than $10 million.*

Fact #4 *The competitive position of U.S. industry in electronic machinery (for automation) in manufacturing applications is a poor second internationally (to Japan).*

Fact #5 *Japan annually spends roughly twice as much as the U.S. on automation.*

Fact #6 *More than 60 percent of the robots installed in American factories in 1986 came from Japan.*

- The U.S. in 1986 had 14,000 robots compared to 67,300 in Japan.

Disappointments—Company Examples

Fact #1 *General Electric in 1980 bet heavily on the factory of the future (a fully automated factory), making grand predictions that never materialized.*

- It invested $500 million to set itself up as America's factory-of-the-future one-stop supermarket, predicting immediate revenues of $1 billion a year and $5 billion of a $25-billion market by 1990.
- In 1982–1984, the project experienced $120 million in losses and, in 1985, they projected $1 billion in revenues by 1988.
- Problems were legion: the products in GE's line-up did not plug together readily; customers hesitated to sign up for automation systems; robots turned out to be hard to sell and still harder to install properly; annual sales of

its numerical controls sank 30 percent and annual losses amounted to nearly $10 million.

Fact #2   GMF Robotics Corporation, owned equally by Japan's Fanuc Ltd. and General Motors, laid off 200 of its 700 employees and mothballed plans for an automated plant where robots would build more robots.

Fact #3   General Motors, with the most ambitious and extensive automation plans, has also scaled back the most.

General Motors—The Automation Story of the 1980s

Fact #1   In the mid-1980s, GM was spending $3 billion a year for research and development and up to $7 billion to introduce automation technologies.

Fact #2   GM's ambitious move into automation runs the gamut of technological investment. By the mid-1980s it was:

- Installing 4,000 robots in mostly revamped old factories, giving it the world's largest population of factory robots.
- Building five new automated plants.
- Pioneering in the establishment of an industry standard computer protocol.
- Entering the uncharted world of artificial intelligence by buying a leading firm in the field.
- Purchasing Electronic Data Systems for $2.2 billion to become a leading player in the new computer software that will run the next generation of factory-automation systems.

Fact #3   Automated equipment is found throughout GM plants and will replace many workers.

For example, in mid-1984, at its three plants in Lansing, Michigan:

- There were 219 welding and painting robots.

- There were 185 automated, guided vehicles, eliminating most human-operated forklifts.

- Other robots replaced the human labor involved in racking door panels, applying vehicle ID numbers, and tightening drive belts.

- Robotgate, a framing station, has eight robots that apply sixty-four precisely located welds to every auto body, thus replacing welders.

- The Master Cube and other computerized checking instruments along the line replaced most human inspectors who used to do that job.

Fact #4   GM revolutionized automation by developing MAP (manufacturing automation protocol), a standardized communications network that allows diverse computers, robots, and controllers to communicate with one another in a common electronic language.

- MAP began to be put into limited use in 1985 at GM and at some Deere, Boeing, and Eastman Kodak plants.

- In 1986, GM's truck-assembly plant in Pontiac, Michigan became the biggest demonstration of GM's massive bid to revolutionize automobile manufacturing through MAP, as all equipment is linked to a single computerized network tying together production, inventory, and quality control.

Fact #5   A number of elements of GM's ambitious plan to automate had to be scaled back beginning in 1986 because there were too many at one time and many managers were simply not ready to handle the full integration of technology.

- Its plan to convert seven plants to produce a new midsize car—involving installing more than 1,000 robots and replacing conventional car assembly lines with the automated guided vehicle (AGV)—was cut back to three plants.

Fact #6   GM's top domestic competitor, Ford, began its serious move into automation much later than GM and with considerably fewer dollars invested.

- Up to 1985, Ford had made only one automation investment, a $2 million investment to purchase 16 percent of Synthetic Vision Systems.
- In 1985, it invested $20 million in American Robot Corporation for a minority stake, in part to fund research and development.

Computer-Integrated Manufacturing

Fact #1   In 1985 a milestone in the application of computer-integrated manufacturing in the U.S. occurred at Allen-Bradley, a Milwaukee-based manufacturer of industrial controls: the ability to make different versions of a product at mass-production speeds in lots as small as a single unit.

- By using automated equipment, it could produce contactors for 60 percent less than it could by relying on a manual assembly line.

Fact #2   Computer-integrated manufacturing, in which shop-floor machines are operated by a central computer, is a reality in only a few plants.

Flexible Manufacturing Systems

Fact #1   Approximately fifty flexible manufacturing systems (FMS)—which bring manufacturers an unparalleled ability to switch from making one kind of part to another very rapidly through a cluster of computer-controlled machines that can *be quickly programmed—had been installed by mid-1986 at a cost of approximately $200 million.*

Fact #2   Labor requirements in an FMS factory are dramatically lower than those for conventional systems.

- At a Vought plant only nineteen workers are needed to run the $10.1 million, eight-machine FMS through three machines compared to twenty-four machines and seventy-two workers to get the same output as with a conventional system.

- At the FMS plant of Japan's largest machine-tool builder, Yamkaki Machinery Works, only 12 operators work on the first and second shift compared with 215 required in a conventional system.

- The most dramatic reductions come in manufacturing overhead where an FMS cuts the number of workers from sixty-four to five.

Fact #3   Efficiency is considerably higher in plants where an FMS has been installed since manufacturers can respond much faster to their markets and custom-tailor their products to a degree never possible before.

- Using FMS technology, it takes a GE locomotive plant in Erie, Pennsylvania sixteen hours rather than sixteen days to make locomotive motor frames.

- Compared with a conventional system, the FMS technology that IBM installed to manufacture, test, and package its new "lap-top" computer at a plant in Austin, Texas, is 75 percent more efficient.

Fact #4   Although American companies were pioneers in FMS development and started making it available to industry in the mid-1970s, by 1986 the Japanese systems were considerably better and in place in many more factories worldwide.

Fact #5   Fifty-five percent of the machine tools introduced in Japan in the 1980s were computer-numerically controlled (CNC) machines (key parts of FMSs) as opposed to only 18 percent in the U.S.

- Over two-thirds of the CNC machines in Japan went to small- and medium-sized companies.

- Compared with U.S. plants, Japanese factories had an average of two and one-half times as many CNC machines, four times as many engineers, and four times as many people trained to use the machines.

Table 2
Comparison of FMSs* in U.S. and Japan

	United States	Japan
System development time years	2.5 to 3	1.25 to 1.75
Number of machines per system	7	6
Types of parts produced per system	10	93
Annual volume per part	1,727	258
Number of parts produced per day	88	120
Number of new parts introduced per year	1	22
Number of systems with untended operations	0	18
Utilization rate** two shifts	52%	84%
Average metal-cutting time per day hours	8.3	20.2

Source: Ramchandran Jaikumar, "Postindustrial Manufacturing," *Harvard Business Review*, November–December 1986, p. 70.

* Flexible Manufacturing System

** Ratio of actual metal-cutting time to time available for metal cutting.

The Human Side of Automation

Fact #1   In the early 1980s, to realize the full potential of automation, a number of innovating companies began to integrate workers and automation technology in "sociotechnical" systems (STS) that revolutionize the way work is organized and managed.

- The old "control" model is replaced by a new "commitment" model that integrates the psychological and social needs of workers with technological requirements in designing a new plant or redesigning an old one.

Fact #2   At the heart of the new STS concept is teamwork among the employees, now used in several hundred offices and factories (especially new highly automated plants with small work forces of 25 to 500 people) compared with fewer than two dozen manufacturing plants in 1976.

Fact #3   Many plants designed with sociotechnical methods and using the most radical innovation, semiautonomous teams, are 30 percent to 50 percent more productive than their conventional counterparts.

- Procter and Gamble's teamwork plants, first established in the 1960s, were 30 percent to 40 percent more productive than their traditional counterparts and significantly more able to adapt quickly to the changing needs of the business.
- Xerox began using teams in some of its operations in the early 1980s and found them to be "at least 30 percent more productive" than conventionally organized operations.

Reorganizing the Machines, not Automation

Fact #1   For many manufacturers, the key to improving productivity and competitiveness has not been to automate but to simply reorganize the manufacturing flow by moving machinery around in the plant.

- In one company the valves produced on their conventional production line traveled a half-mile back and forth between departments during the two months it took to make them; by regrouping the lathes and drills into U-shaped cells the valves travel a few hundred feet and are produced in two to three days.

- By reorganizing, a machine-parts manufacturer that required twenty-four weeks to produce a product the Japanese could produce and ship in six, got production time down to four weeks, increased labor productivity by 50 percent, cut inventory by 80 percent, and became competitive again.

Interpretation of the Facts

1. Automation and the Future

Perhaps the best place to capture the tremendous optimism and enthusiasm behind the latest automation wave embodied in information technologies is in the pages of leading business magazines. In 1985 and 1986, the following appeared:

High Technology is reinventing the factory. Although computer-integrated factories are still a rarity, they are finally beginning to reshape the US industrial landscape. These plants, which can build a wide variety of flawless products and switch from one product to another on cue from a central computer, herald a new age in manufacturing (*Business Week*, June 16, 1986, p. 100).

Business is beginning to reconfigure things from the ground up—this time with the computer in mind. The result: entirely different approaches to existing markets and whole new product lines that didn't seem a logical extension of the business before (*Business Week*, October 14, 1985, p. 108).

By embracing MAP early, GM and other US manufacturers hope to leapfrog Japan, until now the pacesetter in factory automation (*Fortune*, October 28, 1985, p. 102).

Yet squarely in the middle of parched Texas scrubland, a quantum leap is being taken toward the workerless factory of tomorrow. . . . The technology employed by Vought is on the cutting edge of a recent bid by American industry to rethink the way many of its products are made—from the giant war horses of national defense to farm tractors and tiny electric meters (*U.S. News and World Report*, July 14, 1986, p. 44).

Powerful words and phrases keep popping up in these accounts and many others: "reinventing the factory," "reshape the US industrial landscape," "a new age in manufacturing," "reconfigure things from the ground up," "leapfrog Japan," "a quantum leap," "rethink the way many of its products are made."

Peter Drucker, the well-known business/management advisor and author, does not use such flamboyant expressions but he nevertheless extols the virtues of automation. In an article entitled "Automation Payoffs are Real" in *The Wall Street Journal* (Sept. 20, 1985) he argued that the payoff from automation is high and fast. He went so far as to state that automation, wherever installed in a manufacturing plant, has paid for itself within three years and often much faster. He cites three major economic benefits to help substantiate this claim: (1) automation builds quality standards and quality control into every step of the process; (2) it considerably reduces the costs of "downtime" when production is being changed from one model to another; (3) this reduction or elimination of downtime gives a plant an entirely new capacity to generate revenues.

Although Drucker does not cite specific examples to illustrate his points, many others who are optimistic about automation's vast potential do. In addition to the numerous examples cited in the Facts section, here are two classic examples from Harvard Business School case studies:

- Merrill Lynch used computers to create one of the most successful new products ever: the Cash Management Account. Since introducing it in 1978, Merrill Lynch lured billions of dollars of assets from other places, resulting in a $85 billion total by 1985 which despite similar offerings by numerous competitors was 70 percent of the market.

- American Airlines used computers and communications technology to develop an entirely new business, the Sabre reservation system, which it provides to 48% of the approximately 24,000 automated travel agents in the U.S. Profit margins are sky high as in 1985 Sabre was expected to earn $170 million before taxes on $338 million in revenues.

Some proponents say that the facts about labor cost savings are compelling. They often point to the cost of an industrial robot to a car manufacturer: $6 an hour compared to the worker's $23–24 an hour. Or they point to GE's factory in which one enormous locomotive engine frame is produced daily in a process that involves no production workers at all—down from sixty-eight workers who produced only one such frame every sixteen days.

Finally, they note that increasingly the more than 100,000 small job shops that form the backbone of American manufacturing are pushing into factory automation. They supply an estimated 75 percent of all the machined metal parts used in products made by bigger companies and they employ the bulk of all blue-collar workers. One estimate is that computer purchases by small plants will increase nearly 30 percent a year through 1990 compared to 23 percent for midsized plants and 18 percent for large companies. Another survey showed that more than a quarter of the companies planning to buy robots in 1986 had annual sales below $10 million.

The pessimists cite their own set of facts or estimates. Their front-line argument is that investment in new technology is not increasing nearly as fast as was predicted in the early 1980s. In late 1986, Dataquest Inc., a market research firm, lowered its estimate of industrial automation sales in 1990 by 13 percent, to $34 billion.

They also stress the point that the millions of computers purchased by U.S. businesses have apparently not brought about any overall improvement in productivity. It is argued this is because computers are often used for applications with low payoffs.

This leads the pessimists to the point cited in the Facts section that the large payoffs do not come from increasing the efficiency with which people perform their old jobs, but from changing the way work is done. Advanced computer technology calls for another advance in traditional work practices. The problem is that teamwork is very difficult to implement and keep working successfully. Changes in plant and corporate management have doomed many a promising teamwork experiment and personality conflicts in teams also cause problems. Thus, the bottom line is that plants that use teamwork constitute only a small minority of U.S. workplaces.

Related to this is the argument that the fixation on computers, robots, and other automation "wonders" causes managers to skip over more fundamental ideas for cost reduction. One example of the tendency to favor the complex, costly, and often less reliable means of automation is found in a major internal study by General Motors that suggested that the bulk of the cost gap between American and Japanese cars is directly attributable to systems complexity. There is an enormous complexity gap between Detroit and Tokyo in overall marketing-manufacturing systems. Japanese cars are "packaged" with few options available. Almost all American cars are custom built with myriad options and thousands of combinations available. For example, the Honda Accord can be purchased in one of 32 possible combinations. There are American models with over 40,000 possible combinations! Detroit's incredible systems complexity results in overmarketing, excessive capital demand, bloated inventories, slow cycle times, and poor quality.

The auto industry is the one most often pointed to by the pessimists (as well as the optimists). The pessimists build their argument around the U.S.-Japanese cost differential. This stood at $1,500 in Japan's favor in 1979 for a small car. Since then, U.S. automakers have spent at least $40 billion to build highly automated plants. The result? The gap actually increased to $2,500 in 1983 and fell to only $1,900 by 1986, a fall almost wholly attributable to the stronger yen. Observers blame Detroit's woes with automation on its assumption that technology would solve all its problems.

As one further illustration, the pessimists point to GM, the automation leader, and its cancellation in early 1986 of several contracts involving robots worth $80 million. This action was quite significant for GM is such a powerhouse in the drive to automate that its decision to slow down affects many other companies both in and out of the automotive industry.

2. The Size of Future Automation Markets

Estimates are being made continually about the future of automation in general and of such specific markets as robotics. A sampling of some of the most recent, and seemingly most reliable, ones follows.

Looking first at the broad automation picture, the consulting firm Arthur C. Little forecast U.S. companies will spend $100 billion over the next ten years (from 1986) to automate their factories. This is a quite conservative estimate in comparison to other leading market analysts. For instance,

Dataquest Inc. projects that purchases of factory automation systems, which doubled to $18.1 billion from 1980 to 1985, would double again by 1990.

Whatever the dollar figure, most observers feel significant job displacement from automation will take place. One leading prediction is that such widespread automation will reduce the total number of manufacturing jobs in the economy by 25 percent to 50 percent over the next decade.

Turning to the robotics market, Wall Street analysts in 1984 expected that to grow into a multibillion-dollar industry by the early 1990s. Because of unexpectedly soft sales in 1985–1987, predictions were scaled back so that by mid-1986, market researchers predicted that a $1 billion market would not emerge until at least 1989. Much of the growth of this market will depend on events in the auto industry and particularly at GM, the world's largest user of robots. In the mid-1980s, GM was planning to have 20,000 robots on its factory floors by 1990—about 20 percent of the total projected robot population in the United States by that year and three times the total number in use in the U.S. when their projection was made. It is said each robot can displace 1.7 to 6 workers.

GM is also instrumental in another major automation market. Experts predict that the market for MAP systems will explode from a base of zero in 1985 to more than $550 million by 1990.

CHAPTER
★ 18 ★
Competitiveness

The Issues

Throughout the 1980s, it has been said repeatedly that America is losing its competitiveness. Some feel it is only temporary; others see it as an inevitable slide. Some say it is just in a few industries; others feel it is across the board. Some argue America is only falling behind Japan; others feel America is losing out to a host of countries. One gauge of how "hot" competitiveness has become since 1985 is that more than 5,000 "competitiveness bills" were introduced in the 99th Congress (1985–1986).

Many key dimensions of the competitiveness issue are beyond dispute: America's global economic leadership has significantly declined; its ability to compete globally has seriously eroded in the past fifteen to twenty years; and for the past twenty-five to thirty years Japan has surpassed the U.S. in one major industry after another.

Why? Although some observers like to point to "one big reason," most experts agree that several factors have contributed to the decline in competitiveness, ranging from the short-run focus of U.S. managers to the controversial charge that American companies are not really interested in production.

The Facts

Overall Measures of Competitiveness

Fact #1   *U.S. global economic leadership has been steadily shrinking for the past 35 years: in 1950, it accounted for about 6 percent of the world's population, 40 percent of its GNP, and 70 percent of world trade. In 1980 the U.S. had 5 percent of the world's population, 21.5 percent of its GNP, and 11 percent of its trade.*

Fact #2   *Analysts cite a wide variety of measures to indicate the United States' ability to compete in the world economy has eroded significantly over the last two decades.*

- The U.S. merchandise trade balance has deteriorated both in absolute terms and as a percentage of GNP—positive from 1893–1970, it turned negative in 1971 and has generally continued downhill.

- A steady across-the-board loss in world market share of industrial exports covering all major sectors.

- U.S. productivity gains since the mid-1960s pale when compared with those of its major trading partners; productivity has been lower in the recovery begun in 1982 than in any other since World War II; from 1965–1981, manufacturing productivity grew twice as fast in Japan and one and one-half times as fast in Germany as in the United States.

- Real wages, which grew steadily from World War II until 1973, have since fallen and the trend is still downward. In real terms, average gross weekly earnings in 1985 were at 1962 levels.

- The Readiness Index, which measures how well U.S. businesses compete against foreign rivals, based on comparative prices of manufactured goods from each nation, declined steadily since 1980, falling 26 percent by late 1985.

Comparison of Key Economic Variables Underlying Competitiveness

Fact #1   *Net fixed investment as a percentage of gross domestic product, 6.6 percent in the United States in the 1970s, was 19.5 percent in Japan and 11.8 percent in West Germany.*

Fact #2   *Companies in Japan and West Germany have considerably larger savings pools to draw on as the United States devotes less than 6 percent of its personal income to savings while Japan devotes 18 percent and West Germany 13 percent.*

Fact #3   *Highly leveraged capital structures, with debt-to-capital ratios nearly double that of U.S. manufacturers, give Japanese and West German manufacturing companies important competitive advantages.*

- By substituting debt (with tax-deductible interest) for higher cost equity it lowers the after-tax cost of capital.

- The higher a company's financial leverage, the faster the rate of growth it can finance at a given return-on-investment level.

Fact #4   *There are sizable differences in the cost of capital for U.S. and Japanese companies, differences which widened in the 1970s.*

- From 1962 to 1969, the average annual inflation-adjusted difference in pretax capital cost was approximately 6 percentage points while from 1974 to 1983, the average differential widened to more than 11 percentage points.

U.S. vs. JAPAN: The Chief Rivalry

Overview of U.S.–Japanese Economic Competition

Fact #1   *For forty years, in one industry after another, the U.S. has invented a product and the Japanese have picked it up and become world leaders in its production.*

- In the mid-1950s, RCA licensed several Japanese companies to make color televisions.
- In 1953, Western Electric licensed the technology for the solid-state transistor to Sony.
- In 1968, Unimation licensed Kawasaki Heavy Industries to make industrial robots; within fifteen years Japan had four times as many industrial robots in place.
- Other technologies "invented in America" but (largely) "made in Japan" are open-hearth furnaces, videocassette recorders, continuous casters for making steel, and automobile-stamping machines.

Fact #2   *Japanese companies in the past twenty-five years have relentlessly moved into Western markets and swept aside the local suppliers.*

- Japan in 1985 produced three-quarters of the world's videocassette recorders, single-lens cameras, and motorcycles.

• In 1985, it made half of the world's ships, two-fifths of its TVs, and one-third of its semiconductors and cars.

Fact #3   *Many American companies have simply ceded business to the Japanese, particularly in tough, high-volume markets where their production efficiencies are difficult to overcome: leading examples are consumer electronics, small cars, textiles, and machine tools.*

Fact #4   *Japan's imports of manufactured goods from the rest of the world has remained constant since 1960, about 2.5 percent of GNP—less than half of the American ratio.*

Fact #5   *Japanese executives have as their number one priority to make their companies the global leader in an industry while this goal is fourth most important to U.S. managers who put increasing shareholder value as the top priority (according to 1984 and 1985 surveys by Booz, Allen & Hamilton and by* Business Week*).*

Fact #6   *For every 10,000 people: the U.S. has 20 lawyers, Japan has 1; the U.S. has 40 accountants, Japan has 3; the U.S. has 70 engineers, Japan has 400.*

Japanese Companies Manufacturing in the U.S.

Fact #1   *In 1986, about 500 Japanese companies were manufacturing or assembling goods in the United States in a wide range of industries, from auto to high technology.*

Fact #2   *Japan's investment in U.S. manufacturing, real estate, and distribution facilities in 1986—$23.4 billion—was far below that of Britain ($51.4 billion) or the Netherlands ($42.9 billion).*

• Japanese investment nearly quintupled from 1980 to 1986 and Japan's Ministry of International Trade and Industry expects the country's U.S. manufacturing investment to grow 14.2 percent each year until 2000, a tenfold increase over the early 1980s level.

Fact #3   The biggest Japanese investments in the U.S. have been in autos.

- Three Japanese auto-assembly plants—Toyota in Fremont, California, Honda in Marysville, Ohio, and Nissan in Smyrna, Tennessee—were producing at the rate of 560,000 vehicles a year in 1986, from zero in 1982.

- A total of ten U.S. plants are planned by Toyota, Mazda, Subaru-Isuzu, and Mitsubishi, either separately or in partnership with U.S. companies which is projected to lead to 2.5 million made-in-the-USA Japanese vehicles in 1990.

- Two dozen Japanese auto parts manufacturers had plants in the U.S. in early 1987 and the number was projected to jump to over 300 before the end of 1988.

- In late 1987, Honda announced plans to export 70,000 cars per year from Ohio to Japan and other countries by 1991.

Fact #4   Hundreds of Japanese high-tech companies are setting up shop in America.

- In just four months of 1984, over 40 new plants were established by such leaders of Japanese high tech as NEC, Fujitsu, and Sony to produce everything from personal computers to cellular mobile telephones.

Fact #5   Japanese-owned companies in the U.S. significantly outperform their American counterparts in key business areas ranging from capital investment to quality control.

- Quality control standards were very stringent, with 95 percent of the companies reporting a defect rate of under 5 percent and about half reporting a defect rate of less than one-half of 1 percent.

Table 1
U.S.–Japan Joint Ventures

Automobiles
GM-Toyota
Ford-Mazda
Chrysler-Mitsubishi Motors

Computers
IBM-Matsushita Electric
Sperry-Univac-Nippon Univac
National Semiconductor-Hitachi
Honeywell-NEC
Tandy-Kyolera
Sperry-Mitsubishi

Copiers, Photographic Equipment
Kodak-Canon

Disc Players, Air Conditioners
GE-Matsushita

Jet Liners
Boeing-Mitsubishi Heavy Industries
Kawasaki Heavy Industries
Fuji Heavy Industries

Lightweight Plastic Composites
Armco-Mitsubishi Rayon

Machine Tools
Bendix-Murata Machinery Company
GM-Fujitsu Fanuc
Houdaille-Okuma
Houdaille-Mayekawa

Programmable Controllers and Sensors
Allen-Bradley-Nippondenso

Robots and Small Motors
Westinghouse-Komatsu, Mitsubishi Electric
IBM-Sanyo Seiko

- Nearly half reported less than a 1 percent absentee rate.
- The firms enjoyed a higher rate of employee growth and capital investment than comparable American firms.

Alliances of U.S. and Japanese Companies

Fact #1   In the early 1980s, American and Japanese companies began uniting in a vast array of private alliances: joint ventures, supplier agreements, and technology licenses.

Fact #2   There is a general pattern to the new joint ventures: the U.S. handles the two ends of the production process—the new innovations and the final assembly and sales—while the Japanese concentrate on the complex manufacturing process in between.

Fact #3   Four of America's seven largest steelmakers have sold equity stakes to Japanese companies or formed joint ventures with them.

- The major entry has been Nippon Kokan taking a 50 percent stake in National Steel Corporation in 1984.

Fact #4   In 1986, the Japanese made about 400 investments in the depressed U.S. electronics industry.

The Japanese Financial Presence in the U.S. and World

Fact #1   Japan in 1986 had the world's largest-ever surplus of liquid funds—$640 billion of external assets held by Japan's banks.

- Its investment abroad more than doubled from nearly $65 billion in 1985 to $130 billion in 1986.

Fact #2   In 1966, the world's seven largest banks (in terms of deposits) were all American; in 1986, the world's seven largest were all Japanese and the highest ranking U.S. lending institution, Citibank, was 17th.

Fact #3 Seven of the world's eight largest commercial banks and four of the world's eight largest investment banks are Japanese.

- Nomura, Japan's largest investment bank, had a market capitalization (what the stock market say all its shares are worth) of $54 billion in mid-1987, ten times that of Merrill Lynch (America's largest).

Fact #4 Japan's banks and securities houses are moving funds into every nook of the U.S.

- The four largest Japanese investment banks dwarf the four largest U.S. investment banks (Salomon, Merrill Lynch, Shearson Lehman, and Goldman Sachs) in most key measures (estimates for late 1987): net income, Japan $4.2 billion vs. $1.7 billion for U.S.; shareholders' equity, $14.8 billion vs. $10.3 billion; market capitalization, $127 billion vs. $16 billion. The only U.S. lead is in revenues: $27.6 billion vs. $19.6 billion.

- In 1986, Japan bought around $55 billion in bonds from the U.S. Treasury and an additional $10 billion in bonds from U.S. corporations (compared to totals in 1981 and 1982 of under $5 billion).

- Japanese banks by 1986 had provided about $200 billion through loans and bond purchases and about $100 billion in loan guarantees and letters of credit to U.S. states, cities, universities, and businesses.

- By 1987, Japanese banks commanded 9 percent of all U.S. business loans and 50 percent of the market for municipal letters of credit.

Fact #5 Japanese purchases in 1987 of U.S. equities were expected to reach $15 billion or more, up from $2.2 billion in 1985.

Fact #6   Tokyo in the spring of 1987 surpassed New York as the world's largest stock market.

Fact #7   The Japanese are becoming major players in U.S. retail banking: in California they own five of the eleven largest banks.

Japanese Presence at U.S. Universities

Fact #1   By 1984, nearly every major Japanese corporation—from NTT to Sony, Mitsui, and Toyota—was funding research at one or more American universities.

Fact #2   In 1984, more than 14,000 students from Japan were studying at U.S. colleges, nearly 30 percent of them in graduate schools.

East Asia's Little Dragons—Big U.S. Rivals

Fact #1   In 1986, the "little dragons' "—Korea, Taiwan, Hong Kong, and Singapore—collective trade surplus with the U.S. was $27 billion.

Fact #2   The economic performance of the East Asian NICs has been nothing short of spectacular in the past quarter century.

- From 1963–1985, while Japanese growth was averaging 5.9 percent a year, Hong Kong was growing by 8.5 percent, Korea by 8.7 percent, Taiwan by 9.2 percent, and Singapore by 9.7 percent.
- The value of their exports in this period grew by 15.2 percent per year in real terms causing their combined share of the nonfuel exports of the developing countries to rise from 5.6 percent to 33.4 percent.

Fact #3 By 1984, East Asia's "little dragons" had half as large a trade surplus with the U.S. as Japan; they exported more manufactured goods to the U.S. than Britain and twice as much as W. Germany; and their manufactured trade surplus with the U.S. was three times that of the entire European Economic Community.

Fact #4 Taiwan and Korea in particular are increasing their trade in computers: while Japan's sales of computer products to the U.S. actually dropped more than 7 percent in 1985, imports from Korea and Taiwan grew 95 percent and were expanding at a rate of 169 percent in the first half of 1986.

Fact #5 More than ever before, companies in these four countries are teaming up with Western companies.

- General Motor's 1987 Pontiac Le Mans came from Korea and Ford has plans to make subcompacts for Canada in Taiwan.

Europe

Economic Performance in
1970s and 1980s

Fact #1 From 1963 to 1973, economic growth of the European Economic Community (EEC) member states averaged 4.6 percent a year while from 1973 to 1983, growth slackened to an average of 2 percent annually.

- In the early 1980s, growth simply stopped and real purchasing power and living standards began to drop for the first time in thirty years.
- In the 1982–1985 recovery, real GNP in Western Europe grew on average at 2.2 percent, one-half the rate in the U.S., Japan, or Canada.

Fact #2   In 1968, average unemployment in the EEC was 2.3 percent; by 1986, the rate was over 10 percent with around 16 million Europeans unemployed.

- In June 1987, the average unemployment rate for the four largest countries (France, Italy, the United Kingdom, and West Germany) was just under 10 percent, nearly double the 1980 rate.

Fact #3   European unemployment is self-perpetuating in that high percentages of the unemployed have been so for more than a year; in 1986, the rates for unemployed men were 63 percent in Belgium, 46 percent in France, 46 percent in the U.K., and 32 percent in Germany.

Fact #4   While the European economies and the U.S. economy both grew at 2 percent a year from 1973 to 1983, the U.S. gained 14 million jobs while the ten countries that make up the European Economic Community lost 1.8 million.

Fact #5   Between 1973 and 1981, industrial output rose by 26 percent in Japan, 16 percent in the U.S., and only 8 percent in Europe.

Fact #6   There is very little labor mobility in many European countries; the average American worker holds 10.5 jobs over a lifetime, five times as many as his or her German counterpart.

Fact #7   Social outlays were boosted by European governments in the 1960s and 1970s from 14 to 26 percent of their gross national products.

Fact #8   The leading European economy—West Germany's —has been particularly sluggish in the 1980s, right up through 1987.

- Its unemployment rate is stuck at 9 percent after climbing almost without interruption since 1970.

- Its 25.7 million jobs in 1987 was 1.2 million fewer than in 1973.
- It absorbed only 28 percent of its unemployed into service industries between 1973 and 1983 compared with 67 percent in the U.S. and 89 percent in Japan.
- In 1986, 27 German companies went public—a record—compared with 184 in London and 955 in the U.S.
- In 1987, there was a pool of only $550 million available for start-up financing and most of that was basically government handouts.

Fact #9 In 1984, fifty-six national regulations impeded free intra-European trade at a cost of $12 billion in lost business, plus a huge hidden cost (estimated at more than $50 billion) in the form of poor efficiency and lost international competitiveness.

Recent Bright Spots

Fact #1 In 1986, employment in Western Europe began to surge at the fastest pace since the late 1970s.

Fact #2 Small businesses are beginning to spark European employment.

- The city of Cambridge, a "Silicon Valley" of Britain, spawned 250 new companies in the first half of the 1980s.
- In 1985, France created 101,000 new companies, 20 percent more than in 1984.

Fact #3 Privatization, the selling of state-owned businesses, is making money for European governments and causing reorganizations in industries that had grown stagnant while nationalized.

- The pioneer is Britain, which has raised $23 billion since 1979 by selling all or part of thirteen companies ranging from utilities (such as British Gas for $7.9 billion, the largest stock offering in the country's history) to industrial companies, including British Aerospace and Britoil, the state oil producer.

- France is the latest and most enthusiastic recruit to privatization, selling in early 1987 $1.9 billion of shares in Saint-Gobain to 1½ million French citizens (a number equal to the total of all French shareholders before the sale), and planning to sell sixty-five companies worth as much as $45 billion by 1991.

- The positive impacts of privatization are: companies can sell stock to finance expansion instead of piling up debt; managers are freer to buy companies and sell subsidiaries, and to slash bloated work forces.

High Tech

Fact #1   *Europe's high tech output from 1972 to 1984 consistently grew less than 5 percent a year compared to 7.6 percent in the U.S. and 14 percent in Japan.*

Fact #2   *High-tech exports of Britain, France, and West Germany declined from 50 percent of total high-tech exports in 1972 to 35 percent in 1985 (while the U.S. boosted its share from 32 to 37 percent and Japan from 13 percent to 25 percent).*

Fact #3   *From 1979 to 1984, the European share of the world electric and electronic market shrunk from 30 percent to around 20 percent; European firms had less than 20 percent of their own market in 1984.*

- In France, the government in the early 1980s poured nearly $14 billion in grants and loans into their program to revitalize the country's electronics industry; in 1984, three of the four major electronics companies nationalized in 1982 lost a total of $140 million.

- In general, European governments spend two thirds as much as the American government backing R&D in electronics and five times as much as the Japanese government yet the average return on investment of the ten largest European electronics companies in 1984 was only half that of their counterparts in Japan and a quarter those in America.

Fact #4   In 1985, a multibillion-dollar, multiyear program called "Eureka" was launched to get companies and research institutes in nineteen European nations to cooperate on high-technology projects from computing to biotechnology.

- By the spring of 1987, Eureka had become a marriage broker, orchestrator, and venture capitalist for more than 600 companies working on 165 high tech industrial projects worth over $5 billion, making it financially Europe's biggest multinational undertaking.

Interpretation of the Facts

1. The Decline of U.S. Competitiveness

Five reasons are the most frequently cited for the decline in the competitiveness of American industry over the past decade, particularly relative to the Japanese: (1) the focus of U.S. managers on the short-run and on maximizing shareholder wealth; (2) the high cost of capital in the U.S.; (3) Japan's deliberate shift in its comparative advantage toward high technology; (4) U.S. industry is financially dominated and does not follow a global strategy; (5) American companies are not really interested in production.

Short-run Focus of U.S. Business and Business Leaders   Of the many individuals who cite the short-run focus as the primary reason, Richard Ellsworth and Pat Choate are particularly interesting.

Richard Ellsworth, once group-level vice president with Kaiser Aetna and now a professor in strategic management at Claremont Graduate School, states the case for many who believe the financial strategies that keep Wall Street happy undermine U.S. companies when they go head-to-head with foreign manufacturers:

> [T]he competitive decline afflicting many *Fortune* "500" companies in large part reflects management's preoccupation with capital-market conventions that divert attention from product-market needs and frustrate efforts to improve competitiveness.
>
> Among those conventions, none is as prominent as management's sense of duty to maximize shareholder wealth—a duty that often becomes, philosophically at least, the linchpin of a company's goals to the detriment of its competitiveness. This is not to say that the goal of maximizing shareholder wealth itself undermines competitiveness nor to suggest that most senior executives consciously defer to stock prices when making investment decisions. But its unquestioned dominance over other corporate goals puts us at a disadvantage over against competitors abroad who focus chiefly on product markets (R. R. Ellsworth, "Capital Markets and Competitive Decline," *Harvard Business Review*, September–October 1985, p. 171. Copyright © 1985 by the President and Fellows of Harvard College).

Much of this is because institutional investors now dominate the stock market. In the fourth quarter of 1980, institutional activity on the New York Stock Exchange represented 65 percent of public share volume compared to 31 percent in 1960 and by the mid-1980s, institutions held more than 35 percent of all equities listed on the NYSE, double their 1960 share.

Pat Choate, Director of Policy Analysis for TRW, points out, "Just when US business needs to be making long-term investments to meet global competition, the new owners—the institutions—are pressing for quick results." To Choate, the sequence runs as follows. First, increasing ownership by institutions. Second, the growing pace of their transactions so that in 1986 institutional trades constituted almost 90 percent of transactions. Third, such hyperactive trading means the fundamental focus of the stock market has been transformed from long-term investing to short-term speculation. Finally, and most importantly to Choate, active trading, speculation, and relentless demands for short-term results are undermining the performance and imperiling the survival of U.S. companies by "fostering several harmful phenomena":

- "[P]aper entrepreneurship" involving speculative mergers and takeovers, "greenmail," and inflation of corporate earnings through accounting transactions.

- The increased use of firms' capital for buybacks of their own stock to make it less attractive to raiders.

- Corrosion of the venture capital market as pension funds and institutions (which now provide a third of all venture capital) transform the funds from providers of long-term money and technical support to speculators demanding quick results.

- The shift of research and development from long-term efforts that can produce major breakthroughs to short-term "safe" projects that can produce quick results (P. Choate & J. K. Linger, "Business and the Short-Term Syndrome," *Washington Post*, June 15, 1986).

Choate also argues that the preoccupation of corporate executives with the short-term is heightened by the way they are compensated. Since pay and promotion decisions are based primarily on immediate financial results, it is not surprising that when corporate leaders were asked in a 1985 survey about their single overriding objective, 51 percent said "creating shareholder value" as opposed to the 18 percent who cited becoming the market or industry leader as their top priority.

Cost of Capital Disadvantage   Former Senator Paul Tsongas and industry chief George Hatsopoulos are equally insistent in their belief that one must look to the high cost of capital in the U.S. to understand the decline in competitiveness:

> A principal cause of the decline in competitiveness of America's industry is the high cost of capital in the United States. In fact, American firms must pay about three times as much for capital as do their Japanese competitors—a differential that placed US industry at a tremendous disadvantage (P. E. Tsongas & G. N. Hatsopoulos, "Cost of Capital Gives U.S. Competitive Disadvantage," *Washington Post*, October 14, 1985, p. H2).

An underlying factor is the structure of financial institutions, which fosters a heavy reliance of American companies on equity rather than debt. The average debt-to-equity ratio for U.S. industrial firms is only one to three while Japanese firms in industries targeted for development have average debt-to-equity ratios of three to one.

Thus, to these observers, the tendency for U.S. managers to focus on short-term objectives simply reflects a national response to the need for quicker payback on costly capital. To illustrate, Japan's far lower cost of capital relative to the United States' justifies its managers' investing five times as much money in a project requiring ten years of development.

The U.S. is a Regulatory State while Japan is a Developmental State   Harvard Business School professor Bruce Scott noted that in the 1965–1980 period the United States was not shifting its comparative advantage toward high technology while Japan was gaining share in high-technology areas and losing it in low-technology sectors. Scott maintained that government can play a very constructive role in making a nation's industrial base globally competitive.

The basic difference between Japan and the United States, according to economist Chalmers Johnson, boils down to the difference between a developmental state and a regulatory state. Thus, a regulatory state like the United States emphasizes the rules and procedures of competition, not substantive outcomes while Japan, a developmental state, has as its dominant feature the setting of economic and social goals.

Bruce Scott agrees with this distinction and observes that the philosophy of a developmental state differs markedly from a regulatory state's laissez-faire belief in the magic of the marketplace. In particular, Scott notes, "it probably requires a government that asks for short-term sacrifices in the standard of living to amass the saving necessary to finance needed investments, and a "MITI" (Japan's Ministry of International Trade and Industry) to protect the home market while helping secure the necessary technologies." (Bruce R. Scott, "National Strategy for Stronger U.S. Competitiveness," _Harvard Business Review_, March–April 1984, p. 88.)

Many U.S. business leaders agree with these academicians. The American members of the Japan-U.S. Business Conference concluded in a 1984 study that past policies of the Japanese government were "critical" to the success of vital industrial segments ranging from high-tech industries such as semiconductors, computers, and telecommunications to the more traditional areas of shipbuilding, steel, and automobiles.

Global Strategy and Financial vs. Market Domination of Industry Peter Drucker sees a clear distinction between the strategies of Japan and the United States that accounts for the decline in U.S. competitiveness. To Drucker, the traditional multinational company, as Americans understand it, is rapidly becoming obsolete and makes a global strategy almost impossible. A "global strategy" for the future, in Drucker's view, requires an understanding of "the two basic tendencies of this century: Economically the world is becoming more integrated, and politically it is becoming more fragmented" (cited in " 'Multinational,' As We Know It, Is Obsolete," *Forbes*, August 26, 1985, p. 30). Economic integration, not geography, should be the foundation of company activities. Business must organize internationally along product lines, not country lines.

Drucker maintains that growth markets can be penetrated only when business is organized in this way. For these markets, he says, you have to be able to do what the Japanese do—use the profits you get from a market in a developed country to subsidize establishment in a developing market. It is this successful Japanese practice in developing export markets that Drucker perceives as the true nature of Japan's economic challenge to the U.S.

The critical question is: Are American multinationals unable to follow a global strategy for a product line? According to Drucker, this is the case at present because American industry "is financially dominated and not market dominated."

Put very simply, Americans think you run a business to make money. Drucker responds, "No, that is why you invest in a business. A business exists to create a customer and to satisfy the customer's needs and wants. And then you will make money."

American Companies Aren't Really Interested in Production

According to Robert Reich, professor at Harvard University, American companies do not want to invest in production experience as much as the Japanese do. Why? In Reich's view, it is because production experience is essentially social, involving the relationships among engineers, technicians, fabricators, and marketers.

Given this, a company has only two basic options: hope the workers stick together or help to build a shared community so they will want to. As Reich sees it, "American managers won't make these social investments because, by and large, they are incapable of—or unwilling to—transform their enterprises into such communities." (Robert Reich, "On Political Books," *The Washington Monthly*, November 1984, p. 54.)

The result is that (as noted) the United States has the investing and marketing ends of the spectrum while the Japanese increasingly occupy the production center. Reich points out that the U.S. makes money by transferring its ideas to Japan and it makes money by selling these ideas back to us encased in terrific products and parts. A nice deal for all concerned, "Except for one thing" argues Reich:

> Along the way, a large number of them gain experience and skill in making products cheaply and well. They learn how to organize themselves for production—integrating design, fabrication, and manufacturing; using computers to enhance their skills; developing new flexibility. They learn how to make the kinds of small, incremental improvements in production processes and products that can make all the difference in price, quality, and marketability. In short, they develop the collective capacity to transform raw ideas quickly into world-class goods.
>
> Such experience in making products generates more social wealth than does inventing them or assembling and selling them (Robert B. Reich, "Japan Inc., U.S.A.," © Reprinted by permission of *The New Republic*, November 26, 1984, p. 21).

2. The Future

A great many shake-ups and restructurings are underway in American industry that experts feel are paving the way toward a more "lean and mean" U.S. in global competition: (1) the drive for better quality; (2) slashing costs; (3) reducing the work force ("trimming the fat"); (4) emphasizing teamwork among employees; (5) major investments in automation. They also point to such basic U.S. strengths as a highly educated work force, a stable political climate, the world's largest market, and leadership in a number of key high-tech fields such as computers and biotechnology.

This does not assure the U.S. of a continued number one economic ranking or even of a tough, globally competitive industry. What is needed?

According to Pat Choate, the most basic need is to be flexible throughout our society:

The urgent message here is that it is time for America to recover the economic agility that was for so long its hallmark. The nation faces a future in which the shift to the technologies, production processes, and management styles of the twenty-first century will proceed with few certainties and in an environment of fierce, often predatory, global competition. The pace of change, already swift, is sure to accelerate, further reducing lead times for preparation and adjustment.

The most practical way to confront the challenges of a fast-paced, sharply competitive, highly uncertain future is to improve America's ability to adapt to that future, whatever it brings. The nation must become a High-Flex Society—in which firms can innovate, invest, and quickly take a product or service from development to production to market domination, and then on to the next generation of product or service; in which workers can secure training, find jobs, be productive, advance, and shift between jobs and occupations with ease and confidence; and in which government can maintain an environment that facilitates whatever adjustments are needed and do so in a common-sense, socially responsible manner.

If the United States will embrace the High-Flex approach and eliminate the barriers that impede the flexibility of its workers, businesses, and government, then the nation can set the pace of change again, bringing to the global economy an unprecedented burst of productivity and aggressive competitiveness. If the obstacles remain, however, if the status quo prevails, if Americans cannot rediscover their national genius, then their economy, social stability, personal opportunities, and place in the world are sure to decline (P. Choate & J. K. Linger, *The High-Flex Society*. New York: A. Knopf, 1986, pp. 9–10).

CHAPTER
★ 19 ★
Agriculture

The Issues

When one thinks about American agriculture the phrase that comes to mind is "breadbasket of the world." Productive, efficient, bountiful, a richly flowing cornucopia are other phrases that quickly come to mind.

All of these phrases are true, but do not tell the whole story. Since 1981, new troubles have come to the American farm. Incomes have declined, debt has soared, land values have plummeted, government subsidies have shot up, foreclosures have multiplied, and even exports have declined significantly. In response to these problems, government subsidies skyrocketed from $4.0 billion in 1981 to nearly $26 billion in 1986.

Such difficulties are not unique to the 1980s. More farms were lost in 1951 alone than in the entire 1981–1985 period. Moreover, farm income has been on a fairly steady decline since the 1940s.

One thing is certain: American farming today, which is dominated by a few, large-scale farmers, is a vastly different enterprise than it was in 1950. And, sizable changes seem a certainty in the future.

The Facts

The Transformation of U.S. Farming

Fact #1   In virtually every aspect—including size, productivity, prices, debt, exports—the American farm has undergone a radical transformation since 1950.

Size and Structure of the Agricultural Industry

Fact #1   Overall, the combined food and fiber system— farming plus farm supply, food processing, and retailing industries—is one of the largest sectors of the economy.

- In 1984, it generated over 18 percent of the GNP and employed over 21 million full-time workers.

- Of the total, farming itself accounted for only 2 percent of GNP, while downstream activities (farmers buying inputs) were 2 percent and upstream activities (processing, transporting, retailing, exporting, etc.) were 14 percent of GNP.

Fact #2   The structure of American agriculture is dominated by a relatively few large-scale farmers, with most farmers running small-scale, part-time operations.

Table 1

Changes in Ten Characteristics of U.S. Farming: 1950–1984

Farm characteristic	1950	1980	1984
Population in agriculture as percent of total population	15%	3%	2.0%*
Number of farms (millions)	5.4	2.4	2.3*
Average size of farms (acres)	216	429	446*
Percent of farm labor that is hired	23%	35%	39%
Value of machinery per worker (1984 dollars)	5303	32934	31263
Crop production per acre (1984 = 100)	52.7	88.4	100
Ratio of prices received to prices paid by farmers (1984 = 1.0)	1.45	1.06	1.0
Farm debt as a percent of assets	9.3	16.5	20.8
Farm exports (billions of 1983 dollars)	12.5	51.9	37.6**
Number of people fed by one farmer	15	76	79**

Sources: Rows 1–3, USDA, *Agricultural Statistics*
Rows 4–9: *Economic Report of the President*, 1985.
Row 10: USDA, Economic Indicators of the Farm Sector, Productivity and Efficiency Statistics, 1983.
* 1985 data   ** 1983 data

Table 2

Characteristics of Large, Medium, and Small Farms: 1983

Item	Large Farms (Over $200,000 Gross Sales)	Medium Farms ($40,000 to $200,000 Gross Sales)	Small Farms (Under $40,000 Gross Sales)
Number	107,000	558,000	1,705,000
Percent of All Farms	4	24	72
Percent of Total Output	48	39	13
Percent of Net Farm Income Earned	67	32	1
Average Assets Per Farm	$2,295,000	$806,000	$197,000
Percent of All Farm Assets	24	43	33
Average Net Worth	$1,561,000	$642,000	$171,000
Average Family Income	$191,869	$27,185	$19,435
Percent of All Off-Farm Income Earned by the Farm Sector	4	16	80

Source: USDA.

Fact #3   The vast majority of farms are family-owned, but the percentage is diminishing rapidly.

- Ninety-seven percent of American farms are family farms.

- Corporate farms, most of which have 10 or fewer stock-holders and are typically family-owned, accounted for roughly 2.5 percent of farms in 1982, 14 percent of agricultural land, and 24 percent of sales.

- The percentage of farms classified as larger than single-family farms rose from less than 1 percent in 1945 to 49 percent in 1980.

Fact #4   Since 1947, the farm population has declined in all but three years. In 1985, at 5.4 million, it was only one-sixth of its 1940 size and comprised only 2.2 percent of the total population (compared to 23 percent in 1940).

Fact #5   The loss of farms has been great in the 1980s, but is much less than the number lost in earlier years.

- In 1985, the number of farms declined by 43,000.

- From 1981 to 1985, the decline in the number of farms was 150,000.

- In 1961, the decline was 138,000 farms, and in 1951, it was 220,000 farms.

Fact #6   Thirty-four states have more than 20,000 farms.

Agricultural Productivity

Fact #1   One farmer could feed fifteen people in 1950, fifty-three people in 1972, and seventy-nine people in 1983.

Fact #2   Since 1940, both average crop yields and overall productivity have more than doubled.

Fact #3   By any measure—(1) farm output per unit of total output, (2) crop production per acre, or (3) farm output per hour of farm work—agricultural productivity was at a record high in 1985.

Fact #4 *From 1940 to 1985 farm output steadily rose, never experiencing more than two years of decline.*

- The near-record harvest of 1985 produced 20 percent more food than American farmers grew in 1975.
- There has been a substantial change in the mix of crops produced as the share of the major export crops—corn, wheat, soybeans, and cotton—rose from 58 percent to 70 percent of total acres of cropland between 1969 and 1980.

Fact #5 *From 1950 to 1985, use of farm labor has gone down dramatically from 265 to 84 (using an index of 1977 = 100) and mechanical power and machinery and chemicals have gone up dramatically (72 to 83 and 19 to 123 respectively), while total crop acreage harvested remained essentially unchanged.*

- The high levels of mechanization and chemical use have contributed to a growing problem of soil erosion as more than 25 percent of all U.S. cropland is eroding at rates exceeding the soil's regenerative capacity.

The Global Marketplace

Fact #1 *Much of U.S. agriculture is significantly dependent on the world market, as about ⅓ of all U.S. cropland is planted for export.*

Fact #2 *The leading U.S. farm exports in 1986 were: soybeans and products ($5.6 billion), feed grains and products ($3.8 billion), livestock products ($3.5 billion), wheat and products ($3.5 billion), and fruits, vegetables, nuts, etc. ($2.7 billion).*

Fact #3   *In 1970, agricultural exports were only $7.3 billion, 14.4 percent of farm cash receipts, while in the peak year of 1981 they were $43.3 billion and 30.4 percent of receipts.*

- By 1986, the value of farm exports had fallen 40 percent, back down to $26 billion, but they began to rise in early 1987 for the first time in years, reaching $28 billion.

Fact #4   *Due to the dismal export performance from 1981 to 1986 farm products in 1986 made up less than 12 percent of the value of all American exports, the lowest level since 1940.*

Fact #5   *The agricultural trade balance always less than $3 billion until 1973, shot up to $26.6 billion in 1981 and then fell sharply to $5.6 billion in 1986; in 1987, it rose to $7.5 billion.*

Fact #6   *The potential U.S. export market has shrunk as many of the countries that only a decade ago were incapable of feeding themselves are doing so today.*

- The People's Republic of China in the early 1980s expanded its agricultural output at record levels (up 40 percent in five years).
- Bangladesh became self-sufficient in food grains in the mid-1980s.
- India doubled its wheat production from 1970 to 1985, becoming a net exporter, and its rice production is up 30 percent.
- Indonesia, formerly a major importer, has become self-sufficient in rice.

Farm Incomes

Fact #1   *From 1945 to 1970, net farm income was remarkably stable ($10.5 to 17.7 billion). Since 1970 it has fluctuated* *wildly: from a base of $14.4 billion in 1970, it skyrocketed to $34.4 billion in 1973; it then steadily declined to $19.9 billion in 1977; through 1982 it was mostly in the mid-20s; then it hit a rock-bottom low of $12.7 billion in 1983 only to be followed by three very strong years from 1984 to 1986 when it ranged from $32 to $37.5 billion.*

Fact #2   In constant (1982) dollars, the 1986 level of $32.8 billion was lower than the level for all but 2 years prior to 1975.

Fact #3   Between 1977 and 1986, the prices received by farmers went up 23 percent, while the prices farmers paid for fertilizers went up 24 percent, wages 59 percent, tractors and other machinery 74 percent, and fuels 65 percent.

Fact #4   The average income of a farm household in 1984 was $23,658 (including income from non-farm jobs), compared to $27,464 for all households.

- This near-parity stands in sharp contrast to the 1930s, when farm household incomes were only 40 percent of nonfarm households.

Fact #5   Average farm income varies greatly by farm size.

- In 1985, non-commercial farmers (sales under $40,000) averaged $19,000.
- For commercial farmers in 1985, the average incomes were $17,000 for small ($40–99,000 in sales), $47,000 for mid-sized ($100–249,000 in sales), and $110,000 for large ($250–499,000 in sales).

Fact #6   From the early 1960s to the early 1980s, off-farm income as a percentage of farmers' total income went from 47 percent to 61 percent and was the greatest source of income for the majority of farmers with gross sales of less than $100,000.

Farm Debt

Fact #1   *After reaching a peak of $202.4 billion in 1983, farm debt has declined to $156 billion in 1987 and is projected to decrease further to $140 billion in 1988.*

Fact #2   *In 1985, at the peak of the farm crisis, nearly one-third of the nation's 630,000 full-time farmers were in danger of financial collapse and one-third of family-sized farms were in severe financial stress.*

Fact #3   *In 1986, about 10 percent of all farm businesses and households were in a vulnerable financial position, when income and solvency criteria are combined; family-sized commercial farms were the most stressed (13 percent).*

Fact #4   *In early 1987, 325,000 farms (22 percent of all farms) were classified as financially stressed—having a debt-to-asset ratio of 40 percent or more—with midsized farms being most stressed.*

- Farms with a ratio of 40 percent or more held about 67 percent of the total sector debt in 1987.
- The debt-to-asset ratio peaked at 25 percent in 1985 and is projected at 19 percent for 1988.
- Family-sized commercial farms (annual sales of $40,000–$499,999) represented 35 percent of all farms but owed 64 percent of all debt in 1987.

Fact #5   *The interest on farm liabilities in March 1985 was more than $20 billion, while total farm income averaged only $23 billion in 1983 and 1984.*

Fact #6   *In the mid-1980s, agricultural bank failures were running at ten times the annual rate for the past thirty years and accounted for two-thirds of all bank failures.*

Fact #7   *Farm land values have been on a roller coaster in the past decade, going from an average 7 percent yearly increase from 1975 to 1980, to a 4 percent yearly decrease between 1980 and 1983, to sharp declines of 13 percent, 12 percent, and 8 percent respectively in 1984, 1985, and 1986.*

- In the five-year period 1982–1986, farm land values dropped 33 percent.
- During the agriculture boom (1974–1981), the average price of farmland rose from $302 an acre to $795, with prime Midwest land soaring to $4,000 an acre.
- In 1986 dollars, real capital gains on farmland during the 1970s totaled about $500 billion while real capital losses during 1980–86 were about $480 billion.
- Farmland values were estimated to rise 3 to 7 percent in 1987.

Fact #8   In 1987, lenders held nearly 8 million acres of farmland acquired through foreclosure and bankruptcy, less than 1 percent of all farmland.

Fact #9   Nearly two-fifths of all farms were debt-free entering 1987 and another 40 percent had debt-asset ratios less than 0.40.

Fact #10   The financial stress of the farm sector was modifying in 1987; lenders' potential losses on farm loans, which peaked at $8.6 billion in 1985, dropped by more than half to around $4 billion in 1987.

Government Farm Subsidies

Fact #1   Government farm subsidies have risen, from less than $1 billion in 1975 (and still only $4 billion in 1981) to nearly $26 billion in 1986.

- The $26 billion exceeded the notoriously expensive European Common Agricultural Policy's total of $23 billion in 1986.

- In 1986, government payments were high enough to pay an equivalent of $42,000 to each commercial farm (sales over $100,000) while median family income was $27,735.

Fact #2   Direct federal payments to farmers provided roughly 20 percent of farmers' net cash income in the mid-1980s.

Fact #3   Less than half (40 percent) of all commercial farms received direct payment from the government in the mid-1980s.

Fact #4   The largest, richest farms receive most of the government payments, while the smaller farms receive very little.

- Thirty-two percent of all farm subsidies in 1985 went to the largest 4 percent of all producers (sales more than $250,000).

Figure 1

Farm Subsidy Increases
with Farm Size—1985
(Average direct government payment)

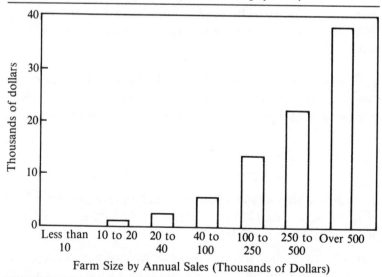

Source: U.S. Department of Agriculture.

Fact #5 Surplus farm products are bought and stored by the government annually at an enormous cost, valued at $6.9 billion in 1985 alone.

Fact #6 The farm programs are extremely costly to consumers and taxpayers, with the cost to these groups far outweighing the benefit to farmers.

- A study by the Department of Agriculture showed that annual net cash to farmers in the 1980s would rise by $4 billion annually, while consumer expenditures for food would increase an average of $5 billion a year and taxpayer expenditures would increase by $16 billion annually.

- Under the sugar program, the average annual transfer from consumers to producers is $120,000 to $145,000 in profit per farm, with another $80,000 per sugar farmer to make the transfer because of inefficiencies associated with the quota system (figures from the *1986 Economic Report of the President*, p. 138).

Interpretation of the Facts

1. Free Market or Government Intervention—Which Course for the Future?

The single major issue is: What should the government's role be in agriculture? Should it be activist, seeking to stabilize and support farmers' income levels? Or, should it be minimal, allowing free-market mechanisms to work as much as possible? Free market versus government intervention is a common, often repeated theme. And, once again, the two sides are represented by the *Economic Report of the President* and the *Economic Report of the People*.

Agriculture's Future

The Free Market

In the 1970s, many saw an "ever-expanding" export market curing the traditional "farm problems" of low relative earning power and excess capacity. American agriculture transformed from a sector using export subsidies and concessional sales to a large competitive exporter. This transformation was accompanied by an expansion in productive capacity financed largely by increased borrowing. Because real agricultural land values rose by as much as two-thirds in the 1970s the expanded borrowing seemed financially prudent to many. Land values, however, were predicated upon strong demand for U.S. exports and expectations of continued inflation. By 1983, however, agricultural export value had fallen from its 1981 peak of $43 billion to $36 billion, and is estimated for 1985 at about $29 billion.

With agricultural export performance faltering and inflation under control, farm debt incurred in the late 1970s became increasingly difficult to manage and service. What had looked like sound business moves in a rapidly growing

Government Intervention

How did the farms and rural communities get into this mess? The Reagan administration argues that the fault lies with farmers, who got greedy during the good years in the 1970s and expanded production beyond what the market could bear. Many farmers blame the government or bankers, claiming they were encouraged to expand and become more mechanized to support the government's foreign policy objectives or the profits of the bankers.

Government policies and the overexpansion they promoted in the 1970s explain part of what happened. But the crisis in American farming is rooted in structural changes in the U.S. economy which could not have been completely avoided by any short-term farm policy. Furthermore, the crisis cannot be solved by new policies unless they address its three basic causes: (1) the "technological treadmill," which prompts increased mechanization, as well as chemical and biological innovation; (2) the increasing control of large agribusiness corporations over food production and distribution; and (3) changes in the farm sec-

sector of a generally inflationary economy of the late 1970s had frequently become unsustainable.

These problems persist despite the existence of Federal Government price- and income-support programs that have cost—and continue to cost—taxpayers billions of dollars a year. Recently, direct Federal payments to farmers have been at record levels and now equal roughly 20 percent of farmers' net cash income. The Federal Government spent more than $60 billion on farm programs in the past 4 years. Yet some of these programs may not help farmers. On the contrary, they can hurt farmers by distorting economic incentives. And some hurt consumers by driving up food prices. Moreover, they use billions of taxpayer dollars in a time of growing fiscal austerity.

A keystone of this Administration's farm policy is that farm programs can distort economic incentives enough to cause some of agriculture's problems. The President recommended in early 1985 that American agriculture be returned gradually to a free-market footing. The Food Security Act of 1985, which the President signed into law in mid-

tor's relations with the international economy.

Far from ameliorating the underlying causes of the farm crisis, Reagan's economic policies have exacerbated them. Shaped with virtually no attention to their consequences for agriculture, conservative economic policies—monetarists, militarist, and supply-side—have helped drown most farmers in red ink and push many off their farms. The farm policies adopted by the Reagan administration to deal with the crisis, consistent with the pattern since the end of the New Deal, are only band-aids: short-term, reactive, and porkbarreled into shape.

All of these features of the farm system indicate that farms can be seriously threatened by forces completely beyond their control. Inflation, the Fed's monetary policy, the value of the dollar, the size of the federal deficit, growth of foreign competition in agricultural products, bad weather, and decisions by monopolistic suppliers and processors all affect the ability of a family farm to earn a decent income.

Conservative economic policies, however, have speeded up the farm crisis exacerbating a long-term trend toward concentration of control over the

December 1985, implemented some of his suggested reforms. But it maintained the traditional structure of American farm programs. Thus, U.S. agriculture has turned toward the free market, but it still remains heavily dependent upon Federal Government programs.

Basically, as the President recommended in 1985, agriculture policy should be shaped to return farming to a freer market. This means separating income supports from production and lowering loan rates or eliminating them. Future agricultural programs should be flexible and should minimize market distortions in achieving their goals (Council of Economic Advisers, *Economic Report of the President*, Washington, D.C.: U.S. Government Printing Office, February 1986, pp. 129–130, 158).

land into fewer and fewer hands. A "solution" to the farm crisis which offers more of the same is bound to fail, at least in the long run. Agricultural surpluses and soil and water depletion will likely continue to get worse if the farm sector is left to "free market" forces.

Furthermore, increasing concentration of land ownership forecloses an economic and cultural option to ordinary people. Solving the farm crisis requires a reorientation of policies and programs toward expanding, rather than contracting, popular access to land. Amidst all the statistics and claims and counterclaims, greater access to the land is the fundamental issue (Center for Popular Economics, *Economic Report of the People*, Boston: South End Press; 1986, pp. 93–94, 111).

CHAPTER
★ 20 ★

Manufacturing

The Issues

During the first seventy years of this century, the American economy was noted for its industrial strength: the muscle of its manufacturing sector. Big business ruled the American market and stimulated similar efforts in other nations that wanted to share in the economic growth that industrialization spawned. This was the Industrial Era and America had inherited the leader's mantle worn by England throughout most of the nineteenth century.

But in the 1970s, the tables began to turn on America. There was increasing talk of deindustrialization, import surges, declining global market shares, the service economy, and even the demise of American manufacturing.

Some of this talk had little factual basis. However, there

is no denying that American manufacturing has been seriously assaulted by foreign competitors in the past two decades (and by the strongly rising dollar in the first half of the 1980s). Although U.S. manufacturing has been brought down, it is far from being "out."

One major result of this assault has been positive, as manufacturers across America are taking an in-depth look at their operations to see how they can become more globally competitive. Many have begun major cost-cutting and productivity-enhancing initiatives. Fifty-six percent of the *Fortune* 500 companies slimmed down in the 1982–1986 period. Many observers argue that the corporate restructuring of the 1980s has been as great as any in American history and has been very beneficial.

The Facts

Overall Performance

Fact #1 *Manufacturing's share of GNP, measured in current dollars, has declined from 30 percent in 1955 to 22 percent in 1986.*

- In contrast to its falling share, the dollar volume of manufacturing in the GNP accounts rose in all but three (1958, 1970, 1982) of the thirty years from 1955 to 1985.

Fact #2 *The number of workers employed in manufacturing remained remarkably stable in the twenty-year period 1966–1986 (19,214,000 in 1966 and 19,187,000 in 1986) but their share of the total American labor force has dropped considerably from 27 percent in 1955 to 16 percent in 1986.*

- Since the peak was reached in 1979, the number of manufacturing workers declined 1,853,000 by 1986.

Fact #3 *From 1979 to 1986, manufacturing employment dropped 9 percent but manufacturing output rose 13 percent.*

Fact #4   The profits of manufacturing companies as a share of total corporate profits has declined significantly over the past thirty years from a 55 percent share to a 30 percent share in 1986.

- The boom period for manufacturing profits was 1974 to 1978 when they more than doubled.
- In 1986, the profits level was still 17 percent below the 1978 peak of $88.7 billion.

Fact #5   Productivity in manufacturing industries has consistently outstripped that of the rest of the nonfarm economy.

- Productivity in manufacturing grew at a sustained 2.5 percent annual pace from 1970 to 1985.
- Productivity in manufacturing averaged 4.1 percent a year, more than 3 times the 1.2 percent rate for the rest of the economy, from 1982 to 1985.

Fact #6   A major change in the 1980s has been the dramatic drop in unit labor costs in manufacturing, from an 11.7 percent increase in 1980 to actual declines in 1983 and 1984.

International Comparisons

Fact #1   Despite the relatively strong showing of manufacturing productivity in the U.S. economy, it has been lower than all its industrial competitors except Canada.

- Despite faster productivity growth rates in recent years, Japan and W. Germany still lag about 20 percent behind the overall level of U.S. industrial productivity.

Fact #2   If unit labor costs are adjusted for the dollar's rise in the early 1980s, America's figures go from an average 1 percent a year to an average 7 percent increase, highest among its major industrial competitors.

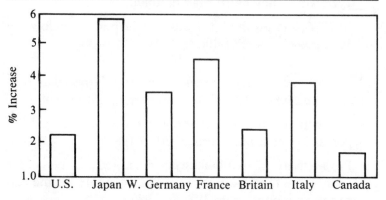

Figure 1

Manufacturing Productivity
in Seven Industrial Nations
(Average annual percentage
increase, 1973–1984)

— Despite faster productivity growth rates in recent years, Japan and
W. Germany still lag about 20 percent behind the overall level of U.S.
industrial productivity.

The Decline of Manufacturing in
Manufacturing Companies

*Fact #1   Manufacturers in many industries are either cur-
tailing their manufacturing operations or shutting them down,
becoming marketing organizations for other, mostly foreign,
producers. The new corporations, which are vertically disaggregated (steps in manufacturing process scattered outside
the company), have been dubbed "dynamic networks" and
"hollow corporations."*

• Kodak and RCA are only two of the many industrial
giants who contract outside their company for manufacturing.

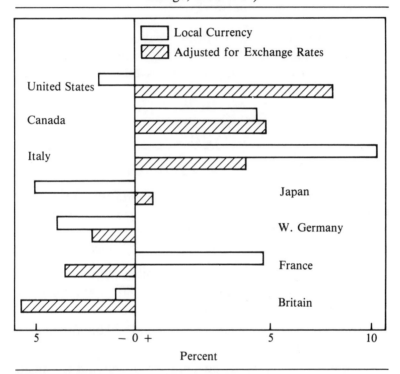

Figure 2

Relative Unit Labor Costs
in Manufacturing
(Average annual percentage
change, 1980–1984)

Source: *The Economist*, April 19, 1986, p. 81.

- Other large companies that continue to do most of their own manufacturing are edging toward disaggregation by (1) turning to foreign sources for finished products (e.g., Firestone, 3M, and GE) and (2) forming joint ventures and temporary alliances overseas (e.g., GM).
- General Electric is a primary example of vertical disaggregation as it is buying TVs and videocassette re-

corders based on its own designs from the Far East; by mid-1986, only 10 percent of the employees in its consumer-electronics units were engaged in manufacturing compared to 60 percent in 1984.

- A sizable number of companies, mostly small-to-midsized, are already networks.

Fact #2 *American Can is a dramatic example of a company that switched in just six years from being a major manufacturer to a $4-billion financial services and retailing company that manufactures nothing.*

Autos

Overall Industry Performance

Fact #1 *Since 1980, the American auto industry has undertaken a wide variety of positive changes to cut costs and become more competitive.*

- Forty-seven facilities were closed from 1980 to 1986.
- The Big Three have built or refurbished eighteen North American assembly plants since 1980, updating their technology as they retooled.
- In 1985–1986 they spent an estimated $20 billion on new high-tech plants.
- A push for quality is reducing scrappage and the need for plant inspectors and repairmen.
- Cheaper, outside suppliers are being used.
- More moderate labor contracts have saved the industry about $6 billion it would have spent if pre-1980 bargaining patterns had continued.
- Ford trimmed around $3.5 billion in overhead costs, including inventories, from 1980 to 1982.
- Dozens of work-rule changes have helped to boost productivity.

Fact #2   *G.M., Ford, and Chrysler were ranked 1, 2, and 6 respectively in terms of 1986 unit sales but their 10-year growth rates are miserable compared with their foreign competitors.*

- 10-year growth rates for GM, Ford, and Chrysler were -1.0 percent, -0.9 percent, and -0.6 percent respectively while the rates for three of their leading competitors—Toyota, Volkswagen, and Honda—were 3.1 percent, 7.2 percent, and 9.0 percent respectively.

Fact #3   *Costs in the auto industry from 1980 to 1986 fell about 12 percent.*

- In 1980 the Big Three in 1980 lost $4 billion on sales of 6.6 million cars while in 1983 they earned $6 billion on only 3 percent higher sales and in 1984 had their highest profits ever ($9.8 billion).

Fact #4   *Auto plants that are not U.S.-owned will account for 11 percent of all North American capacity by 1990, up from only 5 percent in 1986.*

Fact #5   *In the U.S. alone, there could be more than 2 million more cars than buyers annually by 1990.*

Fact #6   *From a low of less than 5 million cars built in 1982, production and sales climbed to about 8.2 million U.S.-made cars in 1986.*

Fact #7   *In the 1985/1986 model year, twelve car companies worldwide had sales increases and eight had sales decreases. Only one U.S. company, Chrysler, had an increase and it ranked twelfth.*

Fact #8   *Japanese car manufacturers are also cutting costs. Despite the yen's 57 percent appreciation against the dollar from the summer of 1985 to the summer of 1986, Japanese cars set a U.S. sales record in July 1986.*

Fact #9   American cars require 3.5 repairs a year while Japanese cars require 1.1 repairs a year.

General Motors

Fact #1   In 1979 GM began a revolution unlike any attempted before by a company of its size.

- GM had three goals: (1) to reward innovative thinking, (2) to develop new methods for making and selling cars, and (3) to decentralize decision-making.

Fact #2   In the first half of the 1980s, GM invested $60 billion in plant and equipment, building six new assembly plants and modernizing twelve others.

Fact #3   Despite its efforts, GM's market share, profits, and production costs were all suffering in 1986 and 1987.

- GM's share of the U.S. auto market went from 48 percent in 1978 to 37 percent in 1987.

- In 1986, GM's profits fell 28 percent while Ford (with about two-thirds of GM's sales) had higher earnings for the first time ever.

- In 1987, its per car production costs were the highest of any major auto maker.

Fact #4   In late 1986, GM announced plans for a major scaling back. It closed eleven plants employing 29,000 workers and producing 730,000 cars and trucks a year (10 percent of GM's total North American capacity) and cut back its new Saturn car project.

- This was part of its plan to cut its work force from 623,000 in 1979 to 470,000 in 1989.

Fact #5   GM's most striking increases in efficiency occurred in plants that organized workers in teams, copying the ap-

*proach at NUMMI (New United Motor Manufacturing Inc.),
a GM-Toyota joint venture.*

- NUMMI, which relies on Japanese-style management
  and a special emphasis on teamwork rather than high
  tech equipment, has a productivity rate twice that of
  most GM plants and its Novas have earned the highest
  customer-satisfaction rating and lowest warranty costs
  of any GM car.

- At one GM stamping plant a die change that used to
  take twelve hours now takes fifteen minutes when performed by workers organized in teams.

Steel

Industry Shrinkage: Output, Jobs, Profits

*Fact #1 In the 1980s (through 1986), a total of 444 mills
closed and more than 200,000 workers left the payroll.*

- The second largest producer, LTV, filed under Chapter
  11 in 1986 and 24 smaller companies have gone belly-
  up since 1977.

*Fact #2 The output and steelmaking capacity of the Amer-
ican steel industry dropped considerably from 1974 to 1986.*

- Capacity went from a peak in 1977 of 160 million tons
  to 112 million tons in 1986 while output dropped from
  110 million tons in 1974 to around 70 million tons in
  1986, drops of 30 percent and 36 percent respectively.

*Fact #3 The greatest shrinkage has come in employment,
as the number of steel workers was more than cut in half,
from 512,000 in 1973 to 163,000 in 1987.*

- Some steel producing areas have been hit especially hard

(e.g., Johnstown, Pennsylvania, had nearly 13,000 steel workers in 1977 and only 2,000 in 1984).

Fact #4   From 1982 to 1986 the steel industry had losses totaling $11.7 billion, with a record $4 billion loss in 1986.

Labor Costs

Fact #1   In 1987, steel wages and fringe benefits averaged $23 an hour in the U.S. and around $3 an hour in S. Korea.

Fact #2   The average steel worker's compensation in 1985 was 67 percent above the market rate for nonunion employees with a similar mix of skills. Relative to the average employee of a manufacturing company, the steel worker in 1983 was paid 98 percent more.

Fact #3   Higher U.S. labor costs can more than offset higher productivity of U.S. steel mills, making the American product noncompetitive.

- One product study on hot-rolled band showed a ratio of 3.6 man-hours per ton in the U.S. to 3.4 in Japan, 5.9 in Brazil, 4.6 in Britain, and 5.5 in Korea; but the $20-plus labor cost in the U.S. meant $84 per ton for that hot-rolled band against $16 for Korea and $38 for Japan.

Imports and Foreign Competition

Fact #1   Imported steel gained more than 20 percent of the American market for the first time in 1982 and has remained above that figure since.

Fact #2   Official statistics showed direct steel imports rising to about 25 percent of the U.S. market in 1985, but they were actually about 50 percent of American consumption if steel in imported products is included.

Fact #3 The number of foreign competitors has increased greatly, from thirty-two countries which produced steel in 1950 to eighty-five countries in 1982.

Steel Industry Getting Out of the Steel Business

Fact #1 Beginning in the mid-1970s, more and more of the major American steel producers began to deemphasize their steel production, to diversify, and in some cases to get out of steel production altogether.

- U.S. Steel, the symbol of steelmaking might through much of this century, had half of its assets out of the business by 1980, spent $6.2 billion to acquire Marathon Oil in 1982, spent $3.6 billion to purchase Texas Oil and Gas in 1985, and dropped Steel from its name in becoming USX in 1986; by then energy accounted for two-thirds of its revenues and all of its profits.
- National Steel got out of the steel business, selling its template plant in Weirton, West Virginia, to the employees and its steel operations to Big Steel.
- Armco Steel dropped "Steel" from its name to reflect the greater diversity of its operations.

Recent Bright Spots for Steel

Fact #1 In 1987, every major steel company was making money and earnings for the six major integrated producers were projected to be $1 billion.

Fact #2 Plant closings and general cutbacks in capacity mean that most of the steel plants that remain are up-to-date; by the end of 1987, the industry had enough continuous casting capability to handle 70 percent of its raw steel, up from 30 percent in 1982.

Fact #3 Productivity in the U.S. steel industry made sizable *advances in the early to mid-1980s, rising 27.4 percent between 1981 and 1986 so that by 1986, American mills were producing steel at fewer man-hours per ton than any foreign competitor.*

- At Bethlehem Steel, productivity in 1983 was up 15 percent, in 1984 up 12 percent, and in 1985 up 5 percent.

Fact #4   The quality of American steel has improved as the reject rate comparison with Japan has gone from 5–10 percent in the U.S. and 1–1½ percent in Japan in the early 1980s to around 2 percent for each in 1986.

Fact #5   The new mini-mills (which differ from the large integrated plants by focusing on one phase of the production process) have become highly competitive, capturing 20 percent of the American market from 1984 to 1986 (compared to 1960 was 3 percent).

Fact #6   The dollar's depreciation in 1985, 1986, and 1987 helped make the U.S. steel industry cost-competitive with steel producers in the European Economic Community and Japan.

- In 1987, major producers' pretax costs were $440 a ton (down 28 percent from 1982) while Japanese steelmakers' costs were $481 a ton (up 17 percent).

Fact #7   Imports in 1987 were projected to be 19 million metric tons, 8 percent less than in 1986 and 27.5 percent less than in 1984.

Interpretation of the Facts

1. American Manufacturers in the Future

Those who believe American manufacturers have a solid and perhaps even bright future have an impressive array of basic facts to draw upon. One is that despite the surge in imports, which began in 1982, manufacturing profits are holding up quite well. This, they feel, is primarily due to the dramatic decline in unit-labor costs and the strong productivity advances of recent years.

In general, they point to a leaner, more efficient industrial base emerging from years of brutal cost reduction and massive consolidation forced by imports. Specifically, key sectors such as textiles, chemicals, and household appliances are rebounding, helped by their slimming down through mergers and bankruptcies. Irwin Kellner, senior vice president of Manufacturers Hanover Trust, feels that as trade improves, "these industries could lead the entire manufacturing sector out of the doldrums." Looking at the broader manufacturing scene, Federal Reserve Governor Wayne Angell says: "We are invigorating the manufacturing sector. This period of adjustment has made us more competitive."

As for the big two—autos and steel—the optimists see a few key bright spots there. In the auto industry, there is primarily the sharp decline in costs since 1980. There can be no doubt that each of the Big Three is considerably more productive than it was in 1980.

Another bright spot is the new, innovative contract that GM and the United Auto Workers (UAW) forged for the Saturn Project. The contract, signed in July 1985, left both labor and management feeling they had won. In it, the UAW agrees to give up restrictive work rules that hamper productivity and to accept guaranteed salaries—not hourly wages—of only 80 percent of the average wage paid to workers in the rest of the industry. The remainder of their compensation would come from profit-sharing and an incentive plan based on workers' performance. In exchange, GM promised lifetime job security to 80 percent of Saturn's workers and offered them a greater voice in decision-making than they have had at GM or elsewhere.

As for the steel industry, the most important fact is that for the first time in a long while, U.S. producers are once again cost competitive. And many feel that they will remain cost-competitive as highly efficient, low-cost mini-mills increase their share of total U.S. production. Robert Crandall, a senior fellow at the Brookings Institution, predicts that by the end of the century, mini-mills will account for fully 40 percent of all American steel production.

Among the leading pessimists are those adherents to the "hollow corporation" thesis. They argue that U.S. companies, by shifting production overseas or shopping abroad for parts and components, are whittling away at the core of what is essential to a strong industrial base.

The cries of alarm are not coming just from academics or government bureaucrats but from top business leaders. Robert A. Lutz, the chairman of Ford of Europe Inc., says: "You're seeing a substantial deindustrialization of the U.S. and I can't imagine any country maintaining its position in the world without an industrial base."

Deindustrialization in the 1980s is of an entirely different, and considerably more fundamental, character than the deindustrialization of the 1960s and early 1970s. Then many companies exported blue-collar jobs to low-wage countries, a trend that continues. But what sets today's deindustrialization apart is that U.S. companies are now shifting far more valuable things overseas: fundamental technology, management functions, and even the design and engineering skills that are crucial to innovation. If this trend continues, warns Jack D. Kuehler, senior vice president of IBM, companies will gradually become less adept at understanding how new technology can be exploited and eventually "lose the ability to design."

Perhaps the other major fact underlying the pessimists' arguments is that the steep plunge in the dollar from 1985 to 1987 did not lead to a sharp rebound in competitiveness and a sharp reversal in the declining merchandise trade deficit. One reason is that foreign competitors displayed an extraordinary penchant for shaving profit margins to hang to on their customers in the U.S. and elsewhere. They did not raise their prices nearly enough to reflect the rise in their currencies against the dollar, and in some cases they did not raise prices at all. They were restrained, in part, by fierce competition from low-cost competitors in newly industrialized countries such as South Korea, Taiwan, and Brazil, which enjoy a special advantage—their currencies are linked to the dollar, so their low export prices hardly budged.

Regarding the auto industry, perhaps the chief factor causing concern is U.S. management. Many feel that by comparison with Japanese automakers, U.S. car companies have long been top heavy, bureaucratic, and shot full of antagonism between management and labor. "Seventy percent of the problem with American auto companies isn't technology related. It's management related," according to James Harbour, a Michigan consultant who has extensively studied U.S. and Japanese automaking costs. As a specific example, David E. Cole, director of the Office for the Study of Automotive Transportation at the University of Michigan, figures that leaner, more Japanese-like management alone could slash GM's costs by 30 percent.

The same type of charge is made about the U.S. steel industry's managers. A. Gary Shilling, an economic consultant, puts it this way:

> . . . managements did not use the breathing space provided by the steel trigger price program [a protectionist trade program] to get their houses in order. Rather, they dissipated their resources on buying oil companies and other investments that not only proved dubious but also convinced labor that management didn't really care about backing the steel business (A. G. Shilling, "Steel Industry Must Scrap Cartel Mentality," *The Wall Street Journal*, July 29, 1986).

Shilling also points out how management hardly set a good example during the rough 1980–1985 period when top executives' salaries and bonuses grew 60 percent while production workers' pay rose 16 percent.

The other major point raised is that the U.S. has given

the steel industry more incentives, relief, and protection than any other industry and yet it still is not a first-class world competitor. Trade protection was enacted for carbon steel in 1968 and again in 1978, trade relief was granted specialty steel in 1976 and again in 1983, and export restraint agreements were negotiated with the Common Market in 1982 and 1983. The result? The highest percentage for imported steel ever recorded in 1984 and 1985. Further, in 1978, the Economic Development Administration extended loan guarantees to three troubled steel companies—two went bankrupt and Wheeling-Pittsburgh entered bankruptcy proceedings in 1985.

The pessimists charge: "If they can't make it with all these things going for them, how will they ever make it?"

CHAPTER
★ 21 ★

The Service
Sector

The Issues

The United States has been a service economy for nearly forty years, ever since more than half of its labor force has been in service occupations. When the "service economy" is mentioned, the reaction of many Americans, including leading opinion-shapers, is one of disgust or doom and gloom. To them, the service economy represents a serious softening of the American economy that will lead to the nation's ultimate demise.

Other Americans see nothing wrong with the U.S. being a service economy. To them, it is a natural move from a manufacturing base as the economy matures. Besides, this is where America has its strongest competitive advantage.

The feelings in this debate are pale in comparison to the views held by people who feel that the service economy does not provide decent service. As one of the commentators in the Interpretation section at the end of this chapter observes: "It is one of the more considerable ironies of an ironic age: At a time when the base of our economy is gradually shifting from manufacturing to service, service as it has traditionally been known is gradually disappearing."

Definition: **Services** are defined by the U.S. Department of Commerce as including: information, finance, transportation, health and medicine, accounting, management, education, law, advertising, trade leasing, consulting, public relations, operations and maintenance, and architecture and engineering.

At first glance, these activities have little in common, except perhaps the apparent intangibility of their principal products. Look again and there is an interlocking web of economic agents that share the unique ability to bring about further economic activity:

- Government, social, educational, and legal services that provide and maintain our social fabric.

- Personal services, entertainment, health services, and hospitality and food preparation services that enhance the quality of life.

- Financial, transportation, and distribution services that allow the free circulation of goods, commodities, services, information, and money.

- Business services like accounting, advertising, leasing, data processing, and franchising that increase economic efficiency.

The Facts

Services as a Percentage of GNP

Fact #1 *Services have been the dominant component of GNP since 1950 (a 61 percent share) and its percentage share of GNP has grown slowly but steadily, to 69 percent in 1986.*

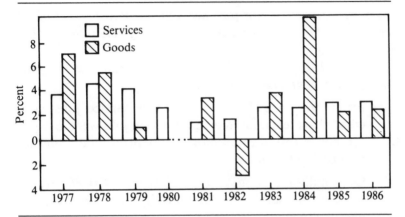

Figure 1

Output of Services and Goods
(Percentage change in
real GNP annually)

Source: The Service Economy, Washington, D.C.: Coalition of Service
Industries, November 1986 and June 1987.

Fact #2 *From 1972 to 1983, output as a share of GNP
increased in all industry groups in the service sector, except
government, while output declined as a share of GNP in all
the industry groups of the goods-producing sector (except
durable goods).*

Fact #3 *The leading annual contributor to GNP from 1980
through 1986 fluctuated back and forth between the services
and goods production sectors.*

Fact #4 *Most major industrialized countries have service
economies. As far back as 1972, services accounted for more
than half of GNP in twelve of the OECD countries. (OECD
countries are all of the industrialized nations of Western Europe, the U.S., Japan, and Canada.)*

Fact #5   Personal services (such as barbers, maids, etc.) account for only about 2 percent of the U.S. GNP.

Service Jobs and Employment

Fact #1   Service sector jobs accounted for 75 percent of all employment in 1986, for a year-end total of 76.2 million jobs.

Fact #2   The vast majority of new jobs created in the past thirty years have been in services.

- From 1978 to 1985, 14 million new service jobs were created while 2 million manufacturing jobs were lost and the goods producing sector experienced a net contraction of 600,000 jobs.

- Of 25 million new net jobs created since 1970, 88 percent were in the service sector and virtually none were in manufacturing.

- From 1959 to 1985 manufacturing jobs increased by 2 million (17 million to 19 million) and service sector jobs increased by 30 million (21 million to 51 million). This means that 15 new service jobs were created for each new manufacturing job throughout the past three decades.

- Of the 2.7 million new jobs created in 1986, services accounted for 2.6 million.

Fact #3   The shift to service employment has been going on for more than a century—for as long as records have been kept on the distribution of the labor force. In 1870 workers employed in the service sector made up 26 percent of the work force; by 1930 they made up 42 percent.

Fact #4   Of the 22 million women added to the labor force in the period 1966–1986, 33 out of 34 found a job in services.

Fact #5   Job growth in services, along with job growth generally, began slowing in 1985. In 1986 service jobs rose by only 3.7 percent, down from 4.3 percent in 1985 and 5.3 percent in 1984.

Fact #6   There are vastly different employment growth rates among various service industries, spanning the spectrum from a few industries in which employment actually declined in the 1981–1984 period, such as railroads and telephone communication, to the explosive growth area of computer and data processing service (up 42 percent).

Fact #7   Service jobs show remarkable resilience in periods of recession: employment in the goods-producing sector declined by 8.3 percent in postwar recessions while service employment actually advanced by an average of 2.1 percent.

Fact #8   The jobs in the service sector are so diverse that they cannot be categorized as either high-wage or low-wage.

- It employs low-paid workers in fast-food restaurants, personal service establishments (such as barbers), and nursing homes.
- It also employs many high-paid workers in legal services, advertising and communications, and computer services.
- It employs 80 percent of America's managerial and professional specialty workers.

Fact #9   The prospects for service jobs over the next decade are mixed.

- Nine out of ten jobs created from 1985 to 1995 are expected to be in services, the fastest growing areas being business and professional services.
- Peter Drucker predicts that new technologies will eliminate 15 million service jobs between 1985 and 1995.

Services and International Trade

Fact #1   Services surpluses have been the major bright spot in U.S. trade statistics for the past decade and help to offset the continual negative trade balance in goods.

Fact #2   Explosive growth in U. S. exports of services in the 1960s and 1970s—with increases of 152 percent and 420 percent respectively—was followed by stagnation from 1982 to 1986 (a 3 percent increase).

- Total service exports were $9.2 billion in 1960, $23.2 billion in 1970, $118.7 billion in 1980, and $152.8 billion in 1986.

Fact #3   U.S. trade in services also shows serious signs of weakness: (1) the surplus in this sector most broadly defined declined from $62 billion in 1981 to $37 billion in 1986 and (2) the U.S. share of services trade worldwide declined from 25 percent in the late 1970s to 20 percent in the mid-1980s.

Investment, Profits, and Prices

Fact #1   The service sector is, and has been for some time, America's dominant purchaser of plants and equipment. Unlike the goods sector, it has not experienced a yearly decline in capital purchases for at least a decade.

- In 1985, service businesses spent $40 billion on new computer and office equipment technology.

Fact #2   Since 1982, the profits of service companies have exceeded those of goods producers.

- For the period 1980–1985, the top five industries in average annual profit growth were all service industries: soft drinks and other beverages, tobacco, health care, oil field services, and publishing.

Figure 2

Corporate Profits
(Billions of current dollars annual)

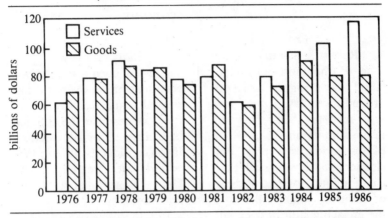

Source: The Service Economy, Washington, D.C.: Coalition of Service Industries, November 1986 and June 1987.

Fact #3   *Between 1979 and 1986, service sector price increases were greater than those in the goods producing sector in every year but 1979.*

Interpretation
of the Facts

1. The Service Economy and U.S. Economic Health

An indication of how deep the rift in opinions on the service economy is seen in these two selections. Robert J. Samuelson

is an economic journalist for *Newsweek* while Barry Bluestone is an economics professor at the University of Massachusetts.

The Service Economy

Pro
Robert J. Samuelson

One of the most misunder-
stood and maligned concepts
around these days is the "service economy." It's frowned
upon, summoning up a vision
of fast-food restaurants, dry
cleaners and bowling alleys—
a nation that produces nothing
of enduring value. All this is
the engaging stuff of cocktail-
party economics. It's also
wrong: the intellectual equivalent of believing, in the 15th
century, that the world was flat.

Popular preconceptions
about the service economy are
generally cockeyed. It is not
inexorably leading to lower
living standards (actually, just
the opposite). It is not dis-
placing the physical production of goods (also, the opposite). It is not polarizing
income between a well-paid
elite of professionals and a
poorly paid proletariat of jan-
itors. And it is not spawning a
nation of laundermats and barbershops.

Mostly, the expansion of the
service sector is a sign of na-

Con
Barry Bluestone

There has been a lot of good
economic news over the last
several years. Relative to Europe, for example, the U.S. has
been a haven for job creation.
If you consider the 1978 to 1984
period, we created in the
United States almost 11 million new jobs.

But, there is also a lot of bad
news. The manufacturing base
continues to decline despite
dramatic reductions in the value
of the dollar and despite significant increases in GNP. We
seem to be stuck somewhere
in the neighborhood of 18 to
19 million jobs in manufacturing and no one expects that
number to increase.

Everyone knows that job
growth has been coming in from
outside the manufacturing sector. But from where in the job
distribution are the new jobs
being created? We found that
no more than 26 percent of 27
million new additional workers in the economy between
1963 and 1978 earned below
half of the low budget stan-

tional wealth, not decay. More workers have been freed to provide services that, when society was poorer, it could not afford or did not want. There are more hotels, amusement parks and professional sports teams because there is more mobility and more leisure. There are more hospitals, doctors and nursing homes because we live longer and can spend more on our upkeep. . . .

Anyone who thinks manufacturing is especially virtuous should also study some comparisons. North Carolina has more of its nonfarm work force in manufacturing (32.8 percent in 1983) than any other state. But its residents' per capita income—the money available to each of them— ranks only 39th. . . . North Carolina is no exception; most states with big manufacturing bases aren't near the top. . . .

Some industries and jobs pay well, others don't. The sloppy assumption that all manufacturing workers are well-paid autoworkers and that every service worker is shoveling french fries at McDonald's obscures this reality. Although goods-producing industries do (on average) pay more than service industries, there's no

dard. However, for the period 1978–84, when we had 11 million jobs created, more than 37 percent were working jobs that paid an annual wage less than that $8,685 figure.

Indeed, we had job creation, but the new jobs have been disproportionately in the low wage sector. This reflects the fact that the new jobs have all been in services and trade where wages are lower than in manufacturing or construction. For instance, in retail trade, the average job pays about 45 percent of the annual wage in manufacturing. The entire "service economy" (including many of the very high wage professional jobs) pays two-thirds of the typical job in manufacturing. Thus, the United States has generated a good number of jobs, but these have contributed much less to income. That's why we have seen stagnating income growth despite the very buoyant employment numbers (B. Bluestone, in *Declining American Incomes and Living Standards*, Washington, DC: Economic Policy Institute, pp. 5–6).

solid evidence—despite claims to the contrary—that the rise of service employment has made income distribution more unequal. . . . The distinction between services and manufacturing is increasingly irrelevant for higher living standards and more jobs. We should encourage efficient firms over the inefficient firms and growth industries over the stagnant—whatever they may be. Old stereotypes are not a good way either to understand the economy or to improve it (R. J. Samuelson, "We're Not a National Laundermat," *Newsweek*, July 9, 1984, p. 61).

2. Does the Service Economy Provide Service?

The answer depends on where you look and who you talk to.

Ask James Haskett, a professor at the Harvard Business School, and he will assure you that the service sector can not only provide service, but service that is better than anything in the past. In particular, he points to Shouldice Hospital Ltd. (in a suburb of Toronto) which has this set of distinctions:

- It is extremely profitable, yet its prices are competitive.

- The surgical care is many times more effective than other hospitals typically provide (based on the success rates of Shouldice's operations).

- Nearly all of its patients walk away from the operating table on the supporting arm of their surgeons.

- Patients seem to love the place since as many as 500 former patients return to the hospital for annual reunions.

According to Haskett, this success is a matter of good strategy. First came a careful strategic decision about the kind of service the hospital would offer—it confines itself solely to repairing abdominal hernias. The external marketing strategy is aimed at the customer and interlocks with an internal operational plan involving employees and managers. The two approaches must reinforce one another. At Shouldice, the way patients are treated results directly from the attitudes that surgeons and staff have about their jobs. Among the many factors contributing to high staff morale are the high success rate of operations, the patients' enthusiasm, and the absence of the most stressful parts of hospital work (especially the long, irregular hours).

Jonathan Yardley, columnist and author, has a very different opinion of the service sector:

> It is one of the more considerable ironies of an ironic age: At a time when the base of our economy is gradually shifting from manufacturing to service, "service" as it has traditionally been known is gradually disappearing. . . . The department stores are scarcely the only culprits when it come to the rapacious pursuit of profits at the expense of service and courtesy. Have you been to the supermarket lately? To an automobile dealer? To that same dealer's "service" department? To a bookstore? A sporting-goods store?
>
> If you have, then you found many things, none of which could be called "service." At the supermarket you found management locked away from you in an aerie by the checkout lane, and your progress through the aisles was impeded by clerks single-mindedly ramming new merchandise onto the shelves. At the auto dealership you found indifferent, even hostile sales personnel, and at the "service" department you found that they were doing you a favor to let you wait three hours in order to give them your money. At the book-

store you found a clerk who knew nothing about books and
regarded special orders as an intrusion on his gum-chewing
time. At the sporting-goods store you found a "shoe sales-
man" who knew nothing about shoes, nothing about feet,
and thus had no helpful counsel about which shoe would fit
you—that's you, your feet—most comfortably (J. Yardley,
"Service and the End of an Era," *Washington Post*, June 3,
1985).

3. Services Are Here to Stay

Although some may not like it, there is widespread agreement that the U.S. will remain a service economy for some
time to come. Indeed, it will consolidate its status since the
vast majority of new jobs will be in services and the great
potential for major advances in U.S. trade is in the service
sector.

We have already mentioned the Bureau of Labor Statistics
(BLS) projection that nine of ten new jobs by 1995 will be
service jobs. Futurologist Marvin Cetron goes so far as to
predict that service jobs will make up 88 percent of total
employment by the year 2000. The fastest growing individual
service industry will be communications, with the BLS estimating 6.2 percent average annual growth from 1984 to
1995.

It is also felt that across the broad spectrum of service
businesses, American companies—at least through the
1990s—will enjoy unparalleled advantages of scale, market
reach, capital depth, and technological prowess. Data Resources projects an immense 280 percent rise over the next
decade in U.S. service exports, leading to a $170 billion
services surplus in the year 2000.

CHAPTER
★ 22 ★
High
Technology

The Issues

Many feel that the nation preeminent in high technology in the twenty-first century will command the world economy. The stakes could not be higher in the race for domination of the four major high tech areas: computers, semiconductors, telecommunications and optical technology, and biotechnology.

The U.S. brings considerable strengths and weaknesses to this race. The U.S. is currently the world leader in computers, semiconductors, and biotechnology. Japan is the world leader in robotics, advanced materials, and fiber optics for telecommunications, and is coming on strong in semiconductors. Particularly worrisome for the U.S. is the fact that its high-technology trade balance swung from a $26.7 billion surplus peak in 1981 to a first-ever deficit in 1986.

In high technology, it is difficult to predict the future accurately. In 1986 superconductors were virtually unknown to the public but by the first half of 1987 they were on the covers of leading newsmagazines and heralded as "transforming the future." The only certainty about high technology is that it is fascinating, fast changing, and the focus of ruthless global competition.

Definitions: There is even controversy about the definition of **high technology**. The National Science Foundation defines it as anything produced by organizations employing 25 or more scientists and engineers per 100 employees and spending over 3.5 percent of net sales on R & D. Economists amend this definition only slightly: high technology products are those that embody an "above average" concentration of scientific and engineering skills. The U.S. Department of Commerce derives its definition from input-output analysis of the total R & D spent on a spectrum of individual products. Thus, high-tech industry is a ranking of the ten most "research-intensive" sectors, where the tenth has at least double the R & D intensity of manufacturing generally:

High-Tech Sector	*Examples of Products*
1. Missiles and space-craft	Rocket engines; satellites and parts
2. Electronics and tele-communications	Telephone and telegraph apparatus, radio and TV receiving and broadcast equipment, sonar and other instruments, semiconductors, tape recorders
3. Aircraft and parts	Commercial aircraft, fighters, bombers, helicopters, aircraft engines, parts
4. Office computing and accounting machinery	Computers, input-output devices, storage devices, desk calculators, duplicating machines, parts

5. Ordnance and accessories	Nonmilitary arms, hunting and sporting ammunition, blasting and percussion caps
6. Drugs and medicines	Vitamins, antibiotics, hormones, vaccines
7. Inorganic chemicals and compounds, special nuclear	Nitrogen, sodium hydroxide, rare gases, inorganic pigments, radioactive isotopes materials
8. Professional and scientific instruments	Industrial process controls, optical instruments and lenses, navigational instruments, photographic equipment
9. Engines, turbines, and parts	Generator sets, diesel engines, nonautomotive petrol engines, gas turbines, water turbines
10. Plastics, rubber, and synthetic fibers	Various chemicals derived from condensation, polycondensation, polyaddition, polymerization and copolymerization; synthetic resins and fibers

The Facts

Overview—Size and Growth of High-Tech Market

Fact #1   *High-tech industries grew at a 14 percent annual pace during the 1977–1984 period.*

Fact #2   *At the end of 1984, high-tech industries accounted for 12.9 percent of U.S. industrial output, more than double their weight in 1977.*

Fact #3   In 1983 there were 193 individual state programs to cultivate high-technology industry and by 1985, 33 states had such programs.

Fact #4   The growth rate for high-tech jobs is fairly strong— the yearly employment growth rate for high tech is 2.0 to 2.2 percent compared with an overall employment growth rate of 1.5 to 1.8 percent—but the number of jobs is not that great.

- Computer makers, for instance, employ less than 1 percent of the workforce.

- Of the 10 occupations that will supply the largest number of jobs through 1995, none is in high tech.

Fact #5   Due to slower growth of the market and greatly increased foreign competition, many high tech companies in 1985 and 1986 took major steps to cut costs.

- AT&T in December 1986 announced it would take a $3.2 billion write-off and lay off 27,400 workers, the largest layoff in its history.

- IBM, seeing its first back-to-back yearly earnings decline since the Great Depression, reorganized, consolidated, and offered extraordinarily generous early retirement settlements in its efforts to reduce its work force.

- MCI Communications cut 15 percent of its workforce and took write-offs totaling $500 to $700 million.

- Wang Laboratories, Data General, Intel, and other leading hi-tech companies have shut down facilities and implemented stringent cost-cutting measures.

U.S. Performance in Global Competition

Fact #1   From 1980–1986, U.S. high-tech exports went up 29 percent while high-tech imports exploded by 250 percent.

Fact #2 While the overall U.S. high-tech trade balance declined 97 percent from 1980 to 1986, the balance with Japan slid 489 percent and declined 2,900 percent with the Southeast Asian NICs.

Fact #3 Of the ten industrial sectors designated high tech (by the Department of Commerce), three made up nearly two-thirds of America's high-tech exports in 1986.

- Aircrafts and parts are America's biggest revenue earner abroad followed closely by office computing and accounting machines and communications equipment.

Table 1

America's High-Tech Exports (1986)

Sector	Value (Billion $)	Percent of total high-tech exports
Aircraft and parts	$18.4	25.4
Office automation	$16.1	22.2
Electronics & telecoms	$14.9	20.6
Professional instruments	$7.8	10.8
Plastics, rubber, etc.	$4.5	6.2
Inorganic chemicals	$3.5	4.8
Drugs and medicines	$3.1	4.3
Engines and turbines	$2.8	3.9
Ordnance	$0.7	1.0
Missiles and spacecraft	$0.6	0.8
Total	$72.5	

- American companies have increased their global market share in only three high-tech industries: communications and electronics; office automation; and ordnance.

Fact #4 Since the mid-1960s, high tech's share of American manufactured goods sold around the world has gone from a little over a quarter to close to a half.

• Manufacturing trade balances experienced volatile swings, going into deficit in seven of the twenty years between 1965 and 1985 but the high-technology trade balance had a steadily ascending surplus until 1981 and remained in a surplus position through 1985.

Fact #5   U.S. high-tech trade moved from a sizable surplus in the 1980s to a first time ever deficit in 1986.

• The high-tech surplus reached a peak of $26.7 billion in 1981. It dwindled to $6 billion in 1984, $3.6 billion in 1985, and a deficit of $2 billion in 1986. In the first half of 1987, it rebounded to a $1.1 billion surplus.

• Every major electronics market—computing equipment, communications equipment, office machines, instruments, semiconductors and components, and consumer electronics—experienced a decline in its trade position each year from 1981 to 1984, leading to a first-ever overall electronics deficit of $68 billion in 1984.

Fact #6   In competition with other leading high-tech export nations, the U.S. share of high-tech exports since 1970 has fluctuated in a quite narrow range of 24 percent to 28 percent.

• From 1970 to 1985, the U.S., West Germany, and Britain all experienced small 2 to 4 percentage point declines in their global market share. Japan was the big winner with a 10 percentage point increase.

Fact #7   The five major high-tech exporting nations (France, Japan, West Germany, United Kingdom, and the United States) devote roughly the same share of GNP to R & D (about 2.2 to 2.8 percent). However, 30 percent of the U.S. total goes for defense projects versus insignificant percentages to defense in Japan and West Germany.

• Since 1980, Federal R & D zoomed from $33 billion in fiscal 1980 to about $60 billion in 1987 but defense R & D accounts for nearly 90 percent of the increase (jumping from $15.4 billion to $38.4 billion), so that it now consumes a record 73 percent of Federal R & D funding.

Fact #8   In many developing nations—Taiwan and Brazil are leading examples—foreign companies are copying U.S. technology and reproducing it with the implicit consent of their own governments.

- It takes roughly three weeks after a new U.S.-made product is introduced before it is copied, manufactured, and shipped back to the U.S.

The High-Tech Sweepstakes: U.S. vs Japan

Fact #1   Japan and the U.S. each have clear areas of high technology leadership.

Table 2	
U.S. vs. Japan—A High-Technology Scorecard	
U.S. as Leader	Japan as Leader
General Technologies	
Computers Semiconductors Telecommunications Biotechnology	Robotics Advanced materials
Specific Technologies	
Lasers Computer software Computer-integrated software Computers	Fiber optics for telecommunications Gallium arsenide memory chips for superfast computers Numerically controlled machine tools and robots Computer disk drives, printers, and magnetic storage media

Fact #2   Japan's breakthroughs in the mid-1980s in gallium arsenide semiconductors, optoelectronics, and superceramics and component materials demonstrated Japanese capability to innovate at the frontiers of knowledge.

Fact #3   Japan has emerged as a major competitor to U.S. leadership in high technology since the mid-1970s.

- Of the 500 breakthroughs in technology considered seminal during the two decades between 1953 and 1973, only 5 percent (34 inventions) were made in Japan compared with 63 percent (315 inventions) in the United States.

Fact #4   The number of U.S. citizens studying engineering in Japan did not exceed 7 a year for the 20 years from 1966 to 1986 while 1,000 Japanese citizens were studying engineering in the U.S. in 1986.

Fact #5   In Japan, 5,000 scientists and engineers routinely process thousands of foreign journals and technical reports while only 19 percent (in 1981) of Japanese scientific and technical publications were even indexed by Western sources.

Fact #6   From 1978 to 1985, American equity markets raised $8 billion for start-ups in electronics alone and $3.3 billion for new biotech companies. In Japan, venture-capital investment in high tech totaled just $100 million.

Computers

Market Size and Growth

Fact #1   Revenues from the worldwide computer industry reached $300 billion in 1986, including software and service.

Fact #2   The U.S. shipped nearly 43 percent of the world's computers in 1981 and 34 percent in 1985.

Fact #3 *The growth in worldwide sales of U.S. computers plummeted between 1984 and 1987. Sales of PCs fell from 51 percent to 9 percent, sales of small computers from 27 to 11 percent, and sales of large mainframes from 11 to 4.5 percent.*

Fact #4 *Growth in total U.S. computer industry revenues dropped from around 30 percent a year in the early 1980s to less than 7.5 percent in 1986; in 1987, they rebounded to a 17 percent growth rate.*

- The real stars of 1987's turnaround were personal computer makers as Apple Computer gained 40 percent in both sales and earnings and Compaq Computer tripled earnings in the first nine months of 1987.

Fact #5 *U.S. computer hardware revenues in 1986 were about $50 billion, divided among types of computers as follows: personal computers, $20 billion; mainframes, $9 billion; departmental computers, $7 billion; engineering and technical systems, $7 billion; superminicomputers, $4 billion; multiuser microcomputers, $4 billion.*

Fact #6 *The computer industry is in the midst of a major transition from mainframes to inexpensive small computers.*

- With booming sales of the new generation of PCs using 32-bit microchips, the combined raw computing power of PCs at year-end 1987 was 20 trillion instructions per second compared to 145 billion instructions per second of all the IBM and IBM compatible mainframes in operation.

Fact #7 *The total computer industry output is less than 2 percent of the GNP.*

Fact #8 *Consolidation has been a major trend, with more than 200 software and service companies being acquired in 1985.*

Fact #9   *As the U.S. computer industry moves from simple number-crunching toward information networks, it is changing the way computers are sold, lengthening the buying process, and creating new organizational and even psychological problems for the people who use them.*

- These networks ease the communication of data and put more reliance on small and medium-sized machines than on giant mainframes.

- The biggest impediment to growth is the lack of a clearly defined set of hardware and software standards on which to build these networks.

Supercomputers

Fact #1   *In 1987, Cray Research Inc. controlled two-thirds of the $1.2 billion market for supercomputers, a market that has had annual growth rates of more than 30 percent.*

Fact #2   *Growth in supercomputer demand in the mid-1980s was three times that of mainframe and personal computers (around 10 percent per year) and rising rapidly.*

- Supercomputers are moving beyond universities and government labs and into corporate research labs in ever greater numbers, including such companies as General Motors, Ford, Dupont, and British Petroleum.

- Supercomputers are still quite limited in number with 35 being sold in 1984, bringing the worldwide total to just over 100.

Fact #3   *The speed and power of supercomputers are enormous: the fastest Cray in 1987 could hit 2,000 megaflops (a megaflop = 1 million complex multiplications a second). ETA has sold four ETA[10] supercomputers with the fastest rated at 3,400 megaflops; Cray will have available by the end of 1988 a 15,000–20,000 megaflops system; not too far off are machines capable of 100,000 megaflops (or 100 billion calculations per second).*

<u>Fact #4</u> *A supercomputer on a single chip became a distinct reality in 1986.*

- This new "superchip," developed by TRW, will have 35 million transistors compared to the most densely packed chips in use now which contain 1 million.
- Such a superchip will be able to perform the work of more than 10,000 ordinary chips, thus eliminating the need to link thousands of chips into a system. This should reduce manufacturing costs and improve the reliability of computers and other products.

<u>Fact #5</u> *Supercomputers are likely to lose market share in the future to massive computers using parallel processing.*

- Instead of solving problems step by step, the new machines break apart computational puzzles and solve their thousands or millions of separate parts all at once by stringing together hundreds or even thousands of microprocessors in a single machine.

Artificial Intelligence (AI) and Expert Systems

<u>Fact #1</u> *Sales of AI technology in 1985 topped $700 million (up 62 percent from 1984) and more than 200 companies were employing it (up over 40 percent from 1984).*

<u>Fact #2</u> *The expertise in AI began to spread out in 1985 from the small start-ups to many major companies, such as GE, Shell Oil, and 3M, which spent around $1 billion in 1985 to maintain in-house AI groups.*

Fact #3 *AI research through 1986 had produced only one major advance—expert systems—computer programs that can act as counselors or advisors on certain subjects. This is still far from AI researchers' ultimate goal of producing "intelligent" computers, which will combine the speed and precision of today's systems with those human deductive abilities not yet replicated.*

• In 1987, barely 100 major expert systems had been installed nationwide, mostly to handle such mundane tasks as production scheduling and equipment diagnosis.

Fact #4 *The two major research efforts in the U.S. are the Strategic Computing Program of the Pentagon's Defense Advanced Research Projects Agency and work being done by the Microelectronics and Technology Corporation (MCC).*

• MCC's twenty-two member companies acknowledge that to get anywhere in AI requires doing decade-long research projects and thus do not expect to meet their goal of solving the problem of replicating human "common sense" until 1994.

Computer Software

Fact #1 *U.S. producers of software have increased their share of the world's software market ($40 billion in 1986) from under 65 percent in the mid-1970s to over 75 percent in the mid-1980s.*

Fact #2 *Software, in the form of writing and "debugging" the programs, accounts for 50 to 80 percent of computer firms' budgets for developing new computers.*

Fact #3 *Software production has been a real weakness of Japan's computer industry but that government's Fifth Generation project envisions instructing 10,000 engineers in the intricacies of software and AI by 1995.*

Semiconductors

Market Size and Growth

Fact #1 In 1986 semiconductors constituted a $26 billion worldwide industry.

- U.S. semiconductor sales in 1986 were $8.5 billion.
- Semiconductor chips are key to computers, telephones, and other electronic gear that accounted for $250 billion of U.S. industrial output in 1986, 15 percent of the total.

Fact #2 Between 1977 and 1984, semiconductor orders had climbed an average of 25 percent annually despite dips in 1977, 1980, 1982 and much of 1984; throughout these years, the annual revenue gains were about 15 percent, peaking at $11.6 billion in 1984.

Fact #3 In 1985, U.S. chipmakers suffered a drop of 30 percent—the most dramatic decline in demand in two decades—despite a relatively healthy economy.

- The semiconductor industry suffered collective losses of $2 billion in 1985 and 1986.

Fact #4 In the 1960s, each $1 of capital generated $10 in annual revenues; in 1986, each $1 invested bought only $1.50 a year in revenues, and the ratio continues to decline.

Fact #5 Application Specific Integrated Circuits (custom-designed chips for specific uses) accounted for an estimated 19 percent of U.S. semiconductor business in 1985 and are becoming an increasingly important segment of the market.

Fact #6 The semiconductor industry in 1985 employed 250,000 people directly and nearly as great a number in the related support industries of equipment and material manufacture, testing and chip measuring, etc.

- Twenty-five thousand jobs were lost in 1985 and 1986 in the semiconductor industry as it went through a major retrenchment.

U.S.-Japanese Competition and the Global Market

Fact #1   From 1975 to 1986, the share of the worldwide market held by U.S. semiconductor companies fell from 57 percent to 44 percent in 1986 while Japan's rose from 19 percent to 46 percent.

- The first year that Japan's share exceeded the U.S. share was 1986.

Fact #2   Japan has taken over the dominant position in three areas: (1) In 1986 the world's top three chipmakers were Japanese firms (NEC, Hitachi, and Fujitsu) which took over the leadership from Motorola and Texas Instruments. (2) Japan in 1986 had the world's largest market for chips: $10.5 billion versus $8.5 billion for the U.S. (3) Japanese chipmakers overtook the U.S. merchant producers in capital spending in 1986.

Fact #3   The U.S. semiconductor market is projected to grow by 19 percent both in 1987 and 1988 while Japan's market is projected to grow at rates of 12 percent and 15 percent.

Fact #4   Despite Japanese advances, U.S. semiconductor manufacturers remain world leaders in all the nonmemory chip segments—microprocessors, logic chips, and linear products—that account for three-fourths of semiconductor sales.

Memory Chips

Fact #1   The Japanese control 67 percent of the $1.65-billion-a-year world market for dynamic random-access-mem-

ory *(DRAM) chips and have a 70 percent share of the DRAM market in America.*

- In 1978, fourteen U.S. chipmakers accounted for the bulk of RAM sales worldwide; in 1980, there were a dozen mass producers, in 1983 there were five, and by 1986 there were only two or three with the capacity to produce the latest generation of memory chips.
- The six Japanese firms that entered the memory chip business back in the early 1970s are still around.
- In 1986, the Japanese had an overwhelming 83 percent of the world market for 256K RAMS while the U.S. had a 13 percent share.

Fact #2   The number and diversity of applications increase tremendously as memory capacity increases and circuit size decreases.

Fact #3   The cost of storing data in memory chips has fallen by 30 to 35 percent a year and the price of the memory chips themselves have dropped on average by 35 percent every year.

- The 64K RAM went from $3.50 in May 1984 to $.75 in May 1985.
- The EPROM went from $17 in early 1985 to less than $4 six months later.
- The 256K RAM went from $25 in the summer of 1984 to $3.50 in the summer of 1985.

Fact #4   The Japanese chips are so much cheaper because of higher quality—typical yields of 256K RAM chips in Japan are triple those in the U.S. According to a study done by Robert G. Graham and Haubrecht Quist Inc., 34 percent of U.S.-made chips and 12 percent of Japanese-made chips do not pass a first quality check; after assembly, only 17 percent of U.S. chips are salable compared to 54 percent of Japanese chips.

Table 3

What Packing More Power on a Chip Will Bring

	1980	1985	1987	1990	1995
Circuit Size:	4 microns	2 microns	1 micron	0.5 micron	0.25 micron
Memory Capacity:	64K	256K	1,024K	4,096K	16,384K
Power Range:	Desktop micro-computer	Minicomputer	Mainframe Computer	Supercomputer	Ultracomputer
Applications:	Digital watches Video games Personal computers	Lap computers Engineering work stations Programmable appliances	Pocket computers, Electronic map-navigators, High-resolution TVs	Robots that can see, Freeze-frame TVs, Computers that recognize and use natural lan-guages	Star Wars Sys-tems, Personal robots Computers with human-like logic

Fact #5 *The capital costs of producing memory chips are high and increasing.*

- The cost of a production plant has climbed well over $100 million.

- In 1975, a RAM fabrication line could be set up for $5 to 10 million whereas in 1985 it was $80 million.

Microprocessors

Fact #1 *In late 1986 the U.S. had 43 percent of the $2.75-billion-a-year world market in microprocessors; Japan had 34 percent, and Western Europe 18 percent.*

Fact #2 *Six American companies dominate the latest generation, 32-bit microprocessors. Motorola, Intel, National Semiconductor, Texas Instruments, AT&T, and Zilog controlled 90 percent of the world market in 1986.*

- A $5,000 desktop machine based on Intel's 80386 32-bit microchip runs as fast as many mainframes costing $500,000.

Fact #3 *In 1985, 99 percent of all microprocessors sold were designed by U.S. companies.*

Telecommunications and Optical Technology

Size and Growth of Markets

Fact #1 *The U.S. telecommunications industry in 1986 was a $145-billion industry; the world telecoms business is worth between $300 to $350 billion.*

- America's overall trade deficit in telecommunications in 1986 was $1.9 billion.

Fact #2 *The largest single market for communication services is the U.S., $123 billion in revenues in 1986 and projected at $209 billion for 1990.*

Fact #3 *A second major market is for telephone equipment, with $57 billion in revenues in 1982 and $83 billion in 1987.*

Fact #4 *Communications and telecommunications are being transformed by optical technology which is rapidly expanding its applications:*

- The first fruits of corporate research efforts in optical technology are found in such products as fiber-optic telephone lines, laser printers, compact disc players, credit cards bearing holograms, and laser price-tag scanners in supermarkets.

- Communications companies have started to lay new transoceanic cables that can easily compete with space satellites.

- Fiber-optic links allow far-flung corporations to install networks of private video hook-ups and connect office buildings into a new kind of "optical city."

Fact #5 *Optics is still an infant commercial field, bringing in $10 billion in revenues in 1986 compared to revenues of $208 billion in electronics.*

Fact #6 *The U.S. market for fiber optics gear totaled about $800 million in 1985 and is projected to jump to $3.6 billion by 1990.*

U.S.—Japanese Competition

Fact #1 *In the telephone equipment market, the United States is the world's dominant supplier (primarily of switching and transmission equipment) as well as its most prolific user of telephone equipment. American manufacturers have 42 percent of the global market while Japanese firms have 8 to 9 percent.*

- In 1986, not a single household telephone was manufactured in the U.S.

Fact #2   *The Japanese clearly lead the world in the research, development, and manufacturing of optical technology.*

- In 1985, the U.S. spent at least $1 billion on optical research and development while Japan spent around $3 billion.

- Since a decision made in the mid-1970s by Japan's Ministry of International Trade and Industry to put money and manpower jointly into this field, teams of up to one hundred scientists and engineers have been working in optoelectronics at each of about ten major Japanese companies, emphasizing the practical implementation of the new technology.

- The U.S. may have more researchers in optoelectronics than Japan does, but for the most part they are scattered in tiny groups doing defense-related work, with only secondary fallout for civilian industry; none of the teams is as production oriented as the Japanese.

- In optoelectronics, only Bell Labs in the United States mounts an effort that matches what a single Japanese company like Hitachi is doing.

Technologies Transforming the Phone System

Fact #1   *Most technologies being employed and developed are centered on the goal of creating a worldwide, homogeneous network that runs entirely on digital equipment—the most popular design being Integrated Services Digital Network (ISDN).*

Fact #2   *Massive communication systems are also being set up by private companies such as Boeing, McDonald Douglas, and General Motors, systems that could compete with local phone companies.*

- GM's new system uses a combination of cable, micro-wave, fiber-optic, and satellite technology to move information among 500,000 terminals, half of them phone and half data terminals.

Fact #3   Phone companies in the U.S. and around the world are laying optical fiber cables as rapidly as possible; in 1986, 45,000 miles were laid in America.

- U.S. Sprint spent by the end of 1987 more than $2.5 billion on an all-optical fiber network 23,000 miles long.

- AT&T by the end of 1987 was expected to have more than 20,000 miles of fiber in place.

- MCI in mid-1986 had 3,000 miles in service with a year-end target of 5,500.

- Lightnet plans to complete by 1987 a 5,000-mile fiber optics system that will link 26 cities east of the Mississippi River.

- Consortiums of telephone companies plan to connect the U.S. and Europe with a 3,700-nautical-mile undersea fiber in 1987.

- AT&T is involved in plans to install a 7,000-plus-mile system by 1989 that will stretch from the West Coast of the U.S. to Turkey.

Biotechnology

Size and Growth of the Market

Fact #1   The market for biotechnology products has been slow to develop from the time it sprang up in the mid-1970s. The market was less than $100 million a decade later in 1984 but had increased to $400 million by 1986.

- In 1983 about 150 small and 100 large corporations were involved in genetic research or manipulation in the United States.

- Looking at fourth-quarter 1984 product sales on an annual basis, only one biotech company (Hybritech) had annual sales of more than $5 million; indeed Hybritech's $20.4 million was 61 percent of the total product revenue of all the entrepreneurial, pure biotech firms.
- In 1984, only about 5,000 people were employed in biotechnology research and development—only one worker in 20,000.

Fact #2　*Most of the small biotech firms formed in the first decade (1975–1984) have formed partnerships with large corporations to finance continued product development and to tap into global distribution networks.*

Fact #3　*Around 1985, American companies began for the first time to turn out a significant number of commercial products and the pace of introduction is quickening.*

- Genentech has a genetically engineered human growth hormone and insulin on the market.
- Cetus Corporation is turning out cancer fighting Interlukin-2 (along with at least 30 competitors in 1987).
- Chinon Corporation developed the first genetically engineered vaccine—for hepatitis B—and is leading (along with Johnson & Johnson) about ten competitors in the development of epidermal growth factor (EGF) which has a wide range of healing applications for wounds, burns, and ulcers.

Fact #4　*The next five years should see a flood of new products.*

- Cetus is preparing a number of immune system regulators.
- Genentech is working on a number of other substances, including ones that fight cancer and dissolve blood clots.
- In agriculture, a host of biotech companies, major seed producers, and such giants as DuPont, Monsanto, and

Ciba-Geigy have under development plants that produce their own fertilizer, resist harsh environments, and are more nutritious.

- Nearly sixty genetically altered plants and organisms, from herbicide-resistant corn to disease-resistant potatoes, will be ready for field tryouts over the next five years.

- In the pharmaceutical industry, more than one hundred therapeutic and diagnostic products based on biotechnology are awaiting FDA regulatory approval.

- Overall, there are 5,500 patent applications in the biotechnology field, with 850 being issued in 1985.

U.S.-Japanese Competition

Fact #1   The U.S. is the world leader in the applications of genetic engineering and in the scope of life sciences research.

- The U.S. spends about $10 billion a year on life sciences and biomedical research, more than all other nations combined.

Fact #2   The Japanese are racing to strengthen their abilities in the life sciences because they believe that biotechnology will be a springboard that will vault Japan into the twenty-first century as the world leader in technology.

- At the National Institutes of Health, the world's principal biomedical research center, 311 Japanese researchers were in residence in 1986, more than from any other country.

- From 1980 to 1983, Japanese companies concluded an astonishing 188 collaborative agreements with small U.S. genetic-engineering companies.

- More than 130 Japanese companies in a variety of industries, including chemical, food-processing, textiles, and paper, are getting involved in biotechnology.

Interpretation
of the Facts

---

1. The Future of New Technologies, New Products, and Their Markets

All the projections and arguments suggest that the world's economies will increasingly be driven by information technologies and biotechnology.

Which one will be predominant over the next ten to thirty years is a matter of intense controversy. Some argue that the markets are so vast and diverse in the information technology arena that it will obviously be predominant. Others argue just as strongly that biotechnology—because it promises to alter life itself—will be by far the most revolutionary, completely transforming entire industries.

Here, sector by sector, are the best projections on that growth and change.

Computers There is a widespread consensus that despite the computer slump of the mid-1980s, a major growth period lies ahead. The key to this optimism has been summed up by Apple Computer Chairman John Sculley: "What people have really been doing with computers up to now is to create information. We've barely scratched the surface of getting access to information."

IBM also sees major growth ahead. They expect the coming together of computers and communications to propel information processing into a $1-trillion-a-year industry sometime in the 1990s.

Since the speed of computers will increase greatly, most observers see supercomputers as a major growth field. Today, the second-generation CRAY 2 supercomputer has a speed of 1.2 billion flops, or gigaflops. To provide the brains for tomorrow's smart weapons, DARPA is driving for an astounding 1 trillion operations a second in the early 1990s—

far faster than the 10 gigaflops that Japan has targeted for 1990. In terms of sales, most projections for 1990 call for annual shipments to soar to 200 supercomputers or more, worth upward of $1.5 billion.

Supercomputers and speed may be fine, but virtually all experts agree that the truly important development lies in the "fifth generation" machines incorporating artificial intelligence. Such machines could greatly extend the reach of computers in two directions: making them far more usable by ordinary people and allowing them to solve a whole new range of problems.

The real visionaries do not stop there, but want to create a "living computer." Specifically, they are working to grow computer circuitry from living bacteria, producing microprocessors with 10 million times the memory of today's most powerful machines. In theory, such tiny supercomputers would find a virtually endless list of applications—from serving as artificial eyes, ear, and voice boxes to a desk-top device that could hold all the information ever recorded by mankind.

Semiconductors   The semiconductor market is generally expected to hit $50 to $60 billion by 1990 and by one estimate $200 billion by the year 2000. However, the stakes are many times higher because integrated circuit technology is the bedrock on which the entire electronics sector rests: Chips are the key to systems worth more than ten times their semiconductor content.

The worldwide market for memory chips is expected to more than double—from $3.7 billion in RAM sales in 1984 to $8 billion by the end of the decade. And, it is anticipated that the growth will continue beyond that. Many industry experts agree that memory capacity will replace raw speed and operating systems in the 1990s as the primary focus for development. Already, Princeton University is building a Massive Memory Machine, or M3, that will support a gigabyte of main memory—a billion characters. Trilogy Ltd. says that it will unveil in 1987 a 2-gigabyte machine.

Even more remarkable is the memory being packed into single chips. In 1985–86, the state of the art was megabit RAMS which stored more than 1 million bits of data in random-access memory. Meanwhile, in development labs chips using half-micron geometrics and holding 4 million transistors were being built. Before the end of the century, gigascale integration—a billion components to a chip—will be possible. All this has led to a new acronym, ULSI, for ultra large-scale integration. USLI will supplant VLSI, very large-scale integration, or chips with 100,000 to 1 million transistors, as the leading edge of semiconductor technology. Such submicron chips will usher in a manufacturing era in which chips make chips.

Translated into real world products, this means that in less than a decade, a single integrated circuit will pack more raw computing power than a dozen of today's $4 million supercomputers. Those circuits are expected to sell initially for just a few hundred dollars.

Biotechnology The worldwide market for biotechnology products is expected to reach $40 billion to $100 billion by the year 2000. As one indication of the spectacular growth, it is expected that the market for genetically modified seed is expected to grow from $165 million in 1990 to $12.1 billion by the year 2005. In general, the market for genetically engineered agricultural products is likely to be at least ten times that of health products, which itself will be delivering a multi-billion-dollar-a-year boost to the pharmaceutical business.

One study concluded that biotechnology will, by the year 2010, touch on industries responsible for 70 percent of the GNP. For reasons such as this, biotechnology's awesome potential for engineering economic growth is being recognized by industrial nations around the world.

Telecommunications and Optical Technology The future for telecommunications in the United States is for new technologies to transform the collection of twenty-two separate local phone systems that used to be the Bell System, plus the millions of miles of computer lines now in big buildings, into one compatible coast-to-coast network that can carry voice and data messages simultaneously over the same line.

The amazing potential of fiber optics was described in *Science*:

> The past 10 years have seen dramatic advances in how much an optical fiber can carry and how fast. The current experimental limit is 4 billion bits—about the information contained in a 30-volume *Encyclopedia Britannica*—transmitted each second over a span of 117 kilometers. With the information-capacity limit still perhaps five orders of magnitude away, it is likely this progress will continue through the coming decade. . . . If the capacities of optical fiber were fully exploited, the entire present telephone voice traffic in the United States could be carried on a single fiber. The contents of the Library of Congress could be transmitted in a few seconds (*Science*, November 1985).

The most ambitious competition is building the first optical computer, considered a practical impossibility only a few years ago. In theory, photons would race through such a machine with near-perfect efficiency, which would make an optical computer 1,000 times as fast as the most advanced of modern electronic supercomputers. AT&T took a significant step toward that faraway goal in June 1986 by producing the first optical equivalent of a transistor. The Japanese, meanwhile, are developing a hybrid microchip that combines the most efficient aspects of electronics and optics.

Superconductors   When I started to write this book, one technology was not included because it was rarely mentioned except in professional scientific journals. By mid-1987, superconductors had become the subject of lead stories in *Time*, *Newsweek*, and *U.S. News and World Report*. The hype seemed too great, as a headline in *Time* shouted about, "The startling breakthroughs that could change our world."

But then Frank Press, president of the National Academy of Sciences, said, "Superconductivity has become the test case of whether the United States has a technological future. That future depends on our ability to commercialize our scientific discoveries. If we lose this battle, it will wound our national pride."

What precisely is this revolutionary technology? Superconductors are simply conductors that offer no resistance whatever to the flow of electricity and hence waste no energy.

The potential applications are endless. Among the leading candidates mentioned are: practical electric cars; electrical lines transmitting power thousands of miles with no loss; trains traveling at hundreds of miles per hour on a cushion of magnetism; smaller, but vastly more powerful computers; safer reactors operating on nuclear fusion rather than fission. In short, everything done with electricity is open to reexamination.

John Robert Schrieffer, who shared the 1972 Nobel Prize in physics for the first successful theory of how superconductivity works, says simply that just as when transformers were first invented it was unimaginable that there would someday be large-scale integrated circuits, so superconductors' most dramatic applications also have yet to be conceived.

2. The High-Tech Competition between America and Japan

There can be no general answer as to whether America or Japan is the high-tech leader or which country will win the high tech sweepstakes. The reason is simple: high tech is too broad a category with vastly different sectors. One must look at each sector and add up the individual industry results to get some overall sense of who generally is the high-tech leader.

To provide some standard of comparison, each sector will highlight a survey by *Fortune* (October 13, 1986) which asked ten scholars, business executives, government officials, and foundation leaders in each high-tech field to rank the state of research and development in the U.S., Japan, Western Europe, and the USSR on a scale of one to ten. In each industry, the U.S. and Japan were the clear leaders, so only their scores will be reported.

Computers   The U.S. score of 9.9 was the highest score in the *Fortune* survey of any country for any high-tech industry. Japan came in second with 7.3. This led *Fortune* to the conclusion that "control of the computer market by American companies seems assured for the immediate future." This is largely due to IBM's dominant position, with 60 percent of the industry's worldwide sales as opposed to Japan's 15 percent.

Another major survey of the high tech competition between the U.S. and Japan by *The Economist* reached a similar conclusion about U.S. dominance:

> American manufacturers have established an almost impregnable position in mainframes and minicomputers—the stuff of corporate sales and accounting departments. And in the push to put a microcomputer on every desk, a handful of American firms (IBM, Compaq, Apple, Atari and Commodore) have been feeding the market a feast of cleverer, faster and (in many cases) cheaper machines that have left Japan's "IBMulators" nibbling on the leftovers of yesterday's lunch. In the personal-computer market, the IBM clone makers having the most impact come mainly from low-cost South Korea and Taiwan rather than Japan ("High Technology," *The Economist*. August 23, 1986, p. 12).

But Japan is not necessarily destined to be number two in computers. The *Fortune* report went on to note that because of the myriad strands that go into computers—particularly the #1 strand of semiconductors—"it is not easy to predict how long U.S. dominance will continue." Many scientists in the field also are wondering if the new stage emerging in computing—parallel processing—may not favor the Japanese. They point to Japanese computer component suppliers who have quietly established a significant position for themselves in the U.S., with their disk-drives, keyboards, monitors, and printers accounting for nearly 30 percent of the market's wholesale value.

Semiconductors Japan has the overall sales lead in semiconductors and certainly a commanding lead in memory chips. U.S. chipmakers still retain the lead in the design of microprocessors and in the world market for the latest generation of 32-bit microprocessors. Furthermore, as *The Economist* reported, with America's new stricter copyright laws making it difficult to imitate American designs, Japanese chip makers are being shut out of all the major markets for microprocessors. Additionally, even Japan's ablest microchip wizards despair at ever matching Silicon Valley's mix of entrepreneurial and innovative flair. "Japan is powerful in only one sub-field of a single application of semiconductors tied to a specific line of products," laments Mr. Atsushi Asada of Sharp Corporation.

Japan enters the future of semiconductors with the sizable advantage of having at least ten firms that are large enough and farsighted enough to pursue research across a broad range of technologies. They cover product development at every stage from the laboratory to the marketplace. Only two American companies—AT&T and IBM—can match this scale of effort and both make chips for internal use only. American manufacturers enter with the sizable advantage that the profitable action is now in the nonmemory segments of the market (three-fourths of the total market) and there they lead. Put simply, price alone does not drive demand. Design, marketing, distribution, and close relationships with a customer are crucial and in all these, U.S. companies have formidable advantages.

Having viewed with alarm Japan's capture of the dominant worldwide market share in 1986, U.S. semiconductor man-

ufacturers in 1987 launched Sematech, a $1.5-billion indus-
try-government program, which the manufacturers claimed
would give them the lead once again in global chipmaking
capability within five years. The goal is the development of
high-volume, low-cost manufacturing technology that will
allow the industry to compete better against Japan.

Telecommunications and Optical Technology   This is the one
high-tech arena that clearly favors Japanese companies. The
Fortune survey gave Japan a score of 9.5 as opposed to 7.8
for the U.S. The higher Japanese score reflected their progress toward combining light and electrons to make speedier
computers. The survey added that in laser research, the U.S.
was the leader.

Despite Japan's leadership in the frontier areas of telecommunications technologies, the U.S. still commands the
lion's share of the telecom market. Will Japan close the
technological gap in telecommunications with America? *The
Economist* answers this question with a "Quite possibly."
But, they added, it will only be through setting up shop in
the United States. The reason, they argue, is that Japanese
firms must pick up the one missing ingredient which is now
as essential in telecommunications as in computing: inge-
nious software.

Biotechnology   The *Fortune* survey awards the U.S. the
leadership position in this field: an 8.9 score versus Japan's
5.7. To combat the U.S. leadership position in genetic engineering and life science research, Japan *is* making a widespread and concerted effort and is likely to close the gap in
the next decade.

Two major government reports released in 1984 both
pointed out the precarious nature of U.S. leadership over
Japan. One, by the National Academy of Sciences (NAS),
pointed out how the U.S. has not invested as heavily as
Japanese companies in biotechnological engineering processes. As one example, Japanese government support of

membrane technology alone amounted to $20 million in 1983 while the National Science Foundation's budget for this important production technology was less than $1 million that year. The Congressional Office of Technology Assessment concurred with the NAS finding, concluding that "U.S. Government funding of generic applied research, especially in the areas of bioprocess engineering and applied microbiology, is currently insufficient to support rapid commercialization."

Both reports also noted the U.S. shortage of trained personnel. As stated in the NAS report: "There are not enough technologically competent biochemical engineers in the U.S. today, nor are there enough faculty to train the engineers, who will be needed by the emerging industry." The same study estimated the annual demand for graduate-level biochemical engineers over the decade as two to three times greater than the available supply.

Finally, a number of observers feel that for biotechnology to march forward in the U.S. it must overcome the many regulatory and legal fiascos that plagued it in 1985 and 1986. Referring to these, Senator David Durenberger said, "Recent events are not reassuring. The process failed completely." Both he and longtime biotech watcher Senator Albert Gore have warned that the government's apparent inability to establish and enforce a coherent regulatory system will inhibit the industry's development.

PART III

American Workers

More Females, More Choices, and More Clout

CHAPTER
★ 23 ★

A Rapidly
Changing
Workforce

The Issues

The most dramatic change in the post-World War II workplace has been the large and rapid influx of women into the labor force, which began in the 1950s and accelerated in the 1960s and 1970s. But there have also been shifts in the work patterns of others: white males, working couples, blacks, the young, the elderly, part-timers, and two-job holders. The picture that emerges is of shifting patterns and attitudes, which make for the most dynamic labor market on earth.

The principal issue, however, deals with the influx of women: Just how revolutionary was it? The opinions here range from "being the nation's most important social development" to a "revolution" that is "largely a statistical illusion."

The Facts

Men

Fact #1 In the 35-year period from 1950–1985, there was a decrease in the adult male labor-force participation rate in every year but one (1978), the rate dropping around 10 percentage points from 88 percent to 78 percent.

Fact #2 In 1983, for the first time, white males comprised less than half of the labor force.

- However, white males did hold 56 percent of full-time, year-round jobs in 1983 because many women work part-time or seasonally.

Women

Fact #1 The adult female labor force participation rate increased from 33 percent to 55 percent from 1950 to 1985. The rate increased every year except 1953 and 1962.

Fact #2 Women of all ages and races have increased their participation in the labor force greatly over this century. White women have increased their participation much more than blacks and other minorities, and women 25 to 34 much more than younger or older women.

- For all women of prime working age (20–64), the increase in labor force participation was steady but slow from 1890–1950 (2 to 4 percentage points a decade), and steady and fast from 1950 to 1986 (8 to 11 percentage points a decade).
- In the period 1890–1920, the percentage of black and other women who worked was more than double that of whites. This difference began to narrow in 1960 (when whites were still 13 percentage points lower) to the point in 1986 where the rates are virtually identical (whites 66.3 percent; black and other 66.4 percent).

Table 1

Labor Force Participation Rates of Women by Age (Percent)

Women 20–64

Year	All	White	Black and Other	All Women 20–24	All Women 25–34
1890	17.4	14.9	38.4	30.2	16.8
1900	19.3	16.5	41.0	31.7	19.4
1920	22.9	20.7	43.1	37.5	23.7
1930	25.4	23.3	44.1	41.8	27.1
1940	29.4	27.9	42.9	45.6	33.3
1950	33.3	32.2	43.2	43.6	32.0
1960	42.3	40.9	54.0	46.1	36.0
1970	50.0	49.1	57.2	57.7	45.0
1980	60.8	60.5	62.8	68.9	65.5
1986	66.4	66.3	66.4	72.4	71.6

Source: There is some controversy over the Census counts of women workers in the 1890–1940 time period. Data here for 1890–1950 are from Bureau of the Census monograph, Gertrude Bancroft, *The American Labor Force*, New York, Wiley, 1958. Data for 1960–1986 are from Department of Labor, Bureau of Labor Statistics.

- From 1890 to 1970, the participation rate of women aged 20–24 was 10 to 15 percentage points greater than for women aged 25–34; by 1986, the difference had all but disappeared (72.4 percent versus 71.6 percent).

Fact #3   While the overall participation rate for women increased by 14 percentage points from 1970–1986, the rate for women with children under 18 years increased by 22 percentage points, to 61.4 percent (according to the Department of Labor).

- Women who maintain families alone participate in the labor force much more than wives with husbands present, with the exception of those with children under three years.

- For wives with husbands present, the overall rate of 61.4 percent covers a range from 49.8 percent for those with children 1 year and under to 68.5 percent for those with children 6–17 years.

- In 1946, 10 percent of mothers with children under 6 worked; in 1986, around 55 percent worked.

- The percentage of mothers returning to work in the first year after childbirth went from 31 percent in 1976 to 48 percent in 1985 (61 percent for college grads).

- Single mothers is one of the only female subgroups to have a decline in the participation rate, from 37 percent in 1969 to 35 percent in 1985.

Fact #4   The 62 percent labor force participation rate for mothers with children under 18 includes a great number of mothers who work part-time; only 29 percent of married mothers work full-time year-round.

Fact #5   Just over half of all working women do not work in full-time, year-round jobs.

- In the 1970–1986 period, approximately one-third of all women who worked in a year worked part-time.

Fact #6   Females have made significant strides in professional positions but still lag far behind men. Numerous occupations that remain heavily dominated by women are generally poor paying.

- More women were employed in professional categories than men in February 1986: 6,938,000 to 6,909,000.

- Women's share of professional jobs increased from 44 to 49 percent from 1972 to 1985.

- In 1987, women made up about one-fourth of all professionals in the Wall Street financial community.

Table 2

Working Mothers, Full-Time
and Part-Time

		With children 0–17	With children under 6
All mothers	Total Number	32,837,000	15,694,000
	Full time	13,527,000 (41%)	5,229,000 (33%)
	Part time	5,395,000 (16%)	2,373,000 (15%)
Married, spouse present	Total Number	25,003,000	12,217,000
	Full Time	9,834,000 (39%)	4,054,000 (33%)
	Part time	4,546,000 (18%)	2,018,000 (17%)
Divorced	Total Number	3,294,000	890,000
	Full time	2,087,000 (63%)	449,000 (50%)
	Part time	353,000 (11%)	123,000 (14%)
Never married	Total Number	2,269,000	1,604,000
	Full time	660,000 (29%)	373,000 (23%)
	Part time	200,000 (8%)	125,000 (8%)
Mothers with children on welfare	Total Number	NA	
	Full time	NA (12%)	NA
	Part time	NA (8%)	NA

Source: Douglas J. Besharov and Michelle M. Delly, "How Much Are Working Mothers Working?" *Public Opinion*, November–December 1986, p. 50.

Table 3

Women in Professional Positions, 1979–1986
(women as percent of all workers)

Profession	1979	1986
Electrical/Electronic Engineers	4%	9%
Industrial Engineers	9	16
Lawyers	10	15
Physicians	11	17
Pharmacists	17	26
Computer Systems Analysts/Scientists	20	30
Computer Programmers	28	40
Accountants/Auditors	34	45

Source: Census Bureau

- Female accountants at Arthur Andersen & Co. went from zero in 1965 to forty-four in 1987 and 35 percent of all recruits are female.

- Women in 1985 made up 97 percent of the 4.9 million secretaries, stenographers, and typists.

- Women made up 79 percent of the 16.9 million clericals; these 13.5 million clericals constitute one-third of all working women.

Fact #7   Females have made significant strides but still lag far behind men in achieving top management positions.

- From 1972 to 1985, women's share of management jobs nearly doubled—from 20 to 36 percent.

- In 1975, one of every eight MBA grads was a woman; in 1985, it was one of three.

- Women drop off the management track more quickly than men; three surveys of different MBA grads showed these dropout percentages after about 10 years: (1) women 30 percent, men 21 percent; (2) women 34 percent, men 19 percent; (3) women 21 percent, men 19 percent.

- At *Fortune* 500 industrial and service companies, women account for only 2 percent of senior executives; more positively in 1986, 83 percent of female officers held the title of vice-president or better while only 35 percent did in 1980.

- From 1977 to 1987, the number of women in commercial bank management jobs rose 68 percent.

Fact #8   Women are increasingly starting their own business. They account for the vast majority of small businesses started in recent years.

- The number of self-employed women increased from 2.1 million in 1980 to 2.6 million in 1985.

- Almost six times as many women as men are starting businesses.

Table 4

Women Owners

Type of Business Owned	Number of Women Owners
Personal services*	419,113
Real estate agencies	225,551
Health services	128,389
Eating and drinking places	66,811
Special trade contractors**	47,219
Food stores	37,635
Apparel and accessory stores	29,132
Wholesale trade, nondurable goods	22,231
Auto dealers and service stations	14,353
Wholesale trade, durable goods	12,021

Source: U.S. Census Bureau data reported in "Women Own One-Fourth of Nation's Firms," *The Washington Post*, August 7, 1986.

* Laundries, beauty shops, photographers, and baby-sitting services.

** Plumbers, heating and masonry contractors, roofers, etc.

- Women in 1983 owned 3.25 million businesses, just over one-fourth of the nation's small businesses.
- About half these small businesses had gross receipts of less than $5,000 and only 0.3 percent had brought in $1 million or more.

Fact #9   A 1979 study found that women in their prime earning years were eleven times more likely to leave the work force voluntarily—if only temporarily—than men were.

Working Couples

Fact #1   The breadwinner husband-homemaker wife household constitutes less than 10 percent of all households.

Fact #2   In 1986, 46 percent of married couples had both spouses working, up from 39 percent in 1982.

Fact #3   Married women have increased their labor force participation dramatically in the past three decades, but the vast majority seek part-time or seasonal work.

- In 1984, only 29 percent of married women held full-time year-round jobs.

- Married women aged 25–44 increased their labor force participation from 26 percent in 1950 to 67 percent in the mid-1980s.

- Married women aged 25–34 increased their labor force participation from 28 percent in 1960 to 65 percent in 1985.

Fact #4   The biggest increase in employment since 1970 has come from mothers in two-parent homes who have young children.

- The participation of married women with children under 6 in the labor force rose from 28 percent in 1969 to 48 percent in 1985.

Fact #5   The news is mixed regarding the incomes of working wives vis-à-vis their husbands' income.

- From 1960 to 1980, the incomes of working wives actually fell in relation to the incomes of working husbands from 40 percent to 38 percent.

- In 1983 4.8 million women earned more than their husbands, almost a fifth of the total 26.1 million married couples where both partners had earnings.

Blacks

Fact #1   Since 1972, the labor force participation rate of blacks has increased by three percentage points and has been one-half to three percentage points lower than the rate for whites.

Fact #2   Blacks' participation in the labor force differs radically from that of whites among major subgroups of teenage and adult males and teenage and adult females.

- Black adult males participation rates run 4 to 5 percentage points lower than those for white adult males.
- Black adult females participation rates run 5 to 9 percentage points higher than those for white adult females.
- Black teenage males participation rates run 14 to 19 percentage points lower than those for white teenage males.
- Black teenage girls participation rates run 16 to 21 percentage points lower than those for white teenage girls.

Fact #3   Since 1959, there has been a growing tendency for black men to drop out of the work force entirely.

- In 1959, the same percentage of black and white men participated in the labor force but by 1984 only 71 percent of black males were either employed or seeking work, compared with 77 percent of whites.
- The projection is that workforce participation by young black men (ages 16–24) will fall from 62 percent in 1986 to 53 percent in 1995, far below the 77 percent for young white men.

Fact #4   Black women have had a much better labor force experience than black men.

- In 1984, black and white female employment percentages were nearly the same (47 percent vs. 50 percent) and employed black women's income was 90 percent of that enjoyed by white women.
- By contrast, only 59 percent of black men had jobs compared with 72 percent of whites and their median income was 32 percent less than that of whites.

The Young

Fact #1 *Teenage participation in the labor force has varied widely: down 7 percentage points from 1950 to 1964; up 13.4 percentage points from 1964 to 1979; down 3.5 percentage points from 1979 to 1985; in December 1985 (at 54.5 percent), it was only 1.5 percentage points higher than in 1948.*

Fact #2 *In recent years (1972–1986), teenage males, both black and white, have decreased their participation in the work force while teenage females, both black and white, have increased their participation substantially to a point where it is just below that of males.*

Table 5

Teenage Labor Force Participation Rates,
By Sex and Race: 1972–1986

	Males		Females	
Year	White	Black	White	Black
1972	60.1	46.3	48.1	32.2
1973	62.2	45.7	50.1	34.2
1974	62.9	46.7	52.7	33.4
1975	61.9	42.6	51.2	34.2
1976	62.3	41.3	52.8	32.9
1977	64.0	43.2	54.5	32.9
1978	65.0	44.9	56.7	37.3
1979	64.8	43.6	57.4	36.8
1980	63.7	43.2	56.2	34.9
1981	62.4	41.6	55.4	34.0
1982	60.0	39.8	55.0	33.5
1983	59.4	39.9	54.5	33.0
1984	59.0	41.7	55.4	35.0
1985	59.7	44.6	55.2	37.9
1986	59.3	43.7	56.3	39.1

Fact #3 Half of the U.S. work force is now under 35, up from just over one-third at the end of the 1950s.

Fact #4 Among young workers, almost two out of five have at least some college training, double the proportion among their parents.

Fact #5 From 1970 to 1986, the proportion of college graduates employed in professional, technical, and managerial positions declined because the number of professional jobs did not keep pace with the number of diplomas; the result is that one out of five college graduates took a job that ordinarily did not require a degree.

The Elderly

Fact #1 There has been a distinct trend toward earlier retirement among men throughout this century.

- In 1900, 63 percent of men over 65 were in the work force, by 1948, it was 47 percent, and by 1985, it had shrunk to 16 percent.
- Participation in the work force of men aged 55–64 dropped from 90 percent in 1948 to 68 percent in 1985.

Fact #2 The trend for older women is distinctly different from that of men, with women ages 50–59 and 60–64 all increasing their participation rates significantly since 1950 and those ages 65–69 decreasing their participation only slightly.

Fact #3 Almost half of those 65 and older who work are working part-time.

Fact #4 The significant increases in pensions—both in number and amounts, public and private—have been a major factor leading to early retirement.

- In 1981, Social Security retirement benefits became available to men age 62 and over.

- The number of employees in private pension plans that specified age 65 for receipt of full benefits dropped from 45 percent in 1980 to 33 percent in 1985.

- From 1973 to 1983, the number of individuals age 50 and over receiving pensions grew by more than 70 percent while among those 50–64, the percentage nearly doubled.

- In 1984, the majority of early pension recipients were not in the workforce and retired individuals 55 and older with pensions tended to work at less than half the rate of those without pensions.

Part-Time Workers

Fact #1   The number of part-time workers grew steadily each year from 1971 to 1981, peaking at 26 million (26.5 percent of all workers); in 1986, there were 25.5 million (23 percent of total workers).

Fact #2   From 1979 to 1986, the number of voluntary part-timers barely increased while the number of largely involuntary part-timers increased by 2.1 million (60 percent); thus, involuntary part-timers accounted for nearly one-fourth of all jobs generated in that period and nearly one-fourth of all part-timers in 1986.

Fact #3   In the retail industry, part-timers accounted for 40 percent of the job growth from 1974 to 1986 and made up more than one-third of all retail employees in 1986.

Fact #4   A 1980 poll by Louis Harris found that working women (unlike the working men surveyed) expressed a preference for part-time over full-time work by a 41 to 17 percent margin.

- The women with the highest earnings capacity—managerial, professional, and executive women—preferred part-time work by a 51 to 19 percent margin.

Fact #5   *Some 70 percent of part-timers have no employer-provided retirement plan and 42 percent have no health insurance coverage.*

Fact #6   *Since the early 1970s, part-time work has risen by about 50 percent in West Germany and Sweden, to 12 percent and 25 percent, respectively, of all jobs.*

Two-Job Workers

Fact #1   *In late 1986, nearly 6 million Americans held two jobs, with the greatest growth among women.*

Fact #2   *In May 1985, 5.4 percent of all employed workers held more than one job—up from 4.9 percent in 1980 and the highest level in more than 20 years.*

- The number of moonlighting women jumped 40 percent between 1980 and 1985, to 2.2 million, three times as many as those holding multiple jobs in 1970.

The Education of Workers

Fact #1   *American workers are among the most highly educated in the world in terms of the percentage of high school graduates and the number enrolling in college.*

- More than three-fourths of workers are high school graduates, up sharply from only half in the early 1960s.
- Almost 40 percent have had at least one year of college.
- A greater percentage of young people are enrolled in higher education in the U.S. than in any other nation.

Fact #2   *Up through high school graduation, Japan clearly provides a more intensive educational effort and their students often score higher in a variety of tests.*

- While 98 percent of Japanese youngsters graduate from high school, only 72 percent of American youngsters do, and the American rate has been falling for a decade.
- Japanese children attend school 240 days per year, compared to 180 days for American children.
- When Japanese teenagers finish twelfth grade, they have the equivalent of three to four more years of school than U.S. high school graduates.

Fact #3   Illiteracy is rampant in the U.S. with the latest government survey (1986) indicating that 17 to 21 million adults— 13 percent of adults—(over age 20) cannot read.

- The majority of illiterates are under age 50 and many have attended high school.
- The illiteracy rate for blacks is 22 percent.
- While 2 million illiterates are helped each year, 2 million more appear each year, about evenly divided between refugees, immigrants, high school dropouts, and sometimes graduates.
- Critics of the study are divided between those who say it overstates the problem and those who say it understates it.

Fact #4   The rates of illiteracy and functional illiteracy for certain groups of the population are shockingly high.

- In some parts of the nation illiteracy afflicts 30 percent of all adults and 46 percent of unemployed adults.
- A 1982 Labor Department study found even higher rates: as many as half and perhaps 75 percent of the unemployed are functionally illiterate.

Fact #5   Many young people now entering the workforce are seriously deficient in basic educational skills.

- The National Center for Education Statistics reports that for 17-year-olds in America in 1985: (1) 14 percent are functionally illiterate: (2) nearly 40 percent cannot draw inferences from written material; (3) 80 percent are unable to write an adequate essay, and almost 55 percent do not understand basic scientific concepts such as gravity.

- The Center projects that if such trends continue, between 900,000 and 2 million of those graduating from high school in 1990 will lack the basic skills necessary for even menial jobs.

Fact #6   The federal government spent $352 million in 1985 and 1986 to educate hard core adult illiterates—about $17 a person.

Interpretation of the Facts

1. Women's Rise in the Labor Force

Among those who maintain that the influx of women into the labor force over the past three decades has constituted a revolutionary change are the major business magazines. George Gilder, author of *Wealth and Poverty*, represents those who see it merely as a statistical illusion.

Has Women's Rise in the Labor Force Been a Revolutionary Change?

Yes	*No*
Business Week and *Fortune*	George Gilder
The Great American job machine is fast becoming the eighth wonder of the world. While employment has declined in most industrial coun-	Every year seems to bring new evidence of radical change in the masculine and feminine role around which most Americans have oriented their lives and

tries, the U.S. is creating jobs at breakneck speed—20 million in the past 10 years. Many experts seem baffled by this phenomenon, but the reason is simple—women.

Women are flooding into the job market, boosting economic growth, and helping to reshape the economy dramatically. Women have seized two-thirds of the jobs created in the past decade. And they had been the linchpin in the shift toward services and away from manufacturing.

Because a rapidly expanding labor force is a principal element in propelling an economy into a fast-growth track, the influx of women into the job market may be the major reason that the U.S. has emerged so much healthier than other countries from the economic shocks of the 1970s (*Business Week*, January 28, 1985, p. 80).

* * * *

When the history of the last quarter of the 20th century in the U.S. is written, scholars may well conclude that the nation's most important social development has been the rise to positions of power and influence of its most vigorous majority: American women. So many women have come flocking into the labor force—

expectations. Yet this "revolution"—for all its numerical weight and anecdotal pervasiveness—is largely a statistical illusion.

Many of the statistics that have been cited in the statistics of the sexual revolution are reflections of the Industrial Revolution. The entrance of women into the work force has accompanied, at a slower pace, their departure from farms. As recently as eighty years ago 36 percent of American families were engaged in agriculture; today fewer than three percent are. This shift is truly a revolution, and it has transformed the official labor statistics for women. Although these statistics show women entering the work force in record numbers, the fact is that women have always worked. Their labor on farms, however—in an array of arduous jobs beyond the hearth and cribside—was never monitored by statisticians.

Current data from the Bureau of Labor Statistics indicate that women work only 70 percent as long for a given employer as men do. According to a study of census data done for the Civil Rights Commission by Solomon Polachek in 1984, the differences in the number of years of continuous service in the work force—and fully 70% of all American women aged 25 to 54 are today at work for pay or actively seeking jobs—that more Americans are now employed than ever before. This is no less than a revolutionary change, one that has created profound shifts not only in the family and the workplace but also in basic U.S. economic policymaking.

The surge of Americans at work—due primarily to the entry of women—has led even liberal economists to conclude that full employment is no longer a 4% rate of unemployment but is now perhaps a 6% rate. Consequently, whether Democrats or Republicans control Congress and the White House in the future, economic enemy No. 1 will not be unemployment (which, after all, affects only a fraction of the population) but inflation (which affects all). So long as the priority problem is inflation, the nation can expect continued pressures to hold down government spending.

Also, because so many women hold paying jobs, future recessions stand to be milder and briefer than they otherwise would have been. If one spouse in a household should lose his or her job, there is a better than 50% chance that the other spouse will con-

resulting differences in training and experience—explain "close to 100 percent of the wage gap" between men and women in the job market.

Although polls show an increasing desire for jobs on the part of women, in a 1986 Roper survey only 10 percent of women declared that a husband should turn down a very good job in another city "so the wife can continue her job." This percentage has not increased since 1980 and offers a reason, beyond maternity, why women leave their jobs so often: they still rate their own employment as less important than their husband's.

The most recent data on occupational trends, released by the Bureau of Labor Statistics for 1985, show little sign that sex roles in the work force are disappearing. The percentage of women in such blue-collar jobs as plumbing, electrical work, and carpentry has scarcely changed. Federal contractors and private firms, including Sears, Roebuck and Co., that have attempted to hire women for jobs traditionally held by men have consistently failed to meet their own goals, for lack of applicants. Yet the government may not be discriminating against women, and private companies may not be

tinue to bring home full-time earnings.

Most important, the rise of executive women promises to give the U.S. a significant edge over its global rivals in the increasingly acute international economic competition of the late 1980s and the 1990s. Whatever America's shortcomings may be, it is ahead of its allies and competitors in at last beginning to admit women to positions of real power and decision making. This should greatly expand the nation's pool of talent and merit, the group from which it chooses its business, political, and academic leaders. With a larger group to choose from, the nation seems destined to select better leaders (*Fortune*, August 18, 1986, p. 16, © 1986 Time Inc. All rights reserved).

either. Let us at least consider the possibility that many women, deliberately rejecting the values of male careerists, are discriminating against the job "rat race" and in favor of their families (G. Gilder, "Women in the Work Force," *The Atlantic*, September 1986, pp. 22–23).

2. A Calmer Future

The labor force will continue to change over the next decade but nowhere near so dramatically as in the past twenty years. Women are expected to increase their participation rate, but only by a few additional percentage points. The decline in the male participation rate is expected to slow, possibly halt, and may even reverse.

The tremendous growth in "contingent workers"—those who work at home, for outside contractors, or involuntarily work part-time, which grew from 8 million to over 18 million from 1980 to 1986, will slow down considerably. There will be many fewer entrants into the labor force and hence it will be a considerably older labor force. The excitement, for now, is over.

This is not to say that challenges do not remain—challenges such as raising the participation rate of black males, improving the education of our youth, and attacking adult illiteracy. These are certainly big challenges to the nation, but they are likely to prove as intractable as they have in the past. This is why the future of the U.S. labor force, relative to the past twenty years, should be "considerably more calm."

CHAPTER
★ 24 ★

Future
Jobs

The Issues

The issue of future jobs involves both the number of jobs and the type of jobs that will be available. The questions are: Will the U.S. economy generate enough jobs to keep unemployment reasonably low and what will the major types of jobs be?

According to projections by the Bureau of Labor Statistics, there will be a sufficient number of new jobs generated. The annual number will not be anywhere near as large as in the 1970s and first half of the 1980s, but the number of new entrants into the labor force will not be as large either.

The vast majority of new jobs will be in service industries. The top six employment categories in terms of number of new jobs generated by the year 2000 are all services. If one is interested in the occupations that will have the fastest *growth* rate, then one must look to high technology, principally computers and electronics.

Even a quick perusal of future job prospects suggests that job retraining is going to become increasingly important. Indeed, it has been estimated that 75 percent of all current workers will need to be retrained by 2000.

The Facts

Current Jobs

Fact #1   In 1985, more than three out of four workers were in "the big four" employment sectors: services, 21.9 million; manufacturing, 19.4 million; retail trade, 17.4 million; and government, 16.3 million.

Fact #2   In the 1980s, two of the "big four" employment sectors—services and retail trade—experienced sizable growth (22 percent and 16 percent respectively) while the other two —manufacturing and government—experienced virtually no growth or even decline (minus 4 percent and 1 percent respectively).

Future Jobs: Official Government Projections

Fact #1   The Bureau of Labor Statistics (BLS) projects that the American economy will create 20,112,000 jobs (nonfarm wage and salary) in the 1986–2000 period. Amazingly, all will come from service-producing industries as goods-producing industries are projected to lose 3,000 jobs by 2000. Nine out of ten new jobs will be filled by women and minorities.

Fact #2   Most of the new jobs fall into low paying, low-level jobs, with three of the top four being retail sales, waiter/wait-

Table 1
Projected Changes in Employment (1986–2000)

Most New Jobs	Number of New Jobs	Percent Change
Retail Sales	1,200,000	33%
Waiter/Waitress	752,000	44
Nursing	612,000	44
Janitor	604,000	23
General Manager	582,000	24
Cashier	575,000	26
Truck Driver	525,000	24
Office Clerk	462,000	20
Food Counter Worker	449,000	30
Nursing Aide	433,000	35

Fastest Growing	Number of New Jobs	Percent Change
Paralegal	64,000	104%
Medical Assistant	119,000	90
Physical Therapist	53,000	87
Physical Therapy Aide	29,000	82
Data Processing Equipment Repair	56,000	81
Home Health Aide	111,000	80
Systems Analyst	251,000	76
Medical Records Technician	30,000	75
Employment Interviewer	54,000	71
Computer Programmer	335,000	70

Most Rapidly Declining	Number of Lost Jobs	Percent Change
Electrical and Electronic Assemblers	−116,000	−54%
Electronic Semiconductor Processors	−14,000	−51
Railroad Conductors and Yardmasters	−17,000	−41
Railroad Brake, Signal, and Switch Operators	−25,000	−40
Gas and Petroleum Plant and System Occupations	−20,000	−34
Industrial Truck and Tractor Operators	−283,000	−34
Shoe Sewing Machine Operators and Tenders	−18,000	−32
Station Installers and Repairers, Telephone	−40,000	−32
Chemical Equipment Controllers, Operators and Tenders	−52,000	−30
Chemical Plant and System Operators	−23,000	−30

Source: Bureau of Labor Statistics, U.S. Department of Labor

ress, and janitor; the fastest growing job categories are all services-high tech while the most rapidly declining are mostly in manufacturing.

Fact #3   *From 1986 to 1995, the percentage of entry-level jobs will remain about the same at 20 percent but the pool of 16-to-24-year-old workers who typically take those jobs will shrink from the current 21 percent of the labor force to only 15 percent.*

Training and Retraining

Fact #1   *It is expected that large numbers of workers will need retraining. The National Commission on Employment Policy estimates that through 1990, 400,000 workers a year may need extensive retraining to find new jobs, and the American Society for Training and Development states that by the year 2000, 75 percent of all workers currently employed will need retraining.*

Fact #2   *Retraining reaches only a relatively small number of workers and an even smaller number use their new skills.*

- From 1977 to 1984, 1 to 2 million workers received basic trade readjustment benefits, only 70,000 began retraining, 28,000 completed their courses, and fewer than 4,500 found jobs that used their new skills.

Fact #3   *Training and retraining costs about $210 billion per year at present.*

- A 1985 study showed that 60 percent of employers had begun new training programs within the previous two years.

- Some companies retrain workers for jobs outside the company if none is available inside. Ford runs a joint training program with the United Auto Workers and retrained some 1,700 displaced Ford workers for other jobs between 1982 and 1986.

Fact #4   The Japanese currently spend about $1,000 more per U.S. worker for training and recruitment than do comparable U.S. companies.

Interpretation
of the Facts

---

1. The Job Outlook for the Future

The former U.S. Secretary of Labor, William Brock, is among the chief proponents of the argument that the future for jobs looks bright. Among those who do not see as bright a future are the members of the Industrial Union Department of the AFL-CIO.

The Future of Jobs

A Bright Future
William Brock

A Bleak Future
Industrial Union
Department

It [the service economy] implies a whole different range of skills that are going to be necessary to hold jobs. The skill base that we've developed in the last 200 years related to agricultural skills or manual skills, craft type skills that came from vocational or apprenticeship type of programs; and skills that are going to be required in the next, basically thinking, reasoning, communicating skills

An important dimension of America's declining living standards and the rise in inequality is the pressures on today's young families and workforce. Their situation is not optimistic. They are earning less than what the previous generation did and are facing higher costs. Many young families will not be able to achieve the income levels that their parents had attained. . . .

that are in a whole different order than those we have thought about and worried about, certainly in the early part of this century, implies a need for much more effective educatonal system, much more emphasis on flexible training that allows people to adapt to technologies as they constantly change around them in the work place.

It implies that the jobs of the next 15 years are going to be much more interesting; cleaner, safer, healthier, more productive and I think, more rewarding jobs. And it's a very nice prospect for those people who are given the opportunity to develop their talents in a fashion that would meet that job requirement. . . .

The work place of the year 2000 is going to be sufficiently diverse that there will be employment for everyone that wants it and has developed their talents to the degree they can. People talk about the informatics age as if everybody is going to be punching into a computer. Services implies a lot more than that, it implies much more personalized skills, much more individualized skills. . . .

From the positive side, the job creation capability of this country is so awesome that we

Perhaps equally as bleak is the fact that it may no longer be possible for young adults to improve their income levels, as did their parents. For instance, the "typical" 30-year-old male in 1949 was able to increase his earning by 63 percent by the time he was 40. Similarly, a male turning 30 in 1959 was able to increase his earning by nearly half by 1969. However, a 30-year-old male in 1973 was not able to raise his standard of living at all by age 40. Will today's young adults, who are earning 1959 levels as it is, be able to achieve greater income in the future? Given the continuous erosion of real wages over the last decade, it appears they cannot expect much wage or salary improvement. . . .

Falling wages and the loss of good jobs are hitting young workers, even more than others. The overall decline in pay levels and good jobs is forcing young workers to start lower and at the same time is removing the rungs on the ladder of upward mobility. . . .

The American Dream is fading, becoming more of a dream than it ever was. (Source: *The Polarization of America*, Washington D.C.: Industrial Union Department of AFL-CIO, 1986, pp. 84–86.)

have in the next seven or eight years a chance to deal with societal problems such as youth unemployment, minority unemployment, that we have failed to deal with in the last 50 years. The job demand is going to be enormous. The demand for people with skills is going to be huge. (Interview with William Brock, "Altering the Face of Work," *Washington Post*, November 30, 1986, pp. 111, 116).

CHAPTER
★ 25 ★

Wages of
American Workers

The Issues

Perhaps the number one wage question is whether the average American worker is better off today than five, ten, or fifteen years ago. A related question concerns the future of real wages (those adjusted for inflation). Specific questions also deal with the relative progress made by women and minorities in the workforce.

The ultimate issue, however, concerns whether there is a general shift in U.S. employment away from well-paying (manufacturing sector) jobs to low-paying (service sector) positions. There is enormous controversy about what changes are taking place and what their effects will be. The result of this shift will determine the place this and future generations of American workers have in the world labor force.

The Facts

General Wage Trends

Fact #1   *Average weekly earnings (measured in 1977 dollars) were $169 in mid-1987, lower than they were in 1962 ($172).*

Fact #2   *Real weekly wages generally rose from 1950 to 1972 ($139 to $198) and have been generally falling since then; they have declined in 8 of the 14 years from 1973 to 1986 to a 1986 level ($171) that is 13.8 percent less than in 1972.*

- Real hourly income also fell, from $5.22 an hour in 1972 to $4.82 an hour in 1986.

- In the 1950s and 1960s, there was only one year (1958) when average real weekly earnings declined; in the 1970s and first half of the 1980s, there were nine years of decline.

- In the 1980s, there has been only one year (1983) when real weekly earnings rose more than one percent.

Fact #3   *There has been a thirty-five-year decline in the rate of real weekly earnings growth.*

Fact #4   *Prior to 1973, young men going from 25 to 35 saw their real earnings grow by 120%, whereas the 25-year-old in 1973 saw real earnings over the next 10 years increase by only 16%. Similarly, a man passing from 40 to 50 experienced a 25% to 30% increase before 1973, and a 14% decrease beginning in 1973.*

Fact #5   *The decline in worker's pay, which began in 1973, has accelerated in the 1980s.*

Fact #6   *In the first four years of the recovery (1983–86), 3 of the 6 groups generating the most new jobs paid above the median weekly earnings of all full-time wage and salary workers ($358).*

Figure 1

The Long-Run Decline in
Real Weekly Earnings Growth
(Change in real average weekly earnings)

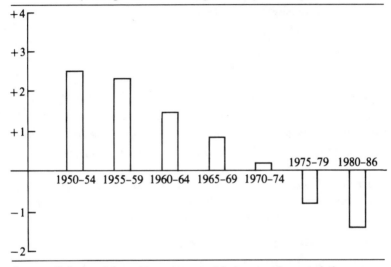

Source: Calculated from Department of Labor earnings statistics

Table 1

Change in Real Average Weekly
and Hourly Earnings (1973–1985)

Pay	1973–1979	1979–1985	1973–1985
Average Weekly Earnings	−7.4%	−7.6%	−14.4%
Average Hourly Earnings	−4.3%	−6.0%	−10.1%

Source: BLS data inflated to 1985 dollars using the CPI.

- The six groups, with percentage of new jobs generated and median weekly earnings, were:
  —executive, administrative, and management, over 20%, $511/week
  —sales, 20%, $351
  —professional, 17%, $500
  —administrative support, 12%, $300
  —service, 11%, $209
  —construction trade, 10%, $401

Fact #7   The private sector jobs lost in the 1979–1985 period were in industries with average pay of $444 per week (36 percent above average) while jobs gained were in industries with average pay of $272 (16 percent below average).

Fact #8   Young men in the 20–24 age group saw their annual real earnings—measured in 1984 dollars—plummet 30 percent from $11,572 to $8,072 over the 1973–1984 period.

- For black men, the drop was 50 percent.
- Educational level was a strong determining factor as the drop in average real earnings was 42 percent for young men without a high school diploma, 30 percent for high school graduates, and only 11 percent for college graduates.
- Overall, real earnings for young women fell just 2 percent between 1973 and 1984.

Fact #9   Nearly half of the new jobs created from 1978 to 1984 paid poverty level wages, resulting in one in four household heads earning poverty-level wages in 1984.

- The trends of poverty level wages for men and women household heads have differed greatly: women were making steady progress from 1967 to 1979 (53 percent to 42 percent) and then had a reversal from 1979 to 1984 while men had been getting steadily worse throughout, with a sharp increase from 1979 to 1984 (20 percent to 26 percent).

- From 1963 to 1978, about 23 percent of all new jobs paid poverty or near poverty level wages, while from 1978 to 1984 the percentage more than doubled to nearly half of all new jobs.

- Of all jobs created between 1979 and 1985, two-fifths paid less than $7,400 a year (in 1986 dollars) compared with one-fifth in the 1968–1978 period.

- In 1986, 5.1 million people worked at or below the minimum wage of $3.35 an hour and an additional 8.4 million earned $3.35 to $4.35; thus 13.5 million people, or a quarter of all hourly workers, made less than $9,000 a year even if they worked full-time, year-round.

Fact #10   *Poverty zone wages (weekly earnings less than 30 percent over the poverty line) were paid in two major sectors—retail trade and health and business services—which in 1986 constituted 49 percent of total private-sector employment and 41 percent of the entire labor force.*

Fact #11   *The median weekly earnings of part-time workers in the fall of 1987 was $105 compared with $371 for full-time workers.*

- Twenty-eight percent of part-time workers earn the minimum wage.

Fact #12   *Many workers are getting bonuses or rewards rather than wage increases.*

- A 1987 study by the American Productivity Center found that 75 percent of firms use bonuses or rewards, the most popular being profit sharing (used by 32 percent) and lump-sum bonuses (used by 30 percent).

Fact #13   *A majority of workers who lost full-time jobs between 1981 and 1985 and were then reemployed experienced a gain in wages.*

- 56 percent of workers who had returned to full-time wage and salary employment were making as much or more than before displacement; more than half of this group were earning 20 percent or more above pay in their previous job.

Manufacturing vs. Services

Fact #1 *Manufacturing wages have generally been about 30 percent higher than service sector wages over the past 10 to 15 years; in mid-1986, the difference was down to 22 percent, with the average hourly pay for manufacturing workers being $9.75 while the average for private service sectors employees was $8.04.*

- Because of a shorter workweek in services, weekly wages in manufacturing are 50 percent higher than in services: $396.01 vs. $265.20 in 1986.

Fact #2 *Real wage growth in manufacturing has been generally declining since 1950 and fell below that of service's real wage growth in the 1980–1985 period.*

Fact #3 *In 1986, the United States slipped from first to third in total manufacturing compensation costs (wages plus fringe benefits); its $13.29 was behind Switzerland's $14.01 and West Germany's $13.85.*

- Japan's hourly compensation costs, even after rising dramatically in 1986, were still only 58 percent of the U.S. level ($7.76).

- Korea, a leading example of a major developing nation competitor in manufacturing, had a level of only $1.53.

Major Industries and Occupations

Fact #1 *Among the major industrial sectors, there is and always has been a vast disparity in wages, from a low in weekly*

Table 2

Average Weekly Earnings in
Major Industries: 1960–1986

Industry	1965	1970	1980	1986	1965–1986 (percent increase)
Goods Producing:					
Mining	$123.52	164.40	397.06	524.97	325
Construction	138.38	195.45	367.78	466.38	237
Manufacturing	107.53	133.33	288.62	396.01	268
Service Producing:					
Transportation and Public Utilities	125.14	155.93	351.25	458.64	267
Wholesale Trade	106.49	137.26	267.96	359.04	237
Retail Trade	66.61	82.47	147.38	176.08	164
Finance, Insurance, and Real Estate	88.91	112.67	209.60	303.94	242
Services	73.60	96.66	190.71	265.20	260

Source: Dept. of Labor, Bureau of Labor Statistics

earnings in 1986 of $176.08 in retail trade to a high of $524.97 in mining.

Fact #2   There is a vast disparity in hourly wages among major American industries, with the wage level in five industries (three in manufacturing) less than half the wage level in basic steel, the industry leader.

Fact #3   Around three-quarters of the 14 million jobs generated in the service sector in the 1979–1986 period were in the two lowest paying categories—retail trade and health and business services; these two areas accounted for 42 percent of all jobs in September 1987.

Fact #4   Among industries, there have been definite winners and losers since 1970 in real wage growth.

Table 3

Hourly Wages for Selected Industries
(July 1986)
Production and Nonsupervisory Workers

Basic steel	$14.08
Railroads	13.82
Motor vehicles, equipment	13.40
Telephone communications	12.80
All construction	12.31
Trucking and terminals	10.79
Machinery	10.57
Stone, clay, glass	10.06
Bakery products	9.91
All manufacturing	9.74
Electrical, electronic equipment	9.68
Hospitals	9.41
All services	8.04
Auto repair	7.51
Banking	7.15
Textile mill products	6.90
Department stores	6.61
Hotels, other lodging	5.81
Apparel, other textiles	5.76
Footwear, except rubber	5.59

Source: Dept. of Labor, Bureau of Labor Statistics.

- Leading winners are hospitals, electrical and electronic equipment, and telephone.
- Leading losers are apparel, construction, trucking, and basic steel.

Fact #5   In the two major sectors of the economy—manufacturing and retail trade—there is a sizable wage gap which has been growing since 1962; the average weekly wage in manufacturing was $96.56 and in retail it was $60.96 in 1962. In 1986 the wage for manufacturing was $396.01 and for retail $176.08.

• The declining ratio from 1962 to 1986 is important in that manufacturing has gone from 30.3 percent to 19.0 percent of total employment while retail trade has gone from 15.1 percent to 18 percent.

Fact #6   Weekly wages among occupations vary considerably, from a low in 1986 of $91 for child care workers in private households to $767 for lawyers.

• The three occupations with the highest weekly pay in 1986 (over $700) were lawyers ($767), chemical engineers ($721), and economists ($704); all are heavily male dominated (75%, 89%, and 62% respectively).

• The three occupations with the lowest weekly pay (under $160) are child care workers ($91), private household cleaners and servants ($147), and food counter, fountain, and related occupations ($152); all are heavily female dominated (99%, 95%, and 80% respectively).

Fact #7   Real earnings in the three decades from 1956 to 1986 went up 132 percent for Fortune 500 CEOs and 23 percent for all employees.

Male and Female

Fact #1   For much of the post-World War II period, full-time women's wages were between 57 percent to 60 percent of men's wages; since 1979, there has been a significant jump, from 62 percent to 70 percent in 1986.

Fact #2   The pay gap between men and women is very small for younger workers but increases significantly with age. According to the Department of Labor, 20-to-24-year-old women earned in 1985 85.7 percent of what similar aged males earned. The percentage for 25-to-34-year-olds was 75.1 percent; for 35-to-44-year-olds 63.2 percent; and for 45-to-54-year-olds 59.6 percent.

Table 4

Earnings for Selected Occupations,
1956 and 1986 (in 1986 dollars)

Job	1956	1986	Percent Change
All Fortune 500 CEOs	$402,110	931,800	+ 132
All employees	16,000	19,750	+ 23
AT&T middle manager	30,350	41,000	+ 35
Average plant manager	75,880	65,000	− 14
School teacher	15,940	25,450	+ 60
Government worker (state or local)	15,210	25,830	+ 70
Private secretary	16,390	23,190	+ 41
Service worker	12,780	17,643	+ 38
Steel worker	20,530	31,360	+ 53
Factory worker	16,000	19,750	+ 23

Source: "Do We Live As Well As We Used To?" *Fortune,* Sept. 14, 1987, p. 33.

Fact #3   *In 1987, for the first time, the hourly earnings of women employed full-time exceeded 75 percent of the earnings of men working full-time of the same age and with the same amount of schooling.*

Fact #4   *The gender gap (the percentage of male wages that women earn) in the fall of 1987 for full-time workers was: whites 69 percent; blacks, 84 percent; Hispanics, 79 percent.*

- For whites, the reduction in the gap from 61.1% in 1979 to 67.3% in 1985 occurred because the female workers suffered only slight real pay reductions while male wages, in real terms, declined 10 to 15 percent.

Fact #5   *From 1979 to 1984, 97 percent of the new jobs filled by white males paid less than $7,000.*

Fact #6   *From 1955 to 1975, women had a strong steady increase in their real earnings; since 1975, there has been virtually no increase.*

Fact #7   In 1984 only 4 percent of working women earned $28,000 or more a year (compared to 26 percent of white men).

Fact #8   In 1985, 14.2 percent of all employed women were professionals while 11.6 percent of all employed men were. Female professionals earned 71 percent of what male professionals earned, the same percentage as 1980.

- In 1985, 64 percent of all female professionals were employed either as teachers or in the "health assessment and treating" occupations compared to 18 percent of all male professionals in these two relatively low-paying categories.

Fact #9   Among the 26.1 million married working couples in 1983, about 4.8 million wives (almost 20%) earned more than their husbands.

- Among working couples, three-quarters of the husbands worked full-time year-round whereas only half the wives did.
- Among the 4.8 million families where the wife earned the most, a higher proportion of women worked full-time year-round than men—3,496,000 to 2,364,000—and the wives tended to be better educated.

Fact #10   In 1983, married women with a graduate education earned 11 percent less than married men with a high school education.

Blacks and Other Minorities

Fact #1   Black men made substantial progress from 1940 to 1980 toward catching up with white men in average weekly earnings, going from 44 percent to 72 percent.

- Black male real weekly wages rose an average of 300 percent in the 40-year period while those of white men rose 163 percent.

Fact #2   Minority women made tremendous progress from 1955 to 1975 toward catching up with white women in average earnings, going from 58 percent to 99 percent; since 1975 the ratio has worsened to 90 percent in 1985.

Fact #3   From 1979 to 1985, all racial wage gaps grew, with the gap for men considerably larger than that for women in 1985.

- In 1985, black and Hispanic men earned 73 percent and 71 percent, respectively, of what white men earned.

- In 1985, black women earned 90 percent and Hispanic women earned 81 percent of what white women earned.

- The white/black wage gap for men was 76.1 percent in 1979 and grew to 72.9 percent in 1985.

Interpretation
of the Facts

1. Present and Future Trends

The AFL-CIO is the strongest proponent of the thesis that there is a significant and serious trend toward low paying jobs. According to their 1986 report *The Polarization of America,*

> This decline in real wages is due to a number of factors, including falling productivity growth and inflation. Probably the single largest factor, however, is the nature of the jobs being created and the shift from generally better paying jobs in goods production and infrastructure—transportation, utility and communication—to lower paying service sector jobs . . . if the mix of employment (proportion of the total workforce in each industry) in 1985 had been the same as it was in 1979, hourly pay would have been 18 cents or 2.0 percent higher and weekly pay would have been 3.5 percent higher in 1985. These estimated effects of industry mix are probably

understated since they do not account for employment changes within the broad 59 industries used in the analysis, including regional shifts.

Of the 6 percent recent decline in real hourly earnings, 2 percentage points are due to a shift in the employment mix. The effect of the changing industry mix on weekly earnings, of 3.5 percent, is almost half (3.5 percent divided by 7.6 percent) of the total 7.6 percent decline.

The $11.46 cut in weekly pay due to employment shifts implies a loss by private sector production workers of, on average, approximately $600 each year. These losses are not shared equally. Rather, they are borne by people not being able to fill the good jobs that were destroyed and by those who had good jobs and lost them. . . .

Average pay has been falling as some industries lose and others gain jobs. That is, if lost jobs pay more than average and gained jobs pay less than average, then average wages fall. This is exactly what's happened . . . new jobs are in industries which pay nearly 40 percent, or $171.91 per week, less than the industries in which jobs were lost.

"How can that be?" one might ask. "Isn't it true that many low wage (textile, apparel) jobs were lost in manufacturing as well as high wage jobs such as in auto or steel?" The answer is yes. Both relatively low and high wage manufacturing jobs were lost. But even low wage manufacturing jobs pay more than many of the new service sector jobs. For instance, for every apparel industry job lost in the last six years there were nearly eight jobs gained in eating and drinking establishments, jobs which on average had weekly wages 40 percent lower than apparel jobs in 1979. Similarly, for every textile job lost, one and a half hotel jobs were created at two-thirds the weekly wage.

This analysis of falling pay due to the employment shifts has focused on production workers who make up two-thirds of the workforce. Unfortunately, trends among the remaining third do not provide ground for optimism. Although there has been a relative increase in nonproduction and supervisory jobs, which implies higher average pay, there has also been a counteracting force—relatively fewer available government jobs.

Neither does the future hold much promise. Recent BLS employment projections for 1995 indicate that retail and wholesale trades and services will provide 75 percent of the net new jobs in the next 10 years and that there will be a continuing fall in the share of jobs in the better paying sectors—goods-producing, infrastructure and government.

The income reductions, or skidding, experienced by dislocated workers is another indication of a deteriorating wage structure and the declining number of good jobs. . . . These figures show substantial skidding among those workers forced from their jobs, particularly if they changed industries or occupations. In fact, this is what happened to those who were lucky enough to find jobs. Over one-third of the displaced workers were still unemployed at the time of the survey or had dropped out of the labor force. If the economy was producing many good jobs in those years, it is clear that most displaced workers were not able to find them (Source: *The Polarization of America*, Washington, D.C.: Industrial Union Department of AFL-CIO, 1986, pp. 17, 22–28).

An equally vigorous proponent of the thesis that there is no general adverse shift toward low paying jobs is Janet Norwood, who has been the commissioner of the Bureau of Labor Statistics since 1979. Here is a part of her analysis of the changing employment mix:

A huge restructuring of industry is under way in this country. Employment is declining in such goods-producing industries as steel, apparel, textiles and leather, but increasing in industries that provide services like health care, banking and merchandising. Both trends are likely to continue. Should that worry us? Not if we understand what is happening and learn to adjust to the trends.

The American factory worker long has been viewed as the backbone of the labor force, the heart of the trade union movement, and a major force in increasing the standard of living in this country. Service jobs, on the other hand, often are thought to be low-skilled, which pay a little more than the minimum wage. Does this mean that we are becoming a nation of low-paid, low-skilled workers?

Let us put our employment growth into perspective. Although the number of factory jobs has not increased since 1970, compared with a whopping 53 percent rise in service sector jobs, there are still 19.4 million factory workers in this country.

Sure, we have lost some high-paying jobs in important manufacturing industries. We know that the workers displaced from these jobs are primarily men who held them for some time, tend to have family obligations, and are not as mobile as younger workers.

But we also have lost jobs in low-paying manufacturing industries like apparel, textiles and shoes. Indeed, in a recent survey of displaced workers, we found more displaced apparel workers than displaced steelworkers. The survey showed that workers who lost jobs in industries like apparel and textiles tended to be disproportionately women and minority group members who always have a difficult time in the labor market.

The widely held notion that all jobs in the service sector are "bad" jobs is not true. Consider, for example, that the sector employs 80 percent of the country's managerial and professional specialty workers. The fact is that the service sector is so diverse that the jobs in it cannot be categorized as either high-wage or low-wage.

It is, in fact, that diversity itself that makes the service sector unique. The sector employs low-paid workers in fast-food restaurants, in personal service establishments and in nursing homes. But the service sector is also the home of computer services, legal services, advertising and communications, where workers, on average, earn fairly high wages. And there are those employed in insurance, wholesale trade and auto repair who earn near-average earnings. The shift to services does not mean that we are becoming a nation of hamburger makers. Many service sector jobs are neither low-paid nor dead end.

Moreover, occupations and earnings as well as industries are shifting. While we need more comprehensive analysis of the interaction of all of these changes, Bureau of Labor Statistics research completed thus far shows some overall shift toward higher-paying and some reduction in lower-paying occupations. And the B.L.S. Employment Cost Index shows that, in recent years, workers in service industry jobs have had larger increases in compensation (wage and fringes) than factory workers have had.

Clearly, both the industrial and occupational mix of employment is changing in this country as well as in other countries. The trends are not so harmful as some have feared. We can live with them if we have the flexibility to minimize the hardship associated with the changes and to capitalize on their potential benefits (J. Norwood, "The Growth in Service Jobs," *The New York Times*, August 28, 1985, p. D-2, © 1985 the New York Times Co. Reprinted by permission).

CHAPTER
★ 26 ★

Changes in
the Workplace

The Issues

American workers today are better educated, more of them
are female, and many have different values and vastly different needs than workers of just a generation ago. The basic
new value is the desire for a greater degree of participation
at the workplace, a greater voice that is heard and treated
with dignity. The greatest new need is for flexibility, so that
a better, more sane, balance between work and family can
be achieved. Companies are being challenged to respond in
order to attract the most productive workers. They are responding in an ever greater variety of ways: participative
management (including quality circles), new labor-management relations, alternative work schedules (involving flex-
time, compressed workweeks, and sabbaticals), child-care
and maternity leave, no-layoff policies, and profit-sharing
and employee ownership.

425

The Facts

Participative Management

Fact #1   In 1984, the estimates of the number of firms that were practicing some form of participative management were: (1) 6,000 companies out of about a million of America's small and mid-size firms (Robert Townsend) and (2) 52 leading corporations that are encouraging workers "to participate more directly in the management of their work and the overall goals of their companies" (the Conference Board).

Fact #2   Companies that practice participative management have better performance than other companies.

- A study of 101 industrial companies found that those that were participatively managed outscored the others on 13 of 14 financial measures.

- A 1983 study by a Yale professor concluded that the key to improving U.S. business is the development of "participation management" skills and environments that incorporate the ideas of the firm's employees.

Fact #3   Most efforts to introduce participation do not succeed. A study by William Cooke, a professor at the University of Michigan, showed that about 75 percent of all programs in the early 1980s failed.

- General Electric's experience over twenty years demonstrates how difficult it is to get management consistently to support participative programs as its twelve plants with work teams in 1975 dwindled to only one by 1985.

Fact #4   In 1985, it was estimated that over 90 percent of the Fortune *500 companies had quality circles (one of the most popular forms of participative management), while a 1982 study showed that 44 percent of all companies with more than 500 employees had quality circle programs.*

- Quality circles usually begin to decline in effectiveness after a number of years due to overt resistance from middle managers and staff, budget cuts, and participants' waning enthusiasm.

New Labor-Management Relations

Fact #1   The first major example of the new style labor-management relations was at New United Motor Manufacturing (NUMMI), a joint venture of GM and Toyota in Fremont, California, in 1984.

- There are only four job classifications in the plant, one covering all production workers—or about 80 percent of the work force—and three covering skilled trades. Some GM assembly plants have more than 100 job classifications.
- On the assembly lines, employees work in teams of eight to ten and each member can perform as many as fifteen separate jobs.
- Hourly and salaried workers use the same parking lot and the same cafeteria.
- A worker can stop the assembly line to correct a defect in a car and the company regularly solicits suggestions from workers.

Fact #2   A study of changing labor-management relations in the U.S. auto industry showed that auto management is shifting decision-making down the ranks in a number of cases, giving hourly workers more responsibility for what happens on the plant floor.

- Worker teams, quality-control groups, and similar bodies are being guided by people who are listed as hourly workers.

Fact #3   In September 1987, Ford and the UAW agreed to a three-year contract that granted unprecedented job security to union workers and adopted a radically different approach to pay in the industry.

- It provides guaranteed employment during the life of the contract for most of the 104,000 workers.

- It would end base pay increases in each year of the contract and give a 3 percent increase in base pay the first year and a 3 percent bonus in each of the last two years.

Fact #4   In 1986, the United Auto Workers (UAW) and GM reached a contract agreement for GM's new Saturn Corp. plant that eliminates distinctions between hourly and salaried workers, a twenty-five year goal of the UAW.

- The switch from hourly pay to annual salaries will give Saturn workers only 80 percent of the average industry pay but they can make up the difference by meeting productivity, profitability, and production goals.

- At Saturn, teams of six to fifteen workers will elect a "counselor" and will be responsible for meeting production schedules and budgets, controlling absenteeism, handling health and safety, and deciding who gets what job.

- Job security is a big element, with guaranteed lifetime employment given to 80 percent of the work force.

Alternative Work Schedules

Fact #1   Flextime, which allows workers to vary their starting and quitting times, is used by one in eight full-time workers.

Fact #2   In the 1973–1985 period, compressed workweeks— in which forty hours of work is done in four or four and a-half days—grew nearly five times as fast as did total employment.

Fact #3   About one out of every ten major companies had some form of sabbatical in 1985.

- These extended leaves, lasting from one month to one year, are provided to attract and keep workers, deal with stress and burnout on the job, broaden professional skills, or simply provide veteran employees with an opportunity for personal growth.

- McDonald's makes available to every full-time employee an extended leave of eight weeks at full pay for every ten years of full-time service.

Child Care and Maternity Leave

Fact #1   *Responding to what perhaps is the most pressing problem for women workers—the acute shortage of day care— 2,500 companies provided some form of child-care aid in 1985, up from 600 in 1982 (150 were on-site centers).*

- More and more companies are realizing that good child care is important to them as childcare problems can short-circuit recruiting efforts, affect staff productivity, and increase absenteeism and turnover.

- IBM has perhaps gone the farthest, spending $1 million in 1984 to set up the first nationwide corporate service for referring employees to community childcare.
  - With an estimated budget of $2 million a year, the service by mid-1986 had referred 16,000 children.
  - IBM has also given money to nonprofit groups that trained 5,000 new providers to care for 13,000 children.

- Some major companies, including Control Data, Merck, and Continental Illinois National Bank, have put computer terminals in some employees' homes so they can work while caring for their children.

- First Bank in Minneapolis lets some employees use sick leave to stay home with an ill child.

- Many employers have added flexible benefit packages so that employees can choose from a menu of optional benefits, selecting day care instead of additional vacation, for instance.

Fact #2   Maternity leave is becoming a major issue and grow-ing practice among companies.

- No more than 40 percent of working women have any form of maternity leave, including those who use sick and vacation leave.

- About 35 percent of 400 major companies surveyed in 1986 had increased the length of paid maternity leave in the past five years.

No-Layoff Policy

Fact #1   A small group of companies, that run the gamut of large and small, high- and low-tech, have either explicit em-ployment guarantee policies or strong implicit traditions that in practice amount to the same thing.

- Some of the best known companies are: Bank of Amer-ica, Delta Airlines, Digital Equipment, Eli Lily, Federal Express, Hallmark Cards, IBM, Materials Research Corp., R.J. Reynolds, William Wrigley.

Fact #2   No-layoff policies are good business, according both to the firms that have them and a major study of them.

- A Work in America Institute study concluded that no-layoff policies pay off in: higher productivity; retention of skilled workers; no delay or expense of hiring and training when demand increases; greater flexibility in deploying people; saving the costs of severance pay, early retirement incentives, and increased unemploy-ment insurance taxes; increased loyalty to the firm and less turnover and absenteeism.

Profit-Sharing and Employee Ownership

Fact #1   Less than 10 percent of American workers see a connection between their pay and any extra effort they make to improve the performance of their firm—whereas 93 percent of Japanese workers think they will benefit personally.

Fact #2   One in seven of America's large corporations in 1982 had some form of pay-for-performance program. These ranged from piecework or commission pay to profit-sharing and employee ownership of the company.

- Seven out of ten corporations reported productivity increases after introducing such incentives.

Fact #3   By 1985, 7,000 firms had created employee stock ownership plans (ESOPs) through which nearly 10 million workers owned all or part of their companies.

Fact #4   Several large corporations link the compensation of all employees to company performance.

- Johnson Wax, Hewlett-Packard, Hallmark Cards, Goldman Sachs, and Reader's Digest pay a portion of pretax profits to all employees.

One Company that Puts It all Together

Merck & Co.:
Blending Family Life and Work

A few years ago, when the number of women at Merck & Co. approached one-third of all employees, the company decided to update its personnel policies. In 1980 the drugmakers helped to open a child-care center near its Rahway (N.J.) headquarters. In 1981 it began letting employees start work at any point from 7 a.m. to 9:30 a.m.—to give parents more flexibility. Two years later it started allowing some parents to work part-time or at home after maternity leave. In 1984, Merck funded a major study on how employees balance work and family life. And last year it created workshops and a counseling program to help parents cope with the double strain of job and family. ("Business Starts Tailoring Itself to Suit Working Women," *Business Week*, October 6, 1986, p. 50.)

Art Strohmer, Merck's director of human resources, planning and development, acknowledges that there is a very basic economic reason for these programs:

It is good business to be interested in an employee's welfare, and do whatever you can to make an employee's existence more fulfilled. If you help take some of the stresses associated with family life, then when an employee comes to work, he or she will be able to put that much more attention to work. . . . We see a definite payback for being responsive. The better you are able to meet the needs of an employee, the more productivity you have. ("Merck Blends Family Life With Work," *The Washington Post*, October 14, 1984, p. H7.)

Interpretation of the Facts

Two workplaces may well exemplify where the U.S. has been, and where it is going. The first workplace is the Jeep division of American Motors in Toledo, Ohio. The second is the Honda of America plant at Marysville, Ohio, just 100 miles away from the Jeep plant—but a world apart.

A Tale of Two Workplaces		
	Jeep	Honda
Outwardly:	An enormous, inner-city-like industrial warren of old buildings and parking lots.	Stretches across a rural landscape of grass and woodlands.

Daily Production:	750	875
Floor Space:	over 5 million square feet	1.7 million square feet
Auto Workers:	around 5,000	2,432
Production lines:	Production lines are broken at several places, requiring carriers and partially assembled car bodies to be dragged manually from one line to the next as assembly proceeds. That not only slows down production but adds employees to the payroll. The Jeep line snakes up and down through most of the factory's maze of 64 interconnected buildings.	From where welding begins until the finished car is fueled and driven off the line, no human moves the car—it is done entirely by hooks or conveyors.
Inventory:	A day or two are required simply to move 12,000 different parts through its labyrinth to the assembly line itself.	Parts inventory is largely stored by its suppliers, which delivers parts to the back dock mere hours before they are needed.
R&D Spending:	1% of sales	4% of sales.
Employee attitudes:	A management frustrated by union intransigence regards new investment skeptically. Why continue to upgrade the plant	Workers are persuaded that automation will not eliminate jobs, but improve quality control, with the result that workers

		see it as an investment in their own job security. Thus, many new automation ideas at Honda come right from the factory floor.
Union work rules and job classification:	The UAW contract calls for three workers, each with a different union job classification, to move parts to the assembly line.	With no union, one person moves parts from inventory to line, where assembly workers pull them up as needed.
Absenteeism:	On a balmy spring Friday, 15% of the plant's second shift beginning at 4:30 p.m. failed to show for work, forcing the plant to close down.	The same day, Honda had an absentee rate of 2%—typical for the firm.
Labor-Management Relations:	The workers are worried about keeping their jobs and they think that hanging tough is the way to do it. A member of management stated: "The union merely exists to protect guys who try to screw the company." In 1985, after management had pressured the UAW local to change some work rules, tension built	By contrast, Honda seems a beehive of camaraderie and fellow-feeling, and the company goes to great lengths to encourage it. All Honda employees, top to bottom, refer to each other as "associates." All wear white coveralls—no neckties—with first names stitched above the pocket. There are no en-

if union work rules frustrate cost savings.

	to the point where a group of shop floor workers abruptly began sabotaging the assembly line, bashing Jeeps with welding tools. The line was intermittently shut down during the week that followed, costing more than $1 million in lost wages.	closed spaces, no executive dining rooms or lounges. In short, democratic.
Profit-Sharing:	None	Added, along with attendance bonuses.

CHAPTER
27
★ 27 ★

Unions

The Issues

Unions. Big labor. One's response to these words tends to depend on one's experience and upbringing. Basically, it depends on whether or not the individual (or his/her family) has been personally involved and helped by a union. If so, unions are great and if not, they are no good.

But aside from these feelings, what role do unions play in the American economy? For most of this century, unions played a very major role; sometimes, as was the case with strikes in the steel industry, they could choke the economy right at the throat. Union membership surged from the 1930s to the 1960s, and along with the increased numbers came increased wages.

But lately, one hears less about unions and certainly there is scant mention of the power of big labor. Has the influence and power of unions passed its peak? The facts suggest the answer is yes.

The Facts

Union Membership: Overview

Fact #1   Since the Depression, union membership has gone through three distinct periods: rapid growth from 1935 to 1945; stability from 1945 to 1975, and rapid decline from 1975 to 1985.

- From 1935 to 1945, the percent of union members in the nonfarm work force went from 13 percent to 30 percent while from 1975 to 1986 it went from 29 percent to 17.5 percent.

- The peak union membership year, in terms of the greatest percentage of the nonfarm work force, was 1,953 with 33 percent.

Fact #2   From 1976 to 1986, the work force expanded by 20 percent but union membership declined by 16 percent (from 24 million to 20 million).

Fact #3   The peak membership years for most major unions were in the 1969–1976 period.

Union Membership–1980s

Fact #1   There was a significant decline in union membership in the first half of the 1980s. The number of union members fell by 2.7 million between 1980 and 1984 (while the total number of wage and salary employees increased by 3.8 million). The percentage of employees who were union members fell from 23 percent to 19 percent.

Table 1

Peak Years of Major Unions
(in thousands)

Union	Peak Year	U. S. Membership in Peak Year	U. S. Membership (1984–1985)	Total Percent Loss
United Mine Workers	1942	595	87	84%
United Steelworkers	1975	1,071	497	45%
United Auto Workers	1969	1,426	904	33%
American Federation of Government Employees	1972	323	218	32%
Hotel Employees and Restaurant Employees	1970	486	312	32%
International Ladies' Garment Workers	1969	387	283	26%
Teamsters	1974	1,946	1,523	20%
National Education Association	1976	1,818	1,444	20%

Source: Union Sourcebook, Leo Troy and Neil Sheflin

- By contrast, in the previous 4-year period (1977–1980) union membership among employed wage and salary workers grew by 800,000.

- Comparing the two major recent recessions, total union membership (including the unemployed) fell by 2.6 million in the 1980–1982 recession and by 147,000 in the 1974–1976 recession.

- In this same 1980–1984 period, union membership in goods-producing industries alone fell by 1.9 million people although these industries had an increase of 1.1 million new jobs.

Fact #2   In the early 1980s, unions' share of the nonfarm, private work force was shrinking annually by 3 percent a year and unions were winning only 0.3 percent of the work force every year in representation elections.

- The union membership share in private industry has been cut in half since 1953, from 35 percent of the work force to just over 17 percent in 1986.

Fact #3   Women are approximately 33 percent of union membership, up sharply from 21 percent in 1972.

- The two unions with the highest percentages of women are the Amalgamated Clothing and Textile Workers (75%) and the National Education Association (62%).
- Still, the 5.8 million female union members represent only 13 percent of all employed women.

Fact #4   Of 16 million clerical workers in 1985, only 2.3 million belonged to a union.

Fact #5   Most union organizing efforts in the 1980s have not gone well.

- In the late 1940s and early 1950s, unions captured almost 75 percent of representation elections, but in the 1980s they are winning less than half.
- After some 250 organizing drives from 1975 to 1984, unions have largely abandoned their efforts to bring high-tech workers into their ranks.
- In 1984, there was not one unionized firm among 1,500 Silicon Valley companies engaged in research, development, and manufacturing.

Fact #6   The number of decertification elections to terminate union representation has more than tripled since 1970 and unions have been losing 75 percent of them.

Fact #7   Unions have had a few successes and gains in the 1980s.

- There have been some gains among government and service workers; the American Federation of State,

County and Municipal Employees, the Communications Workers of America, and the Service Employees International Union had modest membership gains in the early 1980s.

- Unions have won 52 percent of representation elections in firms with less than 500 employees (compared to a 28 percent success rate in firms with 500 or more employees).

- New unions certified by the AFL-CIO in 1984 and 1985 were quite diverse: flight attendants, hospital and health-care employees, school administrators, policemen, and football players.

Fact #8   *More than 80 percent of all workers under 35 have no union members in their households.*

Fact #9   *Government workers accounted for one-third of all union members in 1987.*

Union Wages

Fact #1   *From 1973 to 1984 real wages for union employees dropped.*

Fact #2   *Unions have been forced in the 1980s to make a number of significant wage and benefit concessions—something that did not occur at all in the 1950s and 1960s.*

- In 1983 negotiations, steelworkers took a 9 percent wage cut, airline workers a 15 percent cut, and employees in the construction, rubber, and meat-packing industries made similar concessions.

- The percentage of union members having to accept wage reductions or freezes rose from 0 percent in the 1980 contract negotiations, to 8 percent in 1981, 49 percent in 1982, and 37 percent in 1983.

- Many unions, particularly in the retail, wholesale, food and airline industries, have reluctantly agreed to a two-tiered wage scale which pays new and rehired workers substantially less than existing workers (8 percent of major union settlements in 1984).

Fact #3   Despite the slowdown in their growth, union wages still remain well above nonunion wages; in 1984, the average wage of union workers ($404/week) was 33 percent higher than that of non-union workers ($303/week).

Impact of Unions

Fact #1   Richard Freeman and James Medoff's study, What Do Unions Do? *(1984) concluded that the monopolistic practices of unions cost the economy $5 billion to $10 billion annually but that in their democratic role unions increase the efficiency of the economy by $5 billion to $10 billion annually by reducing training expenses, job search costs, and worker turnover.*

Fact #2   Strikes no longer have a major impact since many capital intensive industries can achieve 90 percent of their usual production during a strike and most other firms attain 50 to 80 percent levels of production.

The Public's Perception

Fact #1   Of all American institutions, public confidence in unions has dropped the most over the past two decades—only 22 percent of the public held unions in high regard in the mid-1980s.

Fact #2   Union leaders, judged in terms of ethical conduct and moral practices, are rated last by Americans, behind lawyers, advertising executives, corporate executives, government officials, and stockbrokers.

Interpretation
of the Facts

1. The Future of Unions

Unions, of course, are familiar with the decline in their numbers and have concluded that some changes will have to be made. The major recommended changes come from the Committee on the Evolution of Work, which was composed of most major union leaders. It is informative to see how their views contrast with those of noted futurist Alvin Toffler. In an article titled "Labor Pains," Toffler offers his vision of a new social contract in which labor plays a key role. Here then are two very different prescriptions for unions.

Organized Labor's Prescription   Basically, there are four major recommendations to make unions more flexible and adaptable.

- Become more active in labor-management worker participation efforts.
- Create new categories of union memberships to provide services and benefits for workers who are not part of organized bargaining entities.
- Devote more resources to the education and training of their officials, stewards, and organizers.
- The AFL-CIO should assist affiliates when they merge and create a mechanism to resolve organizing disputes among unions.

Toffler's Prescription   This brings me to the outlines of a strategic deal—I call it the 5-5-5 plan. A five-point, five-hour, five-year program to fight economic rigidity.

POINT ONE: (And traditional employers will hate this idea—at first).
Today, exactly one century after the start of the eight-hour campaign, unions from the United States to Japan should

begin pressing for the 25-hour week, plus five hours of training time each week. The goal should be a 25-plus-5-hour
week with no loss of pay—to be phased in over a five-year
period. By the early 1990s this 25-plus-5-hour week should
be regarded as full-time work. This means, in concrete terms,
a significant hourly wage increase.

In short, taken by itself, this proposal sounds both naive
and utopian, if not "crazy"—exactly like the "crazy" idea of
the eight-hour day a century ago. Unless, that is, the unions
give something of equal value back to the employer. But
what could possibly be worth so sharp a reduction in hours?
The answer to that is survival—the ability of a firm to make
instant, sharp adjustments to fast-paced changes. The chief
threat to jobs and industrial survival today is not low-
wage foreign competition, but slow organizational adapt-
ation. . . .

POINT TWO: What unions can offer in return for the 25-
hour week, therefore, is the drastic elimination of union-
imposed jurisdictional restrictions, demarcation lines, work
rules, narrow job descriptions and other rigidities that par-
alyze managers in companies and government agencies.

Instead of trying to prevent out-contracting, for example,
unions should recognize that saving a few jobs in the short
run may kill far more jobs in the long run. Why not make
deals that permit, even encourage, contracting out, in return
for bargaining rights or contractual gains in the contractor's
shop—even if that shop happens to be organized by a different union or is located in a different country?

Instead of fighting the use of temporary workers, flextime,
work-at-home (for those who wish it) and other arrangements
that make organizations adaptive, unions should be finding
creative ways to serve—and organize—the new constituen-
cies these arrangements generate.

By freeing the hands of managers to make the firm flexible,
unions would help ensure the survival of jobs, and also help
some of the most vulnerable groups in the work force—such
as single parents—gain entry into the system.

POINT THREE: Unions should end their sometimes blind
resistance to automation. Instead, they should—under negotiated terms—fight for far more radical automation of fac-

tories and offices than most employers of today imagine. . . .

POINT FOUR: Instead of fighting against privatization of government functions, unions should encourage it in many areas. The quid pro quo would be that whenever a government function is transferred to the private sector, the existing unions continue to represent the workers for a minimum of five years, after which, employees will vote on whether they wish to be represented by their present union. This gives unions a half-decade to make the transition and to prove their usefulness to their members.

POINT FIVE: I spoke of five hours for training. I use the number five loosely, and I use the term training loosely. Perhaps five hours are foolish. For some companies and tasks this may be too much. Some training should be done a week at a time or a month, or, who knows, even many months. . . .

This, then, is the basic idea of the five-point strategic deal: a 25-plus-5-hour week in five years; elimination of work-rule rigidity; cooperation in contracting out; and the use of flex-time, and temporary workers; support for radical automation; a transition to privatization; and training, training, training (A. Toffler, "Labor Pains: Giving Birth to a New Social Order," *Washington Post*, August 31, 1986).

CHAPTER
★ 28 ★

Strengths and
Weaknesses

What do all these facts add up to? What do they teach us about the basic health of the American economy? As I stated way back in the Preface, I wanted to leave to you, the reader, such an analysis. With the evidence you have in hand, including the best arguments of many of today's leading economic experts, you are in a good position to render your own judgment.

Now after twenty-six chapters of absenting myself, I will once again exercise some judgments to help you to get a broad overview. Specifically, I have gone through the facts in each chapter, lifting out those that I felt indicated a definite economic strength or weakness. Each fact was judged according to the two standard economic criteria of efficiency or equity—or stated simply, productiveness and fairness.

For convenience, I have grouped the strengths and weaknesses together under each of the three parts of the book: the economy, business, and workers. No attempt is made to assign priorities, a definitely subjective exercise. Each list simply flows chronologically from the first chapter in each part to the last.

Before presenting the lists, I do want one final word—first because some readers may be interested in what my overall judgment is on this fascinatingly diverse and complex entity we call the American economy and second because I can not keep it in me.

I read through the following lists with powerful, yet ambivalent, emotions. On the one hand, I feel great pride and satisfaction in what the American economy has been able to do for the vast majority of Americans—provide standards of living undreamed of for most of the world's people, as well as jobs for more than three out of five working age Americans—and helping to provide many of the nations of the world with the growth, trade, and aid that has brought them enormous, and often much-needed, relief and assistance through difficult periods. And I even feel a bit optimistic when I look at such facts as healthy growth rates in eight of the last eleven years, low inflation rates during the last four years, and America's being by far the greatest job-generating economy in the world. Looking at the U.S. economy, we do have much to be proud of—not only of its past but of its present as well.

BUT, on the infamous other hand (which is the favorite hand of all economists), I must stress that I am deeply troubled when I go through the three lists of weaknesses. Troubled to the point where my heart and soul ache, for many of these numbers are about people—millions of Americans who have to suffer basic, ongoing indignities, such as no job or income too low for basic necessities—in a $4.5 trillion economy.

And, alongside the ache, lies a basic fear for the future. The fear stems from our being blindly willing, as a nation, to live it up and not worry about tomorrow, at least not worry till that day comes. Well, that day is coming and when it does—when we have to pay for those towering twin deficits—it is going to be very painful.

I regret that this is not a very optimistic overall assessment. But then, this is just one person's reading and interpretation of the facts. After going through the following lists, you can make your own judgments.

America's Economy

Strengths

1. Economic growth was quite strong (2.5 percent or greater) in nine of the twelve years from 1976 to 1987.
2. The U.S. economic growth rate was one of the three highest among industrial nations in 1983–1986 (U.S. was 4.1 percent, Canada 4.3 percent, and Japan 3.9 percent).
3. The inflation rate in 1986 was only 1.1 percent, the lowest rate since 1961 and only one-fourth the increase of the previous four years.
4. The United States has had by far the greatest job-generating economy in the world since the mid-1960s.
5. In mid-1987, a record 61.8 percent of the civilian population was employed.
6. Unemployment pressures will shrink considerably as the U.S. heads into the baby-boom shrinkage of the labor force.
7. Manufacturing productivity has been very strong in the 1980s, growing at its fastest rate since the mid-1950s (averaging 4.4 percent annually through mid-1986) and increasing by 3.5 percent in 1986, highest among all major competitors.
8. American families have a very high median family income—$29,458 in 1986.
9. Poverty rates among the aged have been reduced by nearly two-thirds since 1959.

Weaknesses

1. Economic growth averaged 4 percent in the 1960s, 2.8 percent in the 1970s, and 2.2 percent in the 1980s (through 1986).
2. The total debt of $7.2 trillion at the end of 1986 was a record 173 percent of the GNP.
3. The U.S. is living beyond its means; in 1981, total spending came to 98 percent of the GNP so the other 2 percent ($65 billion) could be invested abroad, while in 1986 we spent 104 percent of the GNP, requiring the U.S. to borrow $140 billion from abroad.
4. The U.S. stands last in net national savings among major industrial nations.
5. The U.S. stood last in terms of the misery index, that adds the inflation and unemployment rates, in the 1979–85 period.
6. The U.S. spends a much higher percentage of its GNP on defense than any other industrialized nation; in 1986, it spent 6.7 percent vs. 3.1 percent in W. Germany and 1.0 percent in Japan.
7. In the 1950s and 1960s, inflation's yearly average was 2.1 and 2.4 percent respectively. In the 1970s and 1980s (1980–87), the yearly averages were 7.1 and 5.7 percent, about triple the earlier averages.
8. Inflation in 1986 was barely reduced from the 4 percent plus rates of the previous four years when energy is excluded and was in the 4–5 percent range in 1987.
9. The unemployment rate has steadily increased in each of the past four decades: from 4.5 percent in the 1950s to 4.8 percent in the 1960s, 6.2 percent in the 1970s, and 8 percent in the 1980s (1980–1986).
10. There were serious recession and even depression level rates of unemployment in 1987 for all Americans except white adults.
11. A record low of 25 percent of unemployed Americans received unemployment benefits in the fall of 1987.

12. Budget deficits soared to unprecedented levels around $200 billion in each of the four years from 1983 to 1986.
13. The U.S. has had only one budget surplus in the past twenty-six years.
14. The national debt increased by 43 percent from 1950 to 1969 and by 457 percent from 1970 to 1986, passing the $2 trillion mark in June 1986.
15. Interest payments on the national debt increased by 163 percent from 1980–1986 to a level of $136 billion in 1986. In seven of the eight years from 1978–1985, they exceeded 60 percent of the deficit level.
16. In 1986 Federal taxes were nearly six times higher than in 1966 and state and local taxes were just over seven times higher.
17. The richest Americans will pay relatively less in taxes in 1988 than they did in 1977 while the poor will pay more.
18. Many companies in the mid-1980s paid no corporate income tax and whole industries (airline and financial) had negative tax rates.
19. In the eight years (1979–86), productivity growth was pathetically weak, averaging only 0.4 percent.
20. Productivity growth in the 1980s expansion (1.3 percent) has been less than half that of previous recoveries.
21. The U.S. lead in productivity has shrunk considerably to a level in 1985 just 10 percent higher than in Japan and 15 percent higher than in continental Europe.
22. Personal debt took off in 1976, with consumer credit and mortgage debt levels nearly tripling over the next decade, so that by 1986 the household debt burden was at a record high one-third of disposable income.
23. Twenty to 25 million households are financially overextended.
24. Personal savings as a percent of disposable income has been on the decline for the past twelve years,

reaching a rate of 3.8 percent in 1986, the lowest since 1949.

25. In terms of income and wealth, the U.S. is a two-class society: the median family income of whites is 74 percent greater than that of blacks and their net worth is 12 times greater.

26. The median family income level in 1985 was 5 percent lower than in 1973 (22 percent lower for young families).

27. The gap between the rich and the poor has grown substantially in the 1980s: in the 1980–86 period, the bottom 40 percent of the population had an increase in income of just $199 while the top 40 percent had an increase of $4,418 and the richest 10 percent had an increase of $10,339.

28. In 1985 and 1986, the inequality of the distribution of income was at a record high: the bottom 40 percent received the lowest share (15.4 percent) ever in 1986.

29. Nine million households (11 percent of all Americans) have no net assets or are in debt; nearly one-third have a net worth of less than $10,000.

30. The number of Americans living in poverty has always been greater than 24 million since 1959 and the poverty rate has never gone below 11 percent.

31. The poverty rate declined 10.3 percent in the 1960s, it declined 0.4 percent in the 1970s, and it increased by 1.9 percent in the 1980s (through 1986).

32. The poverty rate for blacks has never fallen below 30 percent; it has generally been three times the rate for whites.

33. A seemingly permanent black underclass has developed in recent years numbering 2.0 to 3.5 million.

34. One of every five children lives in poverty.

35. Two million people in 1986 worked full-time year round but still were in poverty.

36. One of three children lives in a household receiving some form of government welfare.

37. Without government support programs, one in four Americans would fall below the poverty level.
38. The U.S. trade deficit, which never exceeded $10 billion before 1977, has never been less than $25 billion since then and soared to $156.1 billion in 1986.
39. U.S. trade performance from 1982 to 1986 was poor across the board: it worsened in nine of the ten major product groups used to classify trade and it worsened against all of the U.S.'s top ten trading partners and nineteen of the top twenty.
40. The three major areas of trade strength (healthy surpluses) in the early 1980s—agriculture, services, and high tech—all deteriorated badly to only minimal surplus or deficit positions in 1986.
41. For the first time since World War II, the U.S. slipped to second place in total exports in 1986, behind West Germany and only slightly ahead of Japan.
42. Imports, only 13.4 percent of all products sold in 1980, reached 25 percent in summer 1987, their highest share ever.
43. The U.S. in 1986 had a trade deficit of more than $3.5 billion with ten other countries whereas its largest individual surplus was $3.5 billion.
44. The U.S. in 1985 became a debtor nation for the first time since 1914; the $107 billion debt position in 1985 increased to around $400 billion by the end of 1987.
45. Paying back the huge foreign debt will be very costly; in 1986, the U.S. sent overseas a net $10 billion in interest and dividends, a figure that is expected to grow to $50 billion by 1990.

American Business

Strengths

1. Nearly 3.7 million new businesses were started in the U.S. in the 1981–1986 period.

2. Deregulation has brought many new entries into major industries such as airlines and trucking and with them generally lower fares and prices.
3. Many companies both large and small and from all industries have had strong positive performance results from automation.
4. Companies that have developed teamwork in their plants are often 30 to 50 percent more productive than their conventional counterparts.
5. One farmer could feed 15 people in 1950, 53 people in 1972, and 79 people in 1983; by 1985, agricultural productivity was at a record high.
6. Starting in 1980, the auto industry has undertaken a wide variety of positive changes to cut costs and become more productive.
7. Productivity in the steel industry made sizable advances in the early to mid-1980s, rising 20 to 30 percent in 1983 and 1984 so that, by 1986, American mills were producing steel at fewer man-hours per ton than any foreign competitor.
8. In high tech, the U.S. is the leader in a number of key areas: computers, semiconductors, telecommunications, and biotechnology.
9. In 1985, 99 percent of all microprocessors sold were designed by U.S. companies and six companies dominated the latest generation, 32-bit microprocessors.

Weaknesses

1. In nearly all important performance categories, including total revenues and profits, big business fared worse in 1986 than in 1985 (just as 1985 had been worse than 1984).
2. The 500 largest industrial companies have had a generally poor performance in the 1980s: sales declined by 2 percent and profits slid 22 percent from 1981 to 1986, and total employment declined from 1979 to 1986.

3. The overall debt burden of nonfinancial corporations has burgeoned in the 1980s to a total level of $1.7 trillion in 1986.

4. The quality of corporate debt, due primarily to a surge in junk bond financing, declined dramatically in the first half of the 1980s.

5. The number of companies that have installed significant automation systems is quite small: only two dozen come close to the goal of total automation and less than 250 have more than token investments in computer integration.

6. Although American companies were pioneers in the development of flexible manufacturing systems and started making it available to industry in the mid-1970s, the Japanese systems in 1986 were considerably better and they had many more systems installed.

7. Investment by American companies (as a percent of GNP) was only one-third the level of Japanese companies and one-half that of German companies.

8. For forty years, in one industry after another, the U.S. has invented a product and the Japanese have picked it up and become world leaders in its production: color televisions, solid state transistors, robots, VCRs, etc.

9. Japanese executives have as their number one priority to make their companies the global leader in an industry while this goal is fourth most important to U.S. managers who put increasing shareholder value as the top priority.

10. For every 10,000 people: the U.S. has 20 lawyers, Japan has 1; the U.S. has 40 accountants, Japan has 3; the U.S. has 70 engineers, Japan has 400.

11. In 1966, the world's seven largest banks (in terms of deposits) were all American; in 1986, the world's seven largest were all Japanese and the highest ranking U.S. one, Citibank, was seventeenth.

12. Agricultural export performance from 1981 to 1986 was dismal, decreasing each year, so that in 1986 farm

products made up less than 12 percent of the value of all American exports, the lowest level since 1940.

13. In 1985, nearly one-third of the nation's 630,000 full-time farmers were in danger of financial collapse and one-third of family-sized farms were in severe financial stress.

14. Despite manufacturing productivity's relatively strong showing in the U.S. economy, it was lower than all its industrial competitors except Canada from 1973–1984.

15. The steel industry had losses totaling $11 billion in the five-year period 1982–1986 with a record $4 billion in 1986.

16. The explosive growth in U.S. exports of services in the 1960s and 1970s—increases of 152 percent and 420 percent respectively—was followed by stagnation from 1981 to 1986 (a 3 percent increase).

17. In high technology, the U.S. has lost its leadership to Japan in the areas of robotics, advanced materials, and fiber optics.

18. The growth in U.S. computer makers' worldwide sales plummeted between 1984 and 1987 across the board: personal computers from 51 to 9 percent, small computers from 27 to 11 percent, and large-scale computers from 11 to 4.5 percent.

19. The U.S. semiconductor industry suffered collective losses of $2 billion in 1985 and 1986 and saw its share of the worldwide market fall from 64 percent in 1980 to below 40 percent in 1986, while Japan's share rose from 24 to nearly 50 percent.

American Workers

Strengths

1. In the 35-year period from 1950 to 1985, there was an increase in the adult female labor force participation

rate in every year but two, with the rate increasing by 22 percentage points from 33 to 55 percent.

2. American workers are among the most highly educated in the world in terms of the percentage of high school graduates and the number enrolling in college.

3. Women are closing the male-female wage gap; women's wages, which were 57 to 60 percent of men's wages for most of the post-World War II period, had risen by 1986 to 70 percent of men's wages (for full time workers).

4. Companies that engage their workers in participative management have better performance than other companies.

Weaknesses

1. There are numerous occupations that remain heavily dominated by women and are generally poor paying.

2. Women have made significant strides in professional and managerial positions but still lag far behind men in terms of their percentage share, salaries, and reaching the top.

3. Since 1959, there has been a growing tendency for black men to drop out of the work force entirely.

4. From 1979 to 1986, the number of voluntary part-time workers barely increased while the number of involuntary part-timers increased by 2.1 million (60 percent); thus, they accounted for nearly one-fourth of all jobs generated in that period and nearly one-fourth of all part-timers in 1986.

5. Illiteracy is rampant in the U.S. as 17 to 21 million adults (13 percent of adults) cannot read.

6. Many young people currently entering the workforce are seriously ill-equipped in basic educational skills.

7. The ten occupations that will supply the largest number of jobs from 1986–2000 are mostly in services and most pay well below the average for all workers.

8. Retraining reaches only a relatively small number of

workers who need it and those who use their new skills is a still smaller number.

9. Average weekly earnings (measured in 1977 dollars) were $169 in mid-1987, lower than they were in 1962 ($172).

10. The private sector jobs lost in the 1979–1985 period were in industries with average pay of $444 per week (36 percent above average) while the jobs gained were in industries with average pay of $272 per week (16 percent below average).

11. Women, who had been experiencing a strong steady increase in real earnings from 1955 to 1975, have had virtually no increase since then.

12. From 1979 to 1985, all of the racial wage gaps grew with the gap for men considerably larger than that for women in 1985.

13. Less than 10 percent of American workers see a connection between their pay and any extra effort they make to improve the performance of their firm— whereas 93 percent of Japanese workers think they will benefit personally.

APPENDIX

★ 1 ★

People

Policy Economists

---

1. **Barry Bluestone,** Professor of Public Affairs, University of Massachusetts. Bluestone is best known for his analyses purporting to show the decline of the middle class and the massive loss of good-paying jobs. This thesis has made him a favorite economist of organized labor.

2. **Pat Choate,** Director of Policy Analysis at TRW. His two principal books are *America in Ruins* (1981) and *The High Flex Society* (1986). One of a rare breed that advises both Republicans and Democrats.

3. **Martin Feldstein,** Professor of Economics, Harvard University. Professor Feldstein had a relatively short tenure as chairman of the Council of Economic Advisers in 1982–1984 where he became known for his outspoken

differences with various aspects of Administration policy. He frequently contributes articles to major newspapers on taxes, the trade deficit, and a variety of other economic policy issues. A solid, respected, mainstream economist.

4. **Paul Craig Roberts,** Center for Strategic and International Studies, the William E. Simon Chair in Political Economy. One of the original supply-side economic officials in the Reagan Administration, serving as assistant secretary of the Treasury. He writes a regular column for *Business Week* that vigorously defends and upholds supply-side principles, and his latest book is *The Supply Side Revolution*.

5. **Herbert Stein,** American Enterprise Institute. Stein has the record for longest service as a member of the Council of Economic Advisers, serving three years as a member (1969–1971) and nearly three years (1972–1974) as its chairman. He has written numerous books, including *Bedtime Stories for Economists* and *Presidential Economics*. He is among the best of the traditional conservative economists.

6. **Lester Thurow,** Dean, Sloan School of Management, Massachusetts Institute of Technology. He is the author of numerous books, including *The Zero-Sum Society*, *Generating Inequality*, and *Dangerous Currents*. Among the top liberal economic policy analysts and advisers. Tough critic of performance of the American economy and of the discipline of economics; a leading policy advisor.

Economic Reporters and Columnists

1. **Lindley H. Clark,** *The Wall Street Journal*. As the leading economics reporter for *WSJ*, he reaches a vast audience of over 2 million subscribers.

2. **Robert Kuttner,** *The New Republic* and a regular columnist in *Business Week.* The principal left-of-center economics writer for leading magazines.

3. **Hobart Rowen,** *The Washington Post.* The dean of newspaper economic columnists and reporters based in Washington, D.C.

4. **Robert Samuelson,** regular columnist for *Newsweek.* Covers all economic issues, basically from a nonideological perspective.

5. **Leonard Silk,** *The New York Times.* Dean of economic newspaper columnists.

6. **Louis Rukeyser,** *Wall Street Week*, PBS. Leading economics reporter on public television.

Noneconomist Opinion Shapers

---

1. **David Birch,** Professor, Massachusetts Institute of Technology. Birch's name came to the policy forefront in the early 1980s as "Mr. Small Business," due primarily to his studies showing that most new jobs are generated by small business.

2. **George Gilder,** independent writer. Author of the bible of supply-side conservatism, *Wealth and Poverty* (1980), a handbook of the early Reagan Administration. His latest book is *The Spirit of Enterprise* (1985).

3. **Henry Kaufman,** Salomon Brothers. When Henry Kaufman speaks, people listen—literally. In the world of financial markets, where billions of dollars come and go on small movements in interest rates, Kaufman's pronouncements on where interest rates are headed are closely heeded. In recent years, he has issued repeated warnings about the fragility of the U.S. financial system.

4. **Robert Reich,** professor, Kennedy School of Government, Harvard University. A Yale law graduate, Reich

made his reputation in Democratic circles in the early 1980s as "Mr. Industrial Policy." Still focuses most of his writing on American corporations and global competitiveness. Author of *The Next American Frontier* (1982) and *Tales of a New America* (1987).

5. **Ronald Shelp,** vice-president, Celanese Corp. Through his writings and speeches in the first half of the 1980s, he established himself as "Mr. Service Economy." He is the author of *Beyond Industrialization.*

Economic Policy Makers

Congress

1. **Senator Lloyd Bentsen,** chairman, Senate Finance Committee. Bentsen, a long-time member (and chairman for two years) of the Joint Economic Committee, is well-versed in a wide variety of economic issues. His top priority as the new head of the Finance Committee is trade legislation that will get tough with America's foreign competitors.

2. **Senator Lawton Chiles,** chairman, Senate Budget Committee. Chiles was the ranking minority member of the Budget Committee for six years so he knows the intricacies and the politics of the budget and budget process well. He is the quintessential moderate Democrat who shuns extremes or bold, swift solutions. He opposed the Administration's proposed Constitutional amendment to balance the budget.

3. **Senator Paul Sarbanes,** chairman, Joint Economic Committee. Sarbanes has been in the Senate from 1977 and has been with the JEC from 1979 to the present. His top priorities for the Committee under his two-year chairmanship will be foreign trade, the debt crisis, and income distribution.

4. **Senator William Proxmire,** chairman, Senate Banking, Housing and Urban Affairs Committee. Proxmire is by now the Dean of the Senate when it comes to examining the breadth and depth of economic issues. He has been a member (and Chairman for four years) of the Joint Economic Committee for twenty-six years. His special areas of interest have been the military economy and waste in government spending. He has also served on the Banking Committee since 1957, chairing it from 1975–1980 and beginning again in 1987. His current priorities are the regulation of banking, fulfilling the FSLIC insurance commitment to S&Ls, and legislation on corporate takeovers. He has announced his retirement in 1988.

5. **Representative Daniel Rostenkowski,** chairman, House Ways and Means Committee. As leader of what many would consider the most powerful committee in the Congress, he wields considerable leverage over the critical economic areas of trade and tax policy. In the trade arena, he is an advocate of get-tough policies with regard to unfair competition and he wishes to strengthen the international trading system. On the tax front, he favors an increase in taxes to help balance the budget.

6. **Representative William H. Gray III,** chairman, House Budget Committee. Since taking over the chair in 1983 as a relative unknown, Gray has impressed both his colleagues and outside budget watchers with his knowledge of the budget and his political acumen in negotiating the rocky road of the budget process.

7. **Representative Fernand St. Germain,** chairman, House Banking, Finance, and Urban Affairs Committee. He is not an active proponent of deregulation and he does not want to give banks new powers or arenas in which to operate.

Executive Branch

1. **James A. Baker III,** Secretary of the Treasury. Baker, a lawyer by training, has earned generally high marks as Treasury Secretary. He is most noted for his plan to help resolve the debt crisis afflicting many developing countries.

2. **James C. Miller III,** Director, Office of Management and Budget. Miller has brought to OMB a quiet behind-the-scenes style that stands in sharp contrast to his predecessor, David Stockman. Miller is a professional economist who has focused his professional work on regulatory matters. At OMB, his priority is to cut domestic spending and not raise taxes.

3. **Beryl Sprinkel,** chairman, Council of Economic Advisers. In his White House role, Sprinkel (best known as an ardent monetarist) plays a much less active role in economic policy formulation and advice for the president than has generally been the case for the chairman up to 1980. President Reagan does not get involved in very many economic policies and when he does he largely serves as his own adviser.

4. **Clayton Yeutter,** United States Special Trade Representative. Yeutter, an economist, occupies a key position in this time of intense focus on trade issues and U.S. competitiveness. Yeutter has as his top priorities completion of the GATT trade round and beating down the barriers to foreign markets.

5. **C. William Verity Jr.,** Secretary of the Department of Commerce. New to the job in late 1987, Verity, who headed the Armco Steel Corp. till 1982, is a well-respected business leader who is expected to continue the Commerce Department's focus on international trade issues, particularly being quite aggressive in defending the access of U.S. business to foreign markets. He is most noted for his advocacy of increased trade with the Soviet Union.

Independent

1. **Alan Greenspan,** chairman of the Federal Reserve Board. Many consider the Fed chairman to be the most influential and powerful economic policy maker. Greenspan is new to this position but has a long and distinguished career as a private economic consultant and in the government where he served as the chairman of the Council of Economic Advisers from 1974 to 1977.

APPENDIX
★ 2 ★
Publications

Books

---

1. Pat Choate and J. K. Linger, *The High Flex Society: Shaping America's Economic Future.* New York: Alfred A. Knopf, 1986.
This book's thesis is that the most practical way to confront the challenges of a fast-paced, sharply competitive, highly uncertain future is to improve America's ability to adapt to that future, whatever it brings. In short, America must become a "High-Flex Society."

2. Charles Murray, *Losing Ground: American Social Policy 1950–1980.* New York: Basic Books, 1984.
This book quickly became a favorite of the conservatives for its argument that the social programs of the 1960 and 1970s to combat poverty were a dismal failure, a gigantic

waste of money, and, in many instances, either perpetuated poverty or increased it.

3. **Lester Thurow,** *The Zero-Sum Society*. New York: Basic Books, 1980.
   Thurow launched a major economic debate in the 1980s with his thesis that American society resembles a zero-sum game—a game in which losses equal winnings. This means that every economic decision produces losers as well as winners. But, Thurow argues, the rules are changing as economically oppressed groups—women and minorities—demand political and economic equality. The solution: the redistribution of income and a fundamental restructuring of the economy.

4. **Paul Hawken,** *The Next Economy*. New York: Holt, Rinehart and Winston, 1983.
   Hawken, a writer, consultant, and businessman, argues that America has entered a period between two fundamentally different economic structures. Currently we are experiencing the decline of what Hawken calls "the mass economy," the economy of the industrial age. Because of the high cost of energy, he argues that the mass economy is being replaced by "the informative economy."

5. **John Naisbitt,** *Megatrends*. New York: Warner Books, 1982.
   Though not an economics book per se, this book more than any other in the 1980s shaped the thinking of millions of Americans about the U.S. economy. In particular, the first "megatrend" discussed, and the one Naisbitt describes as most "explosive," is the shift from an industrial to an information society. The other major economic trend highlighted is the shift from a national economy to a world economy.

Magazines, Journals, and Newspapers

Among magazines, the three leading business magazines are an excellent source of information not only about the world of business—an integral part of economic activity—but also about broader economic issues such as productivity, unemployment, and economic growth.

1. *Business Week*   Published weekly, it contains such regular economics features as Economic Diary and Economic Watch. It also has periodic Special Reports which recently have focused on such economic issues as U.S. competitiveness and tax reform.

2. *Fortune*   *Fortune* has only one regular economic feature, The Fortune Forecast, but like *Business Week* it has at least one or two lengthier articles in each issue that address a key economic issue or policy arena.

3. *Forbes*   Focusing largely on industrial companies and the corporate world, it is the least economic oriented of the three. Occasional articles on broader economic issues, however, do appear.

4. *National Journal*   This weekly journal focuses on across-the-board national policies and policy makers. Each issue has four to five feature articles, one of which is usually focused on an economic policy issue. The coverage is thorough and highly professional.

5. *Challenge*   This is *the* one and only economic policy journal. Not only does it contain economic issues of broad interest, but it presents them in a way that is easily understood by the nonprofessional economist. By far the best publication for broad ranging, informative, and interesting coverage of key economic policies and programs.

6. *The Wall Street Journal* The newspaper to get for on-going sophisticated coverage of the American economy. Like the business magazines, its focus is on American businesses and the overall corporate environment, but its two front page features often cover an economic topic as do its lead Op Ed pieces.

7. *The Economist* The premier international economic magazine. It regularly covers major economic trends and statistics from nations around the globe as well as general features on politics and other socio-cultural and technological trends.

APPENDIX
★ 3 ★

Institutions

Private-Sector Economic
Think Tanks

Trying to classify a large institution as liberal or conservative, or somewhere in between, is admittedly an imprecise art. Nevertheless, it is often quite clear that some do stand on the left or right ends of the spectrum. The right end far outweighs the left end both in number and particularly in size. The rest by definition are all in the middle. The listing below generally moves from the right end to the left.

Right to Middle Right

1. **Cato Institute** The Cato Institute was established in 1977 but it has really only come into its own in the early 1980s. The most conservative of the major think tanks,

its major recent economics publications are: *National Economic Planning: What is Left?* and *The Search for Stable Money.*

2. **Heritage Foundation**   This is the major conservative think tank that delves heavily into economic issues. Like Cato, it has had a meteoric rise in the 1980s. Their numerous economics publications fall under five main categories: banking and monetary issues, budget and deficit, industrial policy, taxation, and trade and development.

3. **American Enterprise Institute**   Until the rise of the Heritage Foundation in the early 1980s, AEI was basically "the place" for conservatives. Its distinguished roster of economists has included Herbert Stein, Arthur Burns, and Gottfried Haberler. Its coverage of economic issues is very comprehensive, focusing on fiscal and monetary policy, government regulation, and international economics.

4. **The Center for Strategic and International Studies**   Perhaps of all the think tanks listed, this one has the least economics focus. Only one of its six functional programs—International Business and Economics—deals with economics. Its focus is principally international. Its best-known economist is Paul Craig Roberts (see Appendix 1).

The Middle

5. **Institute for International Economics**   This relatively new, but highly respected think tank, is unusual in its focus on a single area of economics: international economics and trade issues. Founded in 1980 by C. Fred Bergsten (a former Carter Administration trade official), it has published numerous definitive studies on the trade deficit, the fall and rise of the dollar, and broad trends in the international economy.

6. **Roosevelt Center for American Policy Studies** Another relative newcomer (founded in 1982), the Roosevelt Center says its goals "are to clarify the policy choices before the nation and to encourage and facilitate the participation of citizens in the decision-making process at all levels of government." Its economic analysis and activities are somewhat limited, one recent publication being *Till Debt Do Us Part.*

7. **The Urban Institute** Despite its name, the Urban Institute examines a wide range of policy issues that are not urban. Many on its professional staff are economists, who specialize in the areas of income distribution, taxes, productivity, and human resources.

The Middle Left and Left

8. **The Brookings Institution** The "granddaddy" of Washington think tanks, Brookings was established in 1927. Clearly identified in the 1960s and 1970s in economics as the Democrat's think tank, it has moved much closer to the middle in the 1980s. Its distinguished roster of economists, most with extensive government service, includes: Alice Rivlin, Joseph Pechman, Charles Schultz, and Robert Crandall. Like AEI, its coverage of economic issues is extensive, the principal areas being: macroeconomic policy, international interrelationships, economic change (productivity and market structure), and social programs.

9. **Center for National Policy** Just as former Ford administration officials flocked to AEI in 1977, so former Carter administration officials congregated around the newly established Center for National Policy in 1981. Since budgetary restraints prevented it from hiring an analytical professional staff in the first half of the 1980s, its published studies largely came from outside experts, who were basically free-of-charge volunteers. It nevertheless

was able to produce high-caliber economic studies in such fields as tax policy, industrial policy, and employment policy.

10. **Center on Budget and Policy Priorities** As its name implies, the focus of this group is the budget, particularly military spending and social welfare spending. Among its major studies are: *Hard Choices: Smaller Slices of the Pie* and *The Military Payoff.*

11. **Economic Policy Institute** Established in 1986 primarily to serve as the major broad-gauged think tank of the left. Still very modest in size, it attempts to leverage itself by publishing studies and hosting seminars and conferences. Founded by a group of economists, including Lester Thurow, Robert Reich, Barry Bluestone, Ray Marshall, Jeff Faux, and Bob Kuttner, its goal is to bring balance to the economic debate by making the case for the public sector's role in making the economy more competitive.

12. **Institute for Policy Studies** The oldest, and most left-wing, of the think tanks. Its critiques of the American economy come from the radical left. Its chief economist for many years has been Richard Barnet.

Congressional Economic Analysis Centers

---

1. **Joint Economic Committee** This is the grandaddy of Congressional think tanks—it is devoted exclusively to economic issues and is the most broadly focused. Its hundreds of reports and hearings cover every conceivable economic issue, policy, and program. Its main publication is the *Annual Report* published each March.

2. **Congressional Budget Office** Founded in 1975 to provide nonpartisan analytical study of the budget, it has

developed a well-respected and highly professional reputation. Its two directors have been Alice Rivlin (1975–1983) and Rudolph Penner (1983–1987).

3. **Joint Committee on Taxation** Despite the "Committee" in its name, the JCT largely functions in a manner analogous to that of the Congressional Budget Office on taxes. Its studies are highly respected and often considered to be the definitive word.

4. **General Accounting Office** Essentially, the GAO, with a large staff of professionals, functions as the general economic watch dog for Congress. Its economic analyses are extensive, ranging from macroeconomic policies to a host of microeconomic policy studies. Its basic focus is on how well government economic programs are doing.

5. **Office of Technology Assessment** Though its focus is technology, OTA has conducted since its founding in 1974 numerous economic studies of major import. Often these deal with specific major industries such as steel or computers, but sometimes broader themes such as U.S. competitiveness and manufacturing technology are conducted. It has three "publication categories" encompassing economic issues: (1) Industry, Technology, and Employment, (2) International Security and Commerce, and (3) Communication and Information Technologies.

Executive Branch
Economic Agencies

---

1. **Bureau of Labor Statistics, Department of Labor** This is the official source of all government statistics relating to employment, unemployment, labor force trends, wages, and so forth.

2. **Census Bureau, Department of Commerce** It issues current reports on manufacturing, retail and wholesale trade, services, construction, imports and exports, and state

and local government finances and employment. It also issues the GNP accounts.

3. **Bureau of Economic Analysis, Department of Commerce** The BEA issues surveys of investment outlays and plans of U.S. business, econometric models of the economy, the leading indicators, the national income and product accounts, personal income statistics, and balance of payments accounts. Its main publication is the *Survey of Current Business*.

4. **Council of Economic Advisers, Executive Office of the President** Most of its analyses are for internal consumption. Its major output for public consumption is the annual *Economic Report of the President*, released in late January, which basically highlights the administration's domestic and international economic policies. It also contains a wealth of economic statistics in over one hundred tables.

5. **Office of Management and Budget, Executive Office of the President** Again, many of its analyses are not for external use. The principal ones available to the public are the Appendices to the budget which go into excruciating detail on the budget.

6. **U.S. Special Trade Representative, Executive Office of the President** The principal publication of this office is its Annual Report, which provides an excellent current summary of trade issues and statistics. It also publishes special studies, including a very helpful primer, called *A Preface to Trade*.

Independent Economic Agencies

1. **The Federal Reserve Board** Most of the Fed's studies are highly analytical and technical. However, it does have some publications for the general public, such as

its Annual Report and its reports to Congress on monetary policy.

Global Institutions

1. **World Bank**   The best source of information on the economies of developing countries, it publishes an annual *World Development Report*, which provides an excellent overview of the latest events and statistics on economic development. It also publishes numerous specialized studies and books on all aspects of the development process, available in its own book store in Washington, D.C.

2. **The International Monetary Fund**   The best source of data on international financial statistics, the IMF publishes *International Financial Statistics* each month and an annual overview. It also publishes *The World Economic Outlook* annually, focusing on OECD policies.

Business Associations

1. **U.S. Chamber of Commerce**   The largest and oldest of all business associations, the chamber publishes two magazines—*Nation's Business* and *Business Advocate*—as well as numerous economic studies in four major areas: private sector initiatives, productivity, international economics, and tax policy.

2. **National Association of Manufacturers**   The NAM is also quite large, with 13,000 member firms. It publishes its own magazine *Enterprise* and issues periodic reports on the economy.

3. **Business Roundtable**   Much smaller, with only about 200 members, the Business Roundtable publishes only a handful of economic studies each year.

4. American Business Conference   The ABC was founded in 1981 and limits its membership to 100 fast-growing small and medium-sized firms. Its studies are limited in number as its focus is mainly lobbying and internal meetings for the benefit of its members. Its two major economic studies are "The High Cost of Capital" and *The Winning Performance: How America's High-Growth Midsized Companies Succeed.*

Organized Labor

1. AFL-CIO   The AFL-CIO is the umbrella organization for most of the country's major unions, encompassing eighty-nine unions at the close of 1986. It publishes a number of economic studies each year on topics related to labor: the declining middle class, loss of manufacturing jobs, unemployment, and the like.

INDEX

★